SECURITY AND PRIVACY IN ADVANCED NETWORKING TECHNOLOGIES

NATO Science Series

A series presenting the results of scientific meetings supported under the NATO Science Programme.

The series is published by IOS Press and Kluwer Academic Publishers in conjunction with the NATO Scientific Affairs Division.

Sub-Series

I.	Life and Behavioural Sciences	IOS Press
II.	Mathematics, Physics and Chemistry	Kluwer Academic Publishers
III.	Computer and Systems Sciences	IOS Press
IV.	Earth and Environmental Sciences	Kluwer Academic Publishers
V.	Science and Technology Policy	IOS Press

The NATO Science Series continues the series of books published formerly as the NATO ASI Series.

The NATO Science Programme offers support for collaboration in civil science between scientists of countries of the Euro-Atlantic Partnership Council. The types of scientific meeting generally supported are "Advanced Study Institutes" and "Advanced Research Workshops", although other types of meeting are supported from time to time. The NATO Science Series collects together the results of these meetings. The meetings are co-organized by scientists from NATO countries and scientists from NATO's Partner countries – countries of the CIS and Central and Eastern Europe.

Advanced Study Institutes are high-level tutorial courses offering in-depth study of latest advances in a field.
Advanced Research Workshops are expert meetings aimed at critical assessment of a field, and identification of directions for future action.

As a consequence of the restructuring of the NATO Science Programme in 1999, the NATO Science Series has been re-organized and there are currently five sub-series as noted above. Please consult the following web sites for information on previous volumes published in the series, as well as details of earlier sub-series:

http://www.nato.int/science
http://www.wkap.nl
http://www.iospress.nl
http://www.wtv-books.de/nato_pco.htm

Series III: Computer and Systems Sciences - Vol. 193   ISSN 1387-6694

Security and Privacy in Advanced Networking Technologies

Edited by

Borka Jerman-Blažič

Laboratory for Open Systems and Networks, Jožef Stefan Institute, Ljubljana, Slovenia

and

Faculty of Economics, University of Ljubljana, Slovenia

Wolfgang Schneider

Fraunhofer Institute SIT, Darmstadt, Germany

and

Tomaž Klobučar

Laboratory for Open Systems and Networks, Jožef Stefan Institute, Ljubljana, Slovenia

and

SETCCE, Ljubljana, Slovenia

IOS
Press

Amsterdam • Berlin • Oxford • Tokyo • Washington, DC

Published in cooperation with NATO Scientific Affairs Division

Proceedings of the NATO Advanced Networking Workshop on
Advanced Security Technologies in Networking
15–18 September 2003
Bled, Slovenia

© 2004, IOS Press

ISBN 1 58603 430 8
Library of Congress Control Number: 2004109511

Publisher
IOS Press
Nieuwe Hemweg 6B
1013 BG Amsterdam
Netherlands
fax: +31 20 620 3419
e-mail: order@iospress.nl

Distributor in the UK and Ireland
IOS Press/Lavis Marketing
73 Lime Walk
Headington
Oxford OX3 7AD
England
fax: +44 1865 750079

Distributor in the USA and Canada
IOS Press, Inc.
4502 Rachael Manor Drive
Fairfax, VA 22032
USA
fax: +1 703 323 3668
e-mail: iosbooks@iospress.com

Foreword

Security and privacy in telecommunications and networking, especially when electronic commerce is involved, are two of the most crucial services offered in the global networks. For the most part, interconnected networks all over the world use a common set of protocols (i.e. the protocol suite TCP/IP), making up the Internet. In general, users of the computer network services are largely unaware of the potential threats to their information, or they choose to ignore such threats. However, the increasing usage of Internet services in all levels of business, education, information, entertainment and every day life has brought the importance of the protection of data, resources and identities to the fore. New applications built up within the paradigm of e-commerce are offering different levels of protection and security. Recently, the Internet has started to spread "over the air" to merge with mobile communication networks, thus making a new broad range of services available to the new economy. Since these new services take place in public and therefore un-trusted networks, there are many security issues involved that are of concern to different communities, e.g.:

- Commercial companies and their clients who want to do business over open networks need protection of resources and exchanged data;
- Administrations, public medical and social services, for whom it is vital that only approved groups are able to participate in their operations;
- Organisations for their external and internal network communication;
- The research community and institutions involved in provision of digital contents related to the cultural heritage.

All these users need security service and an established infrastructure. Lack of established security infrastructure and the knowledge of how to set it up and use it are major obstacles for a better proliferation of secured applications in open networks.

This book provides a broad overview of the basic aspects of technology, services and applications that enable safety, security and privacy in un-trusted networks. The book can be viewed as a sequel of the book Advanced Security Technologies in Networking, published by IOS Press in 2001 and edited by the same editors. While the first book focused mostly on basic security services and mechanisms, network layer security, public key infrastructures and related applications, and secure electronic commerce, this book gives an overview of the most recent security technologies, such as biometrics, mobile networks, intrusion detection systems, and privacy-enhancing technologies.

The first part of the book briefly addresses basic security services and cryptography. The second introduces the notion of security infrastructure in mobile and terrestrial networks. Different infrastructures and networks are dealt with, such as privilege management infrastructure, public key infrastructure, 802.11 wireless networks, exotic wireless networks, active networks and critical infrastructure. The next part gives an overview of firewalls, intrusion detection systems and biometrics. At the end, privacy, applications and legal issues are dealt with.

Most of the papers in this book were prepared on the basis of authors' presentations in the NATO Advanced Networking Workshop on Advanced Security Technologies in Networking that took place in Bled, Slovenia from 15 to 18 September, 2003. In that context we want to express our deep appreciation to all lecturers that made this event a success due to their excellent talks and papers. Special thanks also go to the organising committee members.

Borka Jerman-Blažic and Tomaž Klobucar

Contents

Basic Concepts in Secure Communications

Security and Privacy in Advanced Networking Technologies
B. Jerman-Blažič et al. (Eds.)
IOS Press, 2004

Basic Security Services and Cryptography

Elisabeth OSWALD
Institute for Applied Information Processing and Communications,
TU Graz, Inffeldgasse 16a, A-8010 Graz, Austria
Elisabeth.Oswald@iaik.at

Abstract. In this article, we discuss how basic security services can be realized by cryptographic means. Our discussion includes symmetric primitives as means to ensure confidentiality, data integrity and data origin authentication, and asymmetric primitives, as means to ensure authentication, non-repudiation and as a method to distribute symmetric keys. The last part of this article elaborates on the security of the discussed primitives.

Introduction

During the last century, digital communication has become a major part of people's every day life. Industrialised countries are evolving towards information societies, where bankcards, mobile phones and wireless Internet access are available to every citizen. Moreover, the value of information keeps growing, while it is being subjected to an increased number of threats such as eavesdropping of communication lines and theft of sensitive data. This clearly demonstrates that there is a strong need for techniques to protect information and information systems. Cryptography is the science of protecting information. A cryptographic algorithm is a mathematical function that uses a key to encipher information. Without knowledge of the key, deciphering is not possible. Contemporary cryptography deals with more issues than plain encryption. Mathematical concepts are known which can be used to construct digital signatures or protocols for entity authentication, for example.

1. CIA and Non-repudiation

In the typical scenario, two entities, which are called Alice and Bob, want to exchange messages securely over an insecure channel. The adversary, which is called Eve, can have several goals including eavesdropping the communication or altering it, for example. Eavesdropping is a threat to the *confidentiality* of the messages, i.e., no unauthorized third party can understand the content. Altering is a threat to the *integrity* of the message, i.e., no one can change the message while it is in transit. In addition, Eve could also try imposing one of the communicating parties. Therefore, it is required to *authenticate* (i.e. get assurance of the identity) the communicating parties. The last of the four basic security services deals with *non-repudiation*, i.e., the property, that the sender cannot deny a message was sent. This property cannot be achieved by secret key cryptography alone.

2. Secret Key Cryptography

Numerous applications use (software) implementations of cryptographic algorithms to provide security at low cost. The most important requirement for such algorithms, besides their resistance against attacks, is that the performance of the application itself is reduced as little as possible. Several types of secret key cryptographic primitives are discussed in this section. *Block ciphers* are used to encrypt data. If block ciphers are not fast enough for an application, *stream ciphers* can be used as alternative. In order to ensure integrity of data, modification detection codes (MDC), which are also called *hash functions,* are used. For authentication, message authentication codes (MACs) are used.

2.1 Block Ciphers

Block ciphers are typically used for encrypting large amounts of data. Therefore, they are the encryption primitives, which are used in applications such as PGP, for example.

    A block cipher is defined as a set of Boolean permutations operating on n-bit vectors [1]. This set contains a Boolean permutation for each value of a key k. In other words, a block cipher is a length preserving transformation, which takes an element (a plaintext) from the set of plaintexts and transforms it to an element (the ciphertext) from the set of ciphertexts under the influence of a key.

    Such a block cipher usually consists of several operations (transformations), which form the encryption algorithm. To allow efficient implementations, block ciphers apply the same Boolean transformation several times on a plaintext. The Boolean transformation is then the so-called *round function*, and the block cipher is called an *iterated* block cipher. For each round, a key has to be used. To generate such *round keys* K_i from the cipher key, a *key schedule* algorithm is applied to the cipher key. If the round key is applied in a very simple way, i.e. it is exclusive or-ed (XOR-ed) to an intermediate value, then the cipher is called *key-alternating* block cipher.

    Modern block ciphers are usually based on two different types of designs. In *Feistel ciphers,* the plaintext is split into a right and a left half, L and R. The round function f only acts on one of the halves:

$$L_i = R_{i-1}$$
$$R_i = L_{i-1} + f(R_{i-1}, K_i)$$

    As a consequence from the Feistel structure, it takes two rounds before all plaintext bits have been subject to the round transformation. Decryption can be done in the same way as encryption with the round keys supplied in reverse order. Moreover, the round function f does not have to be a permutation. The *DES* (Data Encryption Standard) [2] consists of an algorithm of that type.

    Another popular construction is called a *substitution permutation network* (short SPN). This construction emphasizes on separating confusion (substitution) and diffusion (permutation) in the cipher. In many recent SPN ciphers, the permutation layer has been replaced by an affine transformation that is chosen in such a way that a high level of diffusion be guaranteed. Rijndael [1], which is the algorithm of the new *AES* (Advanced Encryption Standard) [3], is an example for this design. Feistel ciphers can also be considered as a kind of SPNs.

2.2 Modes of Operation

Whenever a message being longer than the block size needs to be encrypted, the block cipher is used in a certain mode of operation. For the DES, four modes have been standardized [4]. The *electronic code book* (ECB) mode corresponds to the usual use of a block cipher; the message is split into blocks and each block is encrypted separately with the same key. In the *cipher block chaining* (CBC) mode, each ciphertext block is x-ored (chained) with the next plaintext block before being encrypted with the key. In the *output feedback* (OFB) mode and the *cipher feedback* (CFB) modes, a keystream is generated and x-ored with the plaintext. Hence, the latter two modes work as a synchronous additive stream cipher.

There is ongoing work to define new modes. In a special publication [5], five confidentiality modes are specified for use with any approved block cipher, such as the AES algorithm.

2.3 Stream Ciphers

Stream ciphers encrypt individual characters, which are usually bits of a plaintext, one at a time. They use an encryption transformation, which varies with time. Hence, in contrast to block ciphers, the encryption depends not only on the key and the plaintext, but also on the current state. As mentioned before at the end of Section *2.2* , a block cipher can be turned into a stream cipher by using a certain mode of operation (such as CFB or OFB). Except that, there are no stream ciphers that are standardized today. A de-facto standard however is the RC4 stream cipher [1].

Synchronous stream ciphers generate a keystream independently of the plaintext messages and of the ciphertext. Sender and receiver must therefore be synchronized; they must use the same key and operate at the same state within that key. A ciphertext digit that is corrupted during transmission does not influence any other ciphertext bit.

An *asynchronous* stream cipher is a stream cipher in which the keystream is generated as a function of the key and a fixed number of previous ciphertext bits. Because the keystream is dependent on only a few previous ciphertext bits, self-synchronization is possible even if some of the transmitted ciphertext bits are corrupted.

Stream ciphers are often used when block ciphers are not fast enough. This is typically the case when streaming data needs to be encrypted such as in wireless communication.

2.4 MDCs

An MDC (hash function) takes an input of arbitrary length and compresses (digests) it to an output of fixed length, which is called the hash value. Cryptographic hash functions satisfy the following properties in addition:

1. *preimage resistance*: it should be computationally infeasible to find a preimage to a given hash value,
2. 2nd *preimage resistance*: it should be computationally infeasible to find a 2nd preimage to a given input,
3. *collision resistance*: it should be computationally infeasible to find two different inputs with the same hash value.

Hash functions are used to ensure the integrity of data. This can be done by using the data as input to the hash function and storing its output. Later on, to verify that the input data has not been altered, the hash value is recomputed using the data at hand and compared with the original hash value. Another application for hash functions is to use them in digital signature schemes. Hash functions of the SHA family have been standardized in [7].

2.5 MACs

Hash functions, which involve a secret key, are called MACs. The output of such a keyed hash function is also called MAC. They can be used to guarantee data origin authentication (i.e. corroborate the source of information) and data integrity. Most contemporary MACs are constructed based either upon a block cipher or upon a hash function.

In order to ensure authenticity of data, an entity computes a MAC on the data by using the private key. In order to verify the authenticity of the data later on, the MAC can be recomputed by anyone who may access the private key. Standardized MACs are the DAC [8] and the new HMAC [9]. MACs are often used in authentication protocols.

3. Public Key Cryptosystems

In public key cryptography, secret keys are replaced by keypairs consisting of a *private key*, which must be kept confidential, and a *public key*, which is made available to the public by for example publishing it in a directory. Anyone who wishes to send a message to the owner of a certain keypair will take the public key, encrypt the message under this public key and send it to the owner of the keypair. The owner can decrypt the message by using the private key.

This idea works out in practice because the private and the public key are linked in a mathematical way (by a mathematical function) such that knowing the public key does not allow recovering the private key. Several mathematical functions, which are useful for public key cryptography, are known today. Amongst others, the most important hard mathematical problems are:

- *IFP (integer factorization problem):* given a positive integer n, find its prime factorization $n = p_1^{e_1} \cdot p_2^{e_2} \cdots p_k^{e_k}$
- *GDLP (generalized discrete logarithm problem):* given a finite cyclic group G of order n a generator α of G, and an element $\beta \in G$, find the integer $x \le 0 \le n - 1$ such that $\alpha^x = \beta$.
- *GDHP (generalized Diffie-Hellman problem):* given a prime p, a generator α of G and elements α^a and α^b, find α^{ab}

In the subsequent sections, we discuss a reference cryptosystem for each of the above given hard mathematical problems. Thereafter, we sketch two other important applications for public-key cryptography, namely key agreement and digital signatures.

3.1 RSA

The Rivest-Shamir-Adleman (RSA) [10] algorithm was the first public key encryption algorithm invented. Under certain assumptions, the RSA algorithm is based on the IFP. RSA keys are generated as follows: one selects two large secret prime numbers p and q and computes the public RSA modulus $n = p \cdot q$. Then one chooses a public encryption exponent e which satisfies *gcd(e, (p-1)(q-1))=1*. The private key, i.e. the decryption exponent d, can then be calculated by solving $e \cdot d = 1 \,(\mathrm{mod}\,((p-1) \cdot (q-1)))$. Hence, the public key is the tuple *(e,n)* and the private key is the triple *(d,p,q)*.

Suppose that someone wishes to encrypt a message for the entity, which is associated with the public key *(e,n)*. Then, the message needs to be represented as a number $m < n$. The ciphertext is computed by raising m to the power e: $c = m^e \pmod{n}$. The ciphertext can be decrypted by exponentiation with the private key: $m = c^d \pmod{n}$.

3.2 El Gamal

The El Gamal encryption algorithm [11] is based on the GDLP where G is the finite field Z_p^*. An advantage of El Gamal is that a group of users can share some of the public parameters. These so-called *domain parameters* are a large prime p such that *p-1* is divisible by another prime q, and an element $g \in Z_p^*$ of order divisible by q. The private key is chosen to be an integer d. The public key e can then be computed: $g^d \pmod{p}$.

Suppose that someone wishes to encrypt a message for the entity, which is associated with the public key *(e,p,q)*. Then, the message needs to be represented as a number $m < p$. In a first step of the encryption procedure, a random ephemeral key k is generated. The ciphertext c consists of a pair $c = (c_1, c_2) = (g^k, m \cdot e^k)$. To decrypt the ciphertext, $\dfrac{c_2}{c_1^d}$ is computed. Since each message has a different ephemeral key, encrypting the same message twice will produce two different ciphertexts. Cryptosystems with this property are also called *non-deterministic* or *randomized* cryptosystems.

3.3 ECC

An *elliptic curve E* over the field *F* is a smooth curve in the Weierstrassform [12]:
$Y^2 + a_1 X \cdot Y + a_3 \cdot Y = X^3 + a_2 \cdot X^2 + a_4 \cdot X + a_6, a_i \in F$.
We let *E(F)* denote the set of points $(x, y) \in F^2$ that satisfy this equation, along with a "point at infinity" denoted *O*. For finite fields F_p or F_{2^m} the equation can be simplified.

The set of points *E(F)* together with the point at infinity forms an additive group. The group operations are called point addition (two distinct points on the curve are added) and point doubling (a point is added to itself). The GDLP is a hard mathematical problem in this group; it is therefore well suited for cryptography:
If *E* is an elliptic curve over *F* and *B* is a point of *E*, then the discrete log problem on *E* (to the base *B*) is the problem, given a point $P \in E$, of finding an integer $x \in Z$ such that $x \cdot B = P$ if such an integer x exists.

Similar to the El Gamal cryptosystem, several public parameters can be shared amongst a group of users. These parameters are the elliptic curve group itself and the base point. The private key is chosen to be an integer d. The public key is then given by $e = d \cdot B$.

Suppose that someone wishes to encrypt a message for the entity, which is associated with the public key *(e,B,E(F))*. Then, the message needs to be represented as a point on the curve $M \in E(F)$. In a first step of the encryption procedure, a random ephemeral key k is generated. The ciphertext c consists of a pair $c = (c_1, c_2) = (k \cdot B, M + k \cdot e)$. To decrypt the ciphertext, $c_2 - d \cdot c_1$ is computed.

3.4 Key Agreement

A major disadvantage of symmetric key cryptography is that secret keys need to be distributed securely to the users. However, this problem can be solved efficiently using public key cryptography [13].

Suppose that two entities, Alice and Bob, wish to agree on a secret key over an insecure channel. Alice generates a secret random number a and Bob generates a secret random number b. Then, Alice sends g^a to Bob and Bob sends g^b to Alice. Now they can both compute $g^{a \cdot b}$ which is their common secret key.

An adversary who sees the messages g^a and g^b and must reconstruct $g^{a \cdot b}$ from them. This is exactly the DHP considered in the first paragraph of this section. The DHP is a hard mathematical problem in several mathematical structures. In the original version the finite multiplicative group Z_p^* was considered. However, a more efficient version can be produced by taking the group $E(F)$.

3.5 Digital Signatures

A digital signature is the digital equivalent of a handwritten signature; it binds someone's identity to a piece of information. With a digital signature creation algorithm, one produces a digital signature. With a digital signature verification algorithm one verifies that a digital signature is authentic (i.e., was indeed created by the specified entity). A digital signature scheme consists of a signature creation algorithm and an associated verification algorithm.

There are different types of signature schemes. Digital signatures *with appendix* require the original message as input to the verification algorithm. Digital signatures *with message recovery* do not require the original message as input to the verification algorithm. In this case, the original message is recovered from the signature itself.

The DSS is a standardized signature scheme with appendix [14]. The DSS describes an algorithm, called DSA (Digital Signature Algorithm), which is based on the DLP. It has been extended recently and includes now a version of the same algorithm but on elliptic curves, the ECDSA.

In order to sign a message, the owner first computes the hash value of the message. This hash value and the private key are then subjected to the signing algorithm. The output of that algorithm is signature of the input message. Anyone who wishes to verify the signature can simply take the message, the public key and the signature and compute the verification algorithm with these inputs.

4. Security and Attacks

There exist many different types of attacks on cryptographic primitives. The goal of such attacks is typically to deduce the secret key. In this section, we characterize attacks based on the adversary's knowledge and on the adversary's (computational) capabilities.

A *passive* attack is one where the adversary only monitors the communication channel or the side-channels (e.g. electromagnetic emanations of power consumption) of the communication devices. The latter attacks are then called *side-channel attacks* [15]. They do not target the used algorithm itself, but its implementation.

An *active* attack is one where the adversary attempts to alter the transmission on the channel or the computation inside the device. The latter attacks are then called *fault attacks* [16]. They do not target the used algorithm itself, but its implementation.

Side-channel attacks and fault attacks are so called *implementation attacks*. In the last years, it turned out that several types of them pose a serious threat against practical implementations of cryptographic systems.

A widely accepted assumption in modern cryptography is that the adversary knows all the details about the used algorithms and protocols. Only the secret key is unknown to the adversary. This assumption goes back to Auguste Kerckhoffs, a Dutch cryptographer of the 19th century. Based on this assumption, attacks can be classified according to the adversary's knowledge as follows [17]:

1. A *ciphertext-only attack* is one where the adversary tries to deduce the secret key by only observing ciphertext.
2. A *known-plaintext attack* is one where the adversary has a number of plaintexts and corresponding ciphertexts.
3. A *chosen-plaintext attack* is one where the adversary chooses plaintext and gets then the corresponding ciphertext.
4. An *adaptive chosen-plaintext attack* is a chosen plaintext attack wherein the choice of the plaintext may depend on previous ciphertexts.
5. A *chosen-ciphertext attack* is one where the adversary chooses the ciphertext and gets then the corresponding plaintext.
6. An *adaptive chosen-ciphertext attack* is a chosen ciphertext attack wherein the choice of the ciphertext may depend on previous plaintexts.

Encryption schemes, which are vulnerable to ciphertext-only attacks, are considered completely insecure.

4.1 Security Models

The security of a cryptographic primitive can be evaluated under several different models. Practical models are computational security and practical security. The confidence, which we have in the security of a primitive, which is based on computational or practical security, increases with time and investigation of the primitive. Of course, time alone is not enough if only very few people have tried to break the primitive.

Unconditional security: In this model, the adversary is assumed to have unlimited computational power. Unconditional security for encryption schemes is also called *perfect secrecy*. A necessary condition for a secret key cryptosystem to have perfect secrecy is that the key is at least as long as the message. The one-time pad is an example for an unconditionally secure encryption algorithm. Because the key needs to be at least as long as the message to be encrypted, such systems are impractical. None of the modern primitives offers perfect secrecy.

Computational security: Adversaries are assumed to have polynomial computational power. Thus, an algorithm is considered secure if the best algorithm for breaking it requires a superpolynomial or exponential number of steps. State of the art ciphers are supposed to have computational security.

Provable security: A cipher has provable security if the difficulty of breaking it can be shown to be equivalent to solving a well-known and supposedly hard mathematical problem (such as IFP, DLP, etc.). Therefore, the proof of security only holds under certain mathematical assumptions. Public key cryptosystems typically allow constructing such proofs.

Practical security: Practical security is also related to the computational power of the adversary. However, it is concerned with the power computational power, which is needed with respect to previously known attacks. A cipher is considered practically secure if the best-known attack requires at least N operations, where N is a sufficiently large number. State of the art ciphers typically offer practical security.

An attack, which is applicable to all types of keyed cryptographic primitives, is the *exhaustive key search*. Consequently, it is mandatory to choose key sizes to be sufficiently large.

5. Future Trends

Cryptography is an interdisciplinary scientific discipline that has become mature over the last years. Nevertheless, there is a need for further research in the theoretical as well as the practical areas of cryptography. For example, new applications present new challenges such as low cost, i.e. low area and low power, encryption algorithms ("lightweight algorithms") which provide a reasonable security margin and allow for a secure implementation.

During the NESSIE project [18], cryptographic primitives of all types were investigated. The goal of the NESSIE was to put forward a portfolio of strong cryptographic primitives. Therefore, an open call was made and the proposed algorithms were evaluated using a transparent and open process. A result of the evaluation was, that no dedicated stream cipher withstood the analysis. Consequently, no stream cipher could be selected for the portfolio. More research is needed on the design of stream ciphers in the next years.

The STORK project [19] is the link between NESSIE, which was a project with in the 5th Framework Programme of the EU, and ECRYPT, which is the Network of Excellence in the area of Cryptology in the 6th Framwork Programme of the EU. The main objectives of STORK were to identify the gaps between the state of the art in cryptologic research and current and forthcoming requirements for cryptographic algorithms and techniques and to develop a shared agenda for research in cryptology.

ECRYTPT [20] will be the core of European research in the area of cryptology, and will improve communication and collaboration between cryptologic researchers, industrial bodies driving requirements for cryptology, and researchers in fields that influence the development of cryptology.

6. Summary

Basic security services and related cryptographic primitives were considered in this chapter. We gave a survey on secret key cryptography in Section 2. Within this section, we introduced block ciphers, stream ciphers, hash functions and MAC algorithms. Thereafter, in Section 3, we provided a survey on state-of-the art public key cryptosystems. The RSA, El Gamal and ECC cryptosystems were discussed. We discussed the security of modern cryptosystems in Section 4 and gave an outlook on future trends in Section 5.

References

[1] J. Daemen and V. Rijmen. The Design of Rijndael. Number ISBN 3-540-42580-2 in Information Security and Cryptography. Springer, 2002.

[2] FIPS 46-3. Data Encryption Standard. Federal Information Processing Standard (FIPS), Publication 46-3, National Bureau of Standards, U.S. Department of Commerce, October reaffirmed 1999.

[3] FIPS 197. Advanced Encryption Standard. Federal Information Processing Standard (FIPS), Publication 197, Institute of Standards and Technology, U.S. Department of Commerce, November 2001.

[4] FIPS 81. DES Modes of Operation. Federal Information Processing Standard (FIPS), Publication 81, National Bureau of Standards, U.S. Department of Commerce, December 1980.

[5] SP 800-38A. Recommendation for Block Cipher Modes of Operation - Methods and Techniques, National Bureau of Standards, U.S. Department of Commerce, December 2001.

[6] Bruce Schneier. Applied Cryptography. New York: Wiley 1996.

[7] FIPS 180-2. Secure Hash Standard. Federal Information Processing Standard (FIPS), Publication 180-2, National Institute of Standards and Technology, US Department of Commerce, February 2003.

[8] FIPS 113. Computer Data Authentication. Federal Information Processing Standard (FIPS), Publication 113, National Bureau of Standards, U.S. Department of Commerce, May 1985.

[9] FIPS 198. The Keyed-Hash Message Authentication Code (HMAC). Federal Information Processing Standard (FIPS), Publication 198, National Bureau of Standards, U.S. Department of Commerce, March 2002.

[10] R. Rivest, A. Shamir, L. Adleman. A method for obtaining digital signatures and public key cryptosystems. Communications of the ACM, Vol. 21, No.2, pp. 120-126, 1978.

[11] T. El Gamal. A Public-Key Cryptosystem and a Signature Scheme Based on Discrete Logarithms. Advances in Cryptology: Proceedings of CRYPTO 84, Springer Verlag, pp. 10-18, 1985.

[12] N. Koblitz. Elliptic curve cryptosystems. Mathematics of Computation, 48, pp. 203-209, 1987.

[13] W. Diffie, M. E. Hellman. New directions in cryptography. IEEE Trans. Inform. Theory, IT-22, pp. 644-654, November 1976.

[14] FIPS 186-2. Digital Signature Standard. Federal Information Processing Standard (FIPS), Publication 186-2, National Bureau of Standards, U.S. Department of Commerce, January 2000.

[15] P.C. Kocher, J. Jaffe, and B. Jun. Differential Power Analysis. In Michael Wiener, editor, Advances in Cryptology-CRYPTO 1999, volume 1666 of LNCS, pages 388—397, Springer, 1999.

[16] D. Boneh, R. A. DeMillo, and R. J. Lipton. On the importance of checking cryptographic protocols for faults. In Walter Fumy, editor, Proceedings of Eurocrypt'97, volume 1233 of Lecture Notes in Computer Science, pages 37--51. Springer, 1997.

[17] A. Menezes, P. van Oorschot, S. Vanstone. Handbook of Applied Cryptography. CRC-Press, Boca Raton, 1997.

[18] NESSIE. New European Schemes for Signatures, Integrity and Encryption. IST-1999-12324. www.cryptonessie.org.

[19] STORK. Strategic Roadmap for Crypto. IST-2002-38723. www.stork.eu.org.

[20] ECRYPT. European Network for Excellence in Cryptology. IST-2002-507932.

Privilege Management and Public Key Infrastructures

Security and Privacy in Advanced Networking Technologies
B. Jerman-Blažič et al. (Eds.)
IOS Press, 2004

The X.509 Privilege Management Infrastructure

David W CHADWICK

Information Systems Institute, University of Salford, Salford M5 4WT, England

Abstract. This paper provides an overview of the Privilege Management Infrastructure (PMI) introduced in the 2000 edition of X.509. It describes the entities in the infrastructure: Sources of Authority, Attribute Authorities and Privilege Holders, as well as the basic data structure - the attribute certificate - that is used to hold privileges. The contents of attribute certificates are described in detail, including the various policy related extensions that may be added to them. The similarities between PMIs and PKIs are highlighted. The paper also describes how attribute certificates can be used to implement the three well known access control schemes: DAC, MAC and RBAC. Finally the paper gives an overview of how a privilege verifier might operate, and the various types of information that need to be provided to it.

1. Introduction

Although attribute certificates (ACs) were first defined in X.509(97), it was not until the 4th edition of X.509 (ISO 9594-8:2001) [1] that a full infrastructure for the use of attribute certificates was defined. This infrastructure is termed a Privilege Management Infrastructure (PMI), and it enables privileges to be allocated, delegated, revoked and withdrawn in an electronic way. A PMI is to authorisation what a Public Key Infrastructure (PKI) is to authentication.

In order to understand the purpose of an X.509 PMI, it may help if we first consider how privileges are allocated and used today in a paper based privilege management system. A resource owner (e.g. the Financial Director of a company, or a General Manager), called the Source of Authority (SOA) in X.509, will sign a paper form to say that a particular person (the privilege holder) is to be allowed to use a particular resource in a particular way. For example, the Financial Director may say that a Head of Department can sign orders up to the value of ten thousand Euros, or the General Manager may sign a form authorising a user to have access to a particular restricted area of the organisation.

Paper based systems may also support delegation of authority, whereby a privilege holder is allowed to delegate the use of resources to which he has been granted access, to one or more other people. In X.509, such a privilege holder is now termed an Attribute Authority (AA), since the holder has been authorised to assign privilege attributes to other people. For example, a Head of Department may authorise a project manager to sign orders for his project up to a pre-determined sum. The Head of Department is now acting as an Attribute Authority as well as being a privilege holder himself. When performing delegation of authority, the delegator (AA) must not overstep his authority and give the delegatee more privileges than he holds himself. For example, the Head of Departments should not give the project manager authority to spend up to a hundred thousand euros on a project, when the Head of Department is only authorised to spend up to ten thousand euros.

When a privilege is asserted (or exercised) by a privilege holder, someone (the privilege verifier) will need to check that the privilege really does belong to the person claiming the privilege. For example, if a project manager completes an Internal Requisition form in order to purchase a piece of equipment costing five thousand euros, a purchase order clerk (privilege verifier) will need to check such things as:

i)   is this user allowed to sign Internal Requisitions i.e. has he been authorised to do this

ii)   who gave permission for this user to sign Internal Requisitions i.e. what is the delegation chain of authority leading to this user from the Financial Directory (the Source of Authority)

iii)   is this Internal Requisition within the limits of what the user is allowed to purchase i.e. did every delegator act within his limits of authority, and has the user done the same

iv)   are all the signatures valid, both on the original authorisation forms and on this Internal Requisition. This is checking the authenticity of the authorisation chain, and of the Internal Requisition.

v)   has the user's privilege been withdrawn. The privilege verifier will need to check that the authorisation is still current and valid, and has not been withdrawn since the original authorisation forms were signed.

The X.509 Privilege Management Infrastructure is very similar in concept to the existing paper based privilege management infrastructure, and there is direct correspondence between the entities involved.

In X.509 the Source of Authority is the resource owner and is responsible for assigning privileges to other entities. These other entities are Attribute Authorities (if they can delegate their privileges further) and Privilege Holders (if they are not allowed to delegate their privileges to anyone else). An AA is allowed to delegate privileges to other entities (both AAs and privilege holders) but may or may not be able to assert the privileges itself.

The privilege verifier is the entity that checks the asserted privileges and makes a yes/no decision as to whether the privilege may be used or not. The privilege verifier trusts the source of authority (SOA) and checks that the privilege holder has been directly or indirectly authorised by the SOA.

2. Similarities between PKIs and PMIs

Since both PMIs and PKIs are part of the same X.509 standard, one would expect some similarities to exist between the two infrastructures. In fact, there is a significant amount of overlap between the concepts and data structures used by PKIs and PMIs. These are shown in Table 1 below.

Attribute certificates (ACs) are used to hold authorisation information (privileges) in much the same way as public key certificates (PKCs) hold authentication information. The main difference is that a PKC binds a public key to its holder, whilst an AC binds a set of attributes to its holder. Only a CA can issue a public key certificate (being a CA is a very specialised function and there are usually very few of them in an organisation), but anyone holding privileges may be an AA and be allowed to issue attribute certificates to others. This is needed in order to delegate privileges to people and is not such a specialised function as being a CA, so there might be very many AAs in an organisation.

Table 1. A Comparison of PKIs and PMIs

Concept	PKI entity	PMI entity
Certificate	Public Key Certificate (PKC)	Attribute Certificate (AC)
Certificate issuer	Certification Authority (CA)	Attribute Authority (AA)
Certificate user	Subject	Holder
Certificate binding	Subject's Name to Public Key	Holder's Name to Privilege Attribute(s)
Revocation	Certificate Revocation List (CRL)	Attribute Certificate Revocation List (ACRL)
Root of trust	Root CA or Trust Anchor	Source of Authority (SOA)
Subordinate authority	Subordinate Certification Authority	Attribute Authority (AA)

Examples of Sources of Authority might typically be the Financial Director of a company (for allocating financial privileges), or the Network Manager (for allocating networking privileges) etc. An attribute authority could then be a departmental manager, or a project manager etc.

The revocation of certificates is just as important in PMIs as in PKIs, and the certificate revocation list construct is identical for both PKIs and PMIs. It essentially holds the serial numbers of the revoked certificates, and the time of revocation.

3. The Contents of an Attribute Certificate

An attribute certificate comprises a digitally signed SEQUENCE of:

- the version number of this AC (v1 or v2)
- identification of the holder of this AC
- identification of the AA issuing this AC
- the identifier of the algorithm used to sign this AC
- the unique serial number of this AC
- the validity period of this AC
- the sequence of attributes being bound to the holder
- any optional extensions

The holder and issuer can be identified in one of three ways. Firstly by their name (termed a General Name in X.509); secondly by reference to their public key certificate; and thirdly by a hash value of a software object related to them. The General Name of a holder or issuer can be one of:

- otherName – any name of any form (this is catch all to cater for names that are not standardized in the following list)
- rfc822Name – an e-mail address as per RFC 822
- DNSName – an Internet domain name as per RFC 1035
- X.400Address – an O/R address as per X.411
- Directory Name – a directory distinguished name as per X.501
- EDIPartyName – a format agreed between EDI partners, consisting of the name of the EDI naming authority and the name of the EDI party
- UniformResourceIdentifier – a URI as per RFC 1630
- IPAddress – an Internet Protocol address as per RFC 791
- RegisteredID – any OID registered as per X.660|ISO 9834-1

If one wishes to protect the name of the AC issuer and/or holder from being present in the AC, then they can be identified by reference to their public key certificate(s). This form of identification comprises the General Name of the CA issuing the PKC, and the serial number of the PKC that was issued to them. The third way of identifying the holder and/or issuer is by a hash value of a software object related to them. The hash value (message digest) is created from an information object that can be used to directly authenticate the holder or issuer of the attribute certificate. This might be a hash of a public key belonging to the holder or issuer, or of a public key certificate issued to either of them, or of the object itself, for example if the holder is a downloadable program then the hash could be of the program itself, and the AC would then hold the privileges that should be assigned to the program. By rechecking the hash of the downloaded program one can be assured that one has got a copy of the original (virus free) software as intended by the attribute authority. When hash values are used to identify holders or issuers, then the attribute certificate says what software object the hash has been made from, and what hashing algorithm has been used to create it.

Finally, attribute certificates can have any number of extensions added to them. A standard set of extensions are defined in X.509, but other organisations can also specify their own private extensions (as is also the case with X.509 PKCs).

4. X.509 AC Extensions

Extensions to X.509 ACs are concerned with specifying some aspects of policy that govern the use and applicability of the ACs. The extensions can be split up into 5 categories:
– basic extensions
– privilege revocation extensions
– an extension to support roles
– source of authority extensions, and
– delegation of authority extensions

4.1 Basic extensions

There are 4 basic extensions that can be added to X.509 ACs. These are designed to control the time, targets, policies and users of the AC.

The time extension allows the time when the privilege can be exercised to be constrained (e.g. to certain days of the week and certain times of the day etc.)
The targeting extension allows the issuer to control the target resources that the privileges are valid for. Targets may be identified either specifically by naming them using the General Names construct, or generically as a group of servers or services (but how group membership is defined is outside the scope of the standard).

The acceptable privilege policies extension states that the privilege can only be used with these policies that must be known to the privilege verifier associated with the target resource. This extension is always flagged as critical, meaning that if the privilege verifier does not know the policies referred to in this AC extension (or does not even recognise this extension), then it must reject the AC and deny the user access.

The user notice extension is intended to hold a message that is displayed to the holder and/or verifier when the privilege is being used i.e. displayed to the user when he/she is asserting the privilege, and displayed to the privilege verifier when he/she is validating the privilege. A similar extension is defined for public key certificates, and some well known CAs place user notices in the PKCs they issue.

4.2 Revocation Extensions

There are two extensions in this category: the CRL distribution points extension and the 'no revocation' extension.

The CRL distribution points extension points to where the revocation list or lists for this attribute certificate will be found. This allows sets of attribute certificates to have their revocation information posted to different revocation lists. This ensures that revocation lists never become too large. There are two ways of distributing CRL information. The first is by certificate serial number, in which blocks of revoked certificates (say from serial numbers 1 to 500, 501 to 1000 etc.) are posted to different CRLs and each AC in a block will contain the same distribution point extension. The second is by revocation reason, where revoked certificates are posted to different CRLs according to their reason for revocation e.g. compromised certificates list vs. privileges withdrawn list, and all ACs will hold the same set of distribution points.

The 'no revocation' extension tells the privilege verifier that this attribute certificate will never appear on an attribute certificate revocation list. This extension may be useful for short-lived attribute certificates that will never be revoked.

4.3 Extension to support Roles

If an AC is a role assignment attribute certificate (see later), a privilege verifier needs to be able to know what privileges are associated with the role in this AC. If role specification ACs are being used to specify these privileges, then the roleSpecCertIdentifier extension enables the privilege verifier to locate the role specification AC that contains the specific privileges assigned to the role in this role assignment AC. Note that this extension may not be necessary, as privilege verifiers may have their own way of locating role specification ACs, or may not even be using role specification ACs because the role specification information is held in an authorisation policy (as for example in PERMIS).
The roleSpecCertIdentifier extension contains the following fields:
- the role name (this must match the General Name of the holder in the Role Specification AC)
- the role certificate issuer (this must match the General Name of the AA signing the Role Specification AC)
- serial number of the Role Specification AC (optional)
- role certificate locator (a General Name, used to help locate the Role Specification AC)

Note that if the optional serial number is held in this extension, then if the definition of the role specification changes and a new role specification AC is issued, then all role holders will need to be issued with new role assignment ACs (since this extension will no longer be valid). So in general it is not a good idea to include the serial number in this extension.

4.4 Source of Authority Extensions

Privilege verifiers need to know who are the sources of authority for allocating privileges to the resource(s) they manage. This can be achieved in one of two ways. The first method is by out of band means. The privilege verifier in this case needs to be configured (by some trusted means) with the name (and possibly the public key) of the SOA(s) it trusts. This is similar to configuring PKI relying parties with root CAs and trust anchors.

Alternatively, it is possible to leverage the PKI to identify the trusted SOAs on behalf of the privilege verifiers. The public key certificate issued to an SOA can contain the SOA identifier extension (which does not contain any parameters). The presence of this extension in a PKC means that the CA is stating that this subject is an SOA. Thus if the privilege verifier trusts the CA to allocate sources of authority then it can reliably know who is an SOA. The privilege verifier then only needs to be configured by out of band means with the public key of the CA that it trusts (its trust anchor, or root CA).

Privilege verifiers also need to know what privilege attributes will be issued by an SOA, and if these privileges are delegated what rules govern their delegation. This information can be configured into the privilege verifier by some trusted out of band means. Alternatively, the SAO can issue a self signed "attribute descriptor" certificate, that says which attributes it will assign, and what is meant by a delegated privilege being less than a held privilege. An attribute descriptor certificate does not contain any attributes, but instead contains the attribute descriptor extension.

4.5 Delegation of Authority Extensions

There are four extensions that may be inserted into ACs to support delegation of authority.
- The basic attribute constraints extension holds a boolean to control delegation, and if set to TRUE, may contain an integer controlling further delegation
- The delegated name constraints extension restricts the names of subsequent holders of delegated privileges
- The acceptable PK certificate policies extension lists the CA policies under which subsequent delegated holders must have been authenticated
- The AA identifier extension is a back pointer to the attribute certificate of the delegating AA, to help the verifier construct a valid certificate chain

The basic attribute constraints extension comprises a boolean to say if the holder is allowed to delegate the privileges given to him/her. If the boolean is TRUE (i.e. the holder is an AA and delegation is allowed) then it may be accompanied by an integer to say how much further delegation is allowed. A value of zero means that the AA can only issue privilege holder certificates and not AA certificates (no further delegation is allowed after this one), a value of 1 means that the holder of a delegated privilege may also be a AA and delegate privileges one more time. Larger integers correspondingly increase the number of delegations that can take place.

The delegated name constraints extension allows the AA to restrict the names of holders to whom the privilege can be delegated. The constraint consists of either "permitted subtrees" or "excluded subtrees", i.e. the holder name in assigned privileges must be within the permitted namespace or must not be within the excluded namespace.

The acceptable public key certificate policies extension is used to ensure that the holder of delegated privileges has been issued with a public key certificate under an acceptable certification policy. This is to ensure that the delegated holder has been authenticated by a PKI to a required level of trust. This helps to ensure that the PMI is not compromised by weak CAs operating lax authentication policies.

The authority attribute identifier extension is a back pointer to the attribute certificate held by the AA of this attribute certificate. This allows the privilege verifier to check that the privileges held by the AA were sufficient to allow it to assign the privileges in this delegated attribute certificate. By following the entire chain of back pointers, the verifier should eventually end up with an AC issued by a trusted SOA.

5. Applying X.509 PMIs to DAC, MAC and RBAC

5.1 Discretionary Access Controls

Various access control schemes have been devised in the past. The traditional, most popular and well-known model is the Discretionary Access Control (DAC) scheme [2]. This is typically implemented in filestores, file serves, databases etc. In the DAC scheme, users are optionally given access rights to resources by the resource administrator. In traditional systems the access rights are typically held as access control lists within each target resource. This makes it fast to compute the access control decisions. The scheme is also easy to understand, but has the disadvantage that when there are large numbers of users it can be complex to manage. Users have to be given access rights (privileges) to each resource they want to access, and when they leave or change jobs, they have to have their permissions removed from each resource (which isn't always done!).

In an X.509 PMI, the access rights may be held within the privilege attributes of attribute certificates issued to users. Each privilege attribute within an AC will describe one or more of the user's access rights. A target resource will then read a user's AC to see if he is allowed to perform the action that he is requesting.

5.2 Mandatory Access Controls

Another authorization scheme, popular with the military, is the Multilevel Secure (MLS) system, which is a type of Mandatory Access Control (MAC) scheme. In the MLS scheme, every target is given a security label, which includes a classification, and every subject is given a clearance, which includes a classification list. The classification list specifies which type of classified target the subject is allowed to access. A typical hierarchical classification scheme used by the military is: unmarked, unclassified, restricted, confidential, secret, and top secret. A typical security policy, designed to stop information leakage, is "read down and write up". This specifies that a subject can read targets with a lower classification than his clearance, and can write to targets with a higher classification. A user with clearance of confidential, who logs in as such, under this policy could read from unmarked to confidential targets, and write to confidential to top secret targets. The same user could also log in with a lower clearance level, say, unclassified and write to an unclassified target.

The X.509 PMI can support MLS, by allowing subjects to be given a clearance AC. The privilege attribute in the AC now holds the user's clearance. Targets can be securely configured with their own security label and the security policy that is to direct them.

5.3 Role Based Access Controls

More recently, research has focused on Role Based Access Controls (RBAC) [3]. Role based privilege management can simplify the allocation and removal of privileges. In the basic RBAC model, a number of roles are defined. These roles typically represent organizational roles such as secretary, manager, employee etc. In the authorization policy, each role is given a set of permissions i.e. the ability to perform certain actions on certain targets. Each user is then assigned to one or more roles. When accessing a target, a user presents his role(s), and the target reads the policy to see if this role is allowed to perform this action. If the role holder changes, the new person (new role holder) inherits the same privileges as the previous role holder. By removing the role from the original role holder, his privileges are automatically removed. Many people can hold the same role, and have the same set of privileges e.g. all employees may have a basic set of privileges that are not shared by contract members of staff. Project team members may get special privileges associated with their project. When a person leaves an organisation it is usually a simpler task to remove their roles than to remove all their privileges in all the resources given to them by DAC.

The hierarchical RBAC model is a more sophisticated version of the basic RBAC model. With this model, the roles are organized hierarchically, and the senior roles inherit the privileges of the more junior roles. So for example, we might have the following hierarchy:

employee > programmer > manager > director.

If a privilege is given to an employee role e.g. can enter main building, then each of the superior roles can also enter the main building even though their role specification does not explicitly state this. If a programmer is given permission to enter the computer building, then managers and directors would also inherit this permission as well. Hierarchical roles mean that role specifications are more compact.

Another extension to basic RBAC is constrained RBAC. This allows various constraints to be applied to the role and permission assignments. One common constraint is that certain roles are declared to be mutually exclusive, meaning that the same person cannot simultaneously hold more than one role from the mutually exclusive set. For example, the roles of student and examiner, or the roles of tenderer (one who submits a tender) and tender officer (one who opens submitted tenders) would both be examples of mutually exclusive sets. Another constraint might be placed on the number of roles a person can hold, or the number of people who can hold a particular role.

RBAC is supported by the X.509 PMI. X.509 defines role specification attribute certificates that hold the permissions granted to each role, and role assignment attribute certificates that assign various roles to the users. In role assignment ACs, the AC holder is the user, and the privilege attributes are the roles assigned to the user. Further, role assignment may be delegated if wanted.

Role specification ACs on the other hand are a special type of attribute certificate, that define the privileges that go with a role. The holder of the certificate is a role name rather than the name of a person, and the privilege attributes are the permissions granted to the role. Further, role specification certificates cannot be delegated (as can normal attribute certificates). The X.509 PMI also supports hierarchical RBAC by allowing both roles and privileges to be inserted as the privilege attributes in role specification ACs, so that the specified role inherits the privileges of the encapsulated roles.

The X.509 PMI only has a limited number of ways of supporting constrained RBAC. Time constraints can be placed on the validity period of a role assignment attribute certificate, as described earlier. Constraints can be placed on the targets at which a permission can be used, and on the policies under which an attribute certificate can confer privileges (also described earlier). Constraints can also be placed on the delegation of roles. However many of the constraints, such as the mutual exclusivity of roles, have to be enforced by mechanisms outside the standardised PMI e.g. within the privilege management policy enforcement function.

X.509 allows roles to be given to people in one of two ways. You can either put a newly standardised role attribute in the subjectDirectoryAttributes extension of a holder's public key certificate, or you can give the person a role assignment attribute certificate, where the attribute is the role attribute. Typically you would only use the former if the role was as long lived as the holder's public key certificate, otherwise you would need to re-issue their public key certificate when the person's role changes.

The management of the privileges assigned to a role, and the assignment of roles can be administered separately by different AAs if this is needed by an organisation. If this is the case, the *role attribute* can indicate which AA is responsible for allocating privileges to the role.

The newly standardised *role attribute* consists of a sequence of two parameters:
- the role authority (optional), that specifies the name of the AA that allocates the privileges to the role. This parameter will only be present if the role authority is different to the AA assigning roles to users,
- the role name, that specifies the name of the role. The values that this parameter can take are decided by the organisation using the PMI.

6. Verifying Privileges

The X.509 privilege control model is shown in Figure 1, and it comprises the following entities:
- the Privilege Asserter (AC holder) invokes some operation/service request (or object method) on a resource (the object being controlled). E.g. issues an electronic order
- the Privilege Verifier makes a yes/no decision as to whether this privilege holder can access this object in this way, based upon
  - o the Privilege Policy that states precisely when the privilege verifier should conclude that a presented set of privileges is "sufficient" in order that it may grant the requested access (to the requested object, resource, application, etc.) to the privilege asserter,
  - o environmental variables, if relevant, that capture other aspects of policy that are configured into the privilege verifier by some private means e.g. the current time of day, current account balances of customers etc.
  - o the privileges (attribute certificates) held by the privilege asserter and/or a directory service/repository,
  - o the revocation lists held in a directory service or other repository.

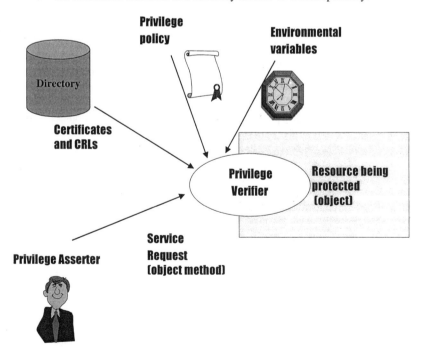

Figure 1. The Privilege Control Model

The privilege verifier needs to have access to the following information before it can verify any claimed privileges:

- the public key of the trusted root CA (this has to be configured into the verifier by some trusted means) so that it can verify signatures on the ACs and PKCs that it will evaluate,
- the name and public key of a trusted SOA, either configured into the verifier by some trusted means or via a public key certificate that can be validated against the root CA's public key, so that the verifier can validate that ACs are issued directly or indirectly by this SOA.
- the policy rules that direct how the verifier can determine that the presented privileges are "sufficient" to access the resource, and how to determine that delegated privileges are less than held privileges (these have to be configured in by some trusted means).
- any local variables used in verifying the claimed privilege e.g. time of day. Again these have to be configured in by some trusted means.
- the attribute certificates of the privilege holder, plus a valid chain back to the SOA, plus the latest revocation information. This information may be obtained from the holder and/or a public directory service. Since the data is digitally signed it cannot be tampered with without detection and therefore does not need to be configured in by trusted means.

One can see that privilege verification is a complex process and involves at least the following steps:

- validating the AC chain back to the SOA, i.e. determining that no AC in the chain has been revoked, that each AA in the chain was allowed to delegate privileges and that the privileges were properly delegated,
- validating all the public keys used to verify the AC chain and the holder's signed request to access the resource. This includes retrieval of all the latest public key CRLs,
- checking that the claimed privilege is valid for this resource at this point in time, by checking any time restrictions, service restrictions and the policy in force,
- checking the privilege against the policy to see if it is sufficient for the mode of access being requested,
- checking the privilege against any local variables such as time of day, or credit balances to see that these are not being exceeded, and finally
- checking that the privilege holder did actually want to exercise the claimed privilege. How this is done is not specified in the standard, but one suggestion is that the request from the privilege holder to the privilege verifier could be digitally signed, and contain the ACs that the holder is wishing to use (or a pointer to them e.g. the AA name and serial number(s) of the AC(s)).

In conclusion, one can see that building a privilege management infrastructure is not a trivial task, but that once it has been built and is in use, we have a very powerful infrastructure for strong authorisation, comparable to that of PKI for authentication.

The EC PERMIS project [4] was one of the first projects to build a functioning X.509 PMI, and information about this can be found in [5][6][7].

References

[1] ITU-T Rec. X.509 (2000) | ISO/IEC 9594-8 The Directory: Authentication Framework

[2] Sandhu, R. and Samarati, P. "Access controls, principles and practice". IEEE Communications, 32(9), pp 40-48, 1994

[3] Sandhu, R.S., Coyne, E.J., Feinstein, H.L., Youman, C.E. "Role Based Access Control Models". IEEE Computer 29, 2 (Feb 1996), p38-43.

[4] The EC PERMIS, see http://www.permis.org and http://sec.isi.salford.ac.uk/permis

[5] D.W.Chadwick, A. Otenko, E.Ball. "Implementing Role Based Access Controls Using X.509 Attribute Certificates", IEEE Internet Computing, March-April 2003, pp. 62-69.

[6] D.W.Chadwick, A. Otenko "The PERMIS X.509 Role Based Privilege Management Infrastructure". Future Generation Computer Systems, 936 (2002) 1–13, December 2002. Elsevier Science BV.

[7] D.W.Chadwick, A. Otenko. "RBAC Policies in XML for X.509 Based Privilege Management" in Security in the Information Society: Visions and Perspectives: IFIP TC11 17th Int. Conf. On Information Security (SEC2002), May 7-9, 2002, Cairo, Egypt. Ed. by M. A. Ghonaimy, M. T. El-Hadidi, H.K.Aslan, Kluwer Academic Publishers, pp 39-53.

Security and Privacy in Advanced Networking Technologies
B. Jerman-Blažič et al. (Eds.)
IOS Press, 2004

Implementing Role Based Access Controls using X.509 Privilege Management - The PERMIS Authorisation Infrastructure

David W CHADWICK, Alexander OTENKO
IS Institute, University of Salford, M5 4WT, England
Email: d.w.chadwick@salford.ac.uk   o.otenko@salford.ac.uk
Telephone: +44 161 295 5351
Fax: +44 161 745 8169

Abstract. This paper describes the PERMIS role based access control infrastructure that uses X.509 attribute certificates (ACs) to store the users' roles. Users' roles can be assigned by multiple widely distributed management authorities (called Attribute Authorities in X.509), thereby easing the burden of management. All the ACs can be stored in one or more LDAP directories, thus making them widely available. The PERMIS distribution includes a Privilege Allocator GUI tool, and a bulk loader tool, that allow administrators to construct and sign ACs and store them in an LDAP directory ready for use by the PERMIS decision engine. All access control decisions are driven by an authorization policy, which is itself stored in an X.509 AC, thus guaranteeing its integrity and trustworthiness. Authorization policies are written in XML according to a DTD that has been published at XML.org. A user friendly policy management tool is also being built that will allow non-technical managers to easily specify PERMIS authorisation policies. The access control decision engine is written in Java and has both a Java API and SAML-SOAP interface, allowing it to be called either locally or remotely. The Java API is simple to use, comprising of just 3 methods and a constructor. The SAML-SOAP interface conforms to the OASIS SAMLv1.1 specification, as profiled by a Global Grid Forum draft standard, thus making PERMIS suitable as an authorisation server for Grid applications.

1. Introduction to X.509 PMIs

Most people familiar with PKIs will know that the standard format for a public key certificate is specified in the X.509 standard [14], published jointly by the ITU-T and ISO/IEC. The primary purpose of a PKI is to strongly authenticate the parties communicating with each other, though the use of digital signatures. But strong authentication on its own is insufficient for a process to determine who is allowed to do what. An authorisation mechanism is needed for this. Edition 4 of X.509 is the first edition of X.509 to fully standardise a strong authorisation mechanism, which it calls a Privilege Management Infrastructure (PMI). PMIs provide the authorisation function after the authentication has taken place, and have a number of similarities with PKIs. This paper assumes the reader is already familiar with the general concepts of PKIs, and these will not be repeated here. Readers wishing to learn more about PKIs may consult texts such as [1] or [12].

The primary data structure in a PMI is an X.509 Attribute Certificate (AC) (see Figure 1.) This strongly binds a set of attributes to its holder, and these attributes are used to describe the various privileges of the holder bestowed on it by the issuer. The issuer is termed an Attribute Authority (AA), since it is the authoritative provider of the attributes given to the holder. Examples of attributes and issuers might be: a degree awarded by a university, an ISO

9000 certificate issued by a QA compliance organisation, the role of supervisor issued by a manager, file access permissions issued by a file's owner. The whole data construct is digitally signed by the AA, thereby providing data integrity and authentication of the issuer.

Figure 1. Attribute Certificate

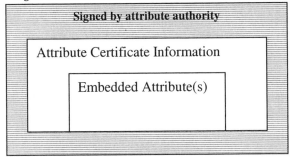

The attributes are embedded within the Attribute Certificate Information data construct (see Figure 2). This contains details of the holder, the issuer, the algorithms used in creating the signature on the AC, the AC validity time and various optional extensions. Anyone familiar with the contents of an X.509 public key certificate (PKC) will immediately see the similarities between a PKC and an AC. In essence the public key of a PKC has been replaced by a set of attributes. (In this respect a public key certificate can be seen to be a specialisation of a more general attribute certificate.) Because the AC is digitally signed by the issuer, then any process in possession of an AC can check its integrity by checking the digital signature on the AC. Thus a PMI builds upon and complements existing PKIs.

Figure 2. Attribute Certificate Info

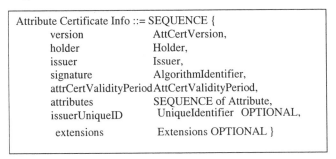

Since a PMI is to authorisation what a PKI is to authentication, there are many other similar concepts between PKIs and PMIs. Whilst public key certificates are used to maintain a strong binding between a user's name and his public key, an attribute certificate (AC) maintains a strong binding between a user's name and one or more privilege attributes. The entity that digitally signs a public key certificate is called a Certification Authority (CA), whilst the entity that signs an attribute certificate is called an Attribute Authority (AA). Within a PKI, each relying party must have one or more roots of trust. These are CAs who the relying party implicitly trusts to authenticate other entities. They are sometimes called root CAs1 or trust anchors. Popular Web browsers come pre-configured with over 50 PKI roots of trust. The root of trust of a PMI is called the Source of Authority (SOA). This is an entity that a resource implicity trusts to allocate privileges and access rights to it. The SOA is ultimately responsible

---

[1] Unfortunately early versions of X.509 did not standardise the term root CA or any term for the root of trust. Because of this, disparate meanings for the term "root CA" have now evolved.

for issuing ACs to trusted holders, and these can be either end users or subordinate AAs. Just as CAs may have subordinate CAs to which they delegate the powers of authentication and certification, similarly, SOAs may have subordinate AAs to which they delegate their powers of authorisation and attribute assigning. For example, in an organisation the Finance Director might be the SOA for allocating the privilege of spending company money. But (s)he might also delegate this privilege to departmental managers (subordinate AAs) who can then allocate specific spending privileges (ACs) to project leaders.

When a problem occurs in a PKI, a user might need to have his signing key revoked, and so a CA might issue a certificate revocation list (CRL) containing the list of PKCs no longer to be trusted. Similarly if a PMI user needs to have his authorisation permissions revoked, an AA may issue an attribute certificate revocation list (ACRL) containing the list of ACs no longer to be trusted. The similarities between PKIs and PMIs are summarised in Table 1.

Table 1. A Comparison of PKIs and PMIs

Concept	PKI entity	PMI entity
Certificate	Public Key Certificate (PKC)	Attribute Certificate (AC)
Certificate issuer	Certification Authority (CA)	Attribute Authority (AA)
Certificate user	Subject	Holder
Certificate binding	Subject's Name to Public Key	Holder's Name to Privilege Attribute(s)
Revocation	Certificate Revocation List (CRL)	Attribute Certificate Revocation List (ACRL)
Root of trust	Root Certification Authority or Trust Anchor	Source of Authority (SOA)
Subordinate authority	Subordinate Certification Authority	Attribute Authority (AA)

Further details about X.509 PMIs can be found in [17].

2. Implementing RBAC with X.509

Recent research has focussed on Role Based Access Controls (RBAC) [22] [11], culminating in the publication of RBAC as an American National Standard (ANSI INCITS 359-2004) in February 2004. In the basic RBAC model, a number of roles are defined. These roles typically represent organisational roles such as secretary, manager, employee etc. In the authorisation policy, each role is given a set of permissions i.e. the ability to perform certain actions on certain targets. Each user is then assigned to one or more roles. When accessing a target, a user presents his role(s), and the target reads the policy to see if this role is allowed to perform this action. RBAC has the advantage of scalability over traditional discretionary access control (DAC) schemes such as access control lists (ACLs), and can easily handle large numbers of users as there are typically far fewer roles than users.

X.509 supports simple RBAC by defining role specification attribute certificates that hold the permissions granted to each role, and role assignment attribute certificates that assign various roles to the users. In the former case, the AC holder is the role, and the privilege attributes are permissions granted to the role. In the latter case the AC holder is the user, and the privilege attributes are the roles assigned to the user.

The hierarchical RBAC model is a more sophisticated version of the basic RBAC model. With this model, the roles are organised hierarchically, and the senior roles inherit the privileges of the more junior roles. So for example we might have the following hierarchy:

employee > programmer > manager > director.

If a privilege is given to an employee role e.g. can enter main building, then each of the superior roles can also enter the main building even though their role specification does not explicitly state this. If a programmer is given permission to enter the computer building, then managers and directors would also inherit this permission. Hierarchical roles mean that role specifications are more compact. X.509 supports hierarchical RBAC by allowing both roles and privileges to be inserted as attributes in a role specification attribute certificate, so that the latter role inherits the privileges of the encapsulated roles.

Another extension to basic RBAC is constrained RBAC. This allows various constraints to be applied to the role and permission assignments. One common constraint is that certain roles are declared to be mutually exclusive, meaning that the same person cannot simultaneously hold more than one role from the mutually exclusive set. For example, the roles of student and examiner, or the roles of tenderer (one who submits a tender) and tender officer (one who opens submitted tenders) would both be examples of mutually exclusive sets. Another constraint might be placed on the number of roles a person can hold, or the number of people who can hold a particular role. X.509 only has a limited number of ways of supporting constrained RBAC. Time constraints can be placed on the validity period of a role assignment attribute certificate. Constraints can be placed on the targets at which a role can be used, and on the policies under which an attribute certificate can confer privileges. Constraints can also be placed on the delegation of roles. However many of the constraints, such as the mutual exclusivity of roles, have to be enforced by mechanisms outside the attribute certificate construct e.g. within the policy enforcement function.

Of course, every target that relies on X.509 ACs to confer privileges, also needs to be configured with a policy, or a set of rules, that will tell it which access methods are to be granted by which privileges. Unfortunately X.509 does not standardise any type of policy and leaves this up to the applications using the X.509 PMI. This is one of the biggest challenges for anyone deciding to build an X.509 PMI.

3. The PERMIS PMI Architecture

The PERMIS PMI is, according to Blaze's definition in RFC 2704 [3], a trust management system. Consequently it must have the following five components:

i)   A language for describing `actions', which are operations with security consequences that are to be controlled by the system.

ii)   A mechanism for identifying `principals', which are entities that can be authorized to perform actions.

iii)   A language for specifying application `policies', which govern the actions that principals are authorized to perform.

iv)   A language for specifying `credentials', which allow principals to delegate authorization to other principals.

v)   A `compliance checker', which provides a service to applications for determining how an action requested by principals should be handled, given a policy and a set of credentials.

X.509 attribute certificates specify mechanisms for ii) and iv). Principals are the holders and issuers of ACs and can be identified by their X.500 General Name (usually an X.500/LDAP distinguished name (DN) [16], IP address, URI or email address) or by reference to their public key certificate (issuer name and serial number) or if the principal is a software object by a hash of itself. Credentials are specified as X.500 attributes, which comprise an attribute type and value. Defining the policy (iii) and action (i) languages were significant tasks of the PERMIS project [5], as was building a privilege allocation subsystem that creates X.509 ACs, and a compliance checker (v) that validates them.

4. Defining the Policy Language

The authorisation policy needs to specify who is to be granted which roles, and what types of action on which targets are to be granted to the roles (optionally under which conditions). Domain wide policy authorisation is far more preferable than having separate access control lists configured into each target. The latter is hard to manage, duplicates the effort of the administrators (since the task has to be repeated for each target), and is less secure since it is very difficult to keep track of which access rights any particular user has across the whole domain. Policy based authorisation on the other hand allows the domain administrator (the SOA) to specify the authorisation policy for the whole domain, and all targets will then be controlled by the same set of rules.

Significant research has already taken place in defining authorisation policy languages. The Ponder language [7] is very compact and very powerful, but does not have a large set of supporting tools. The Keynote policy language [3] is also very comprehensive and covers many of our requirements, but is focussed on DAC rather than RBAC. Also, the policy assertions are very generic and are not related specifically to X.509. For example, the authoriser and licensees fields are opaque strings whereas we wanted them to have structure and meaning. Further, it does not seem to be possible to control the depth of delegation allowed from one authoriser to a subordinate. Finally, the syntax, comprising of ASCII strings and keywords, is specific to Keynote. The PERMIS project wanted to specify the authorisation policy in a well-known language that could be both easily parsed by computers, and read by the SOAs (with or without software tools). We decided that XML was a good candidate for a policy specification language, since there are lots of tools around that support XML, it is fast becoming an industry standard, and raw XML can be read and understood by many technical people. Shortly after we started our work, Bertino et al published a paper [2] that showed that XML was indeed suitable for specifying authorisation policies. Later, the OASIS consortium began work on the eXtensible Access Control Markup Language (XACML) [18], and this is now an OASIS standard for specifying policies.

We needed a language tailored to X.509 and RBAC, so we specified a Data Type Definition (DTD)2 for our X.500 PMI RBAC Policy. The DTD is a meta-language that holds the rules for creating the XML policies. Our DTD comprises the following components:

- RBAC Policy – this specifies the unique number for the policy, using a globally unique Object Identifiers (OID)
- SubjectPolicy – this specifies the subject domains i.e. only users from a subject domain may be authorised to access resources covered by the policy
- RoleHierarchyPolicy – this specifies the different roles and their hierarchical relationships to each other
- SOAPolicy – this specifies which SOAs are trusted to allocate roles. By including more than one SOA in this policy, the local SOA is effectively cross certifying remote authorisation domains
- RoleAssignmentPolicy – this specifies which roles may be allocated to which subjects by which SOAs, whether delegation of roles may take place or not, and how long the roles may be assigned for

---

[2] We used a DTD rather than an XML schema, since XML schemas were still under development when we started our work, and few tools were available to support schemas. We are currently migrating towards the use of an XML schema.

- TargetPolicy – this specifies the target domains covered by this policy
- ActionPolicy – this specifies the actions (or methods) supported by the targets, along with the parameters that should be passed along with each action e.g. action Open with parameter Filename
- TargetAccessPolicy – this specifies which roles have permission to perform which actions on which targets, and under which conditions. Conditions are specified using Boolean logic and might contain constraints such as "IF time is GT 9am AND time is LT 5pm OR IF Calling IP address is a subset of 125.67.x.x". All actions that are not specified in a Target Access Policy are denied.

A full description of the PERMIS X.500 PMI RBAC policy can be found in [4]. The policy DTD has been published by XML.ORG (http://www.xml.org) and is also available from our web site at http://sec.isi.salford.ac.uk/permis/Policy.dtd.

Table 2. The Role Assignment DTD

```
<!ELEMENT RoleAssignmentPolicy (RoleAssignment)+ >
<!ELEMENT RoleAssignment  (SubjectDomain,Role,Delegate,SOA,Validity) >

<!ELEMENT SubjectDomain EMPTY>
<!ATTLIST SubjectDomain ID IDREF #REQUIRED>

<!ELEMENT Role EMPTY >
<!ATTLIST Role Type IDREF #IMPLIED
            Value IDREF #IMPLIED >

<!ELEMENT SOA EMPTY>
<!ATTLIST SOA ID IDREF #REQUIRED>

<!ELEMENT Validity (Absolute?, Maximum?, Minimum? ) >
<!ELEMENT Absolute EMPTY>
<!ATTLIST Absolute Start CDATA #IMPLIED
            End CDATA #IMPLIED >
<!ELEMENT Maximum EMPTY>
<!ATTLIST Maximum Time CDATA #IMPLIED >
<!ELEMENT Minimum EMPTY>
<!ATTLIST Minimum Time CDATA #IMPLIED >

<!ELEMENT Delegate EMPTY >
<!ATTLIST Delegate Depth CDATA #IMPLIED >
```

Table 2 shows a portion of the DTD that specifies the rules for the Role Assignment Policy, and Table 3 it is an example Role Assignment Policy for an electronic tendering application built by Salford City Council.

Table 3. An Example Role Assignment Policy

```
<RoleAssignmentPolicy>
  <RoleAssignment>
<!-- Role assignment for tender officers.
They must be employees of Salford City Council.  Valid only from close of tender.
Delegation not permitted -->
        <SubjectDomain ID="Employees"/>
    <Role Type="permisRole" Value="TenderOfficer"/>
    <Delegate Depth="0"/>
    <SOA ID="Salford"/>
    <Validity>
      <Absolute Start="2001-09-21T17:00:00"/>
    </Validity>
  </RoleAssignment>
  <RoleAssignment>
<!-- Role assignment for tenderers.
They must be dot com or co.uk companies.  Valid only until close of tender.
Delegation not permitted -->
        <SubjectDomain ID="Companies"/>
    <Role Type="permisRole" Value="Tenderer"/>
    <Delegate Depth="0"/>
    <SOA ID="Salford"/>
    <Validity>
      <Absolute End="2001-09-21T17:00:00"/>
    </Validity>
  </RoleAssignment>
  <RoleAssignment>
<!-- Role assignment for companies who are ISO9000 Certified.
They must be dot com or co.uk companies.  Valid only for a maximum of one year, as
companies have to be annually re-accredited. Certificates are issued by BSI.
Delegation not permitted -->
        <SubjectDomain ID="Companies"/>
    <Role Type="ISOCertified" Value="ISO9000"/>
    <Delegate Depth="0"/>
    <SOA ID="BSI"/>
    <Validity>
      <Maximum Time="+01"/>
    </Validity>
  </RoleAssignment>
</RoleAssignmentPolicy>
```

The SOA creates the XML authorisation policy for the target domain and stores this in a local file, say MyPolicy.XML. This will be used later by the Privilege Allocator tool to create the policy AC. However, creating XML files using generic XML editors such as IBM's Xeena, or text editors such as Notepad, is not intuitively easy, especially for non-technical managers. Consequently we are currently working on a joint project between the University of Salford and UCL to create a user-friendly graphical interface (GUI) to allow non-technical managers to easily create PERMIS policies. A screen shot from this is shown in Figure 3 below.

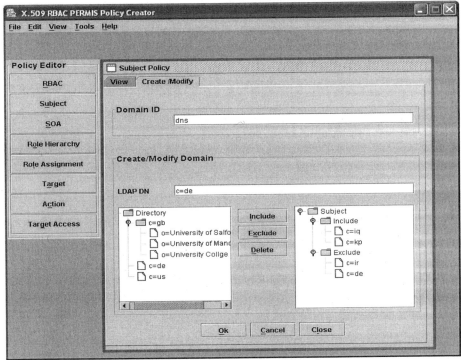

Figure 3. A screenshot from the PERMIS Policy Management GUI tool

4.1 Storing the policy

Policies are stored as digitally-signed authorisation policies, in a X.509 policy ACs. The policy AC is a standard X.509 AC with the following special characteristics: the holder and issuer names are the same (i.e. that of the policy issuer SOA), the attribute type is pmiXMLPolicy and the attribute value is the XML policy created as described above. The policy AC is signed by the root of trust of the PMI, and is similar to the self-signed public key certificate of the root CA of a PKI. Policy ACs are created using the Privilege Allocator (PA) tool (see later). The PA prompts the SOA for the name of the policy file (e.g. MyPolicy.XML) and then it copies the contents into the attribute value. After the SOA has signed the policy AC, the PA stores it in the SOA's entry in the LDAP directory. Each authorisation policy is given an Object Identifier [13], which is a globally unique number. This ensures that the PERMIS API (see later) always runs with the correct policy for the domain.

5. Role Assignment

A role in PERMIS is simply defined as an attribute type and value. We usually use the attribute type permisRole whose values are IA5 strings. Administrators (SOAs or AAs) can then put any value in the IA5 string to identify a specific role. Note however that there will have to be negotiation between the role allocating SOAs and the target site SOA to ensure they use exactly the same attributes for the same roles. This is one reason that the Internet2 consortium has defined the EduPerson LDAP object class [23], so that all universities can use the same attribute types and values to mean the same things.

PERMIS provides two tools for assigning roles to individuals: the Privilege Allocation (PA) graphical user interface tool, and the bulk loader tool. The PA allows an administrator (SOA or AA) to assign one or more attributes (roles) to an individual, to digitally sign the encompassing AC, and then store the AC in the user's entry in an LDAP directory (see Figure 4). The bulk loader comprises a Java API and a sample program which searches an LDAP directory for entries that have a particular object class. For each retrieved LDAP entry, the sample program assigns a particular attribute to its Distinguished Name (DN), then calls the Java API which embeds the attribute in an X.509 AC, signs the AC using the private key of the SOA, and stores the AC in the entry of the given DN. In this way every person, e.g. student, manager, accountant etc. can be automatically assigned different role ACs.

In real life, role assignment can only be done by an authorised person. For example, allocating the role of professor to an academic may be decided by a university appointment's panel and the chair of the panel may inform the Registrar's department to assign the role to a particular individual. In the electronic world, the Registrar would need to issue and digitally sign an X.509 AC to the individual containing the professor role attribute. Within a university department, the head of school may assign the role Undergraduate Course Leader to a member of staff, and similarly issue an X.509 AC to this individual. The X.509 AC always provides the name of the assigning person (the AA), and this is bound to the AC through his/her digital signature, thus X.509 ACs cannot easily be forged.

In PERMIS, anyone is allowed to run the PA or bulk loader tools, i.e. to issue role ACs, but only authorised individuals will be trusted by the PERMIS decision engine, according to the PERMIS trust model (see later). Since all the ACs are digitally signed by their assigning authorities, the PERMIS decision engine can easily determine trusted ACs from non-trusted ACs. Since ACs are digitally signed by the AA which issued them, they are tamper-resistant, and therefore there is no modification risk from allowing them to be stored in a publicly accessible LDAP directory. This also means that authorities who issue digital ACs can store them locally, but give global access to them (just as they might for X.509 public key certificates).

The attribute certificate revocation lists (ACRLs) of revoked certificates (if any), also need to be stored in a publicly accessible place, such as the local LDAP directory, so that relying parties can have easy access to them. Thus there is little advantage in general of distributing the ACs to their holders, rather than keeping them centrally stored in an LDAP directory, since a relying party will still need to access the issuing authorities LDAP directory in order to retrieve the latest ACRL. On the other hand, if the ACs are not distributed to their holders, but are retained in the local LDAP directory, then there is no need for ACRLs to be issued, since the administrator simply needs to delete a user's ACs from their entry in order to "revoke" the AC. We thus believe that the so called "pull" model for AC retrieval [10], where ACs are fetched by PERMIS from various LDAP directories, rather than the user pushing them to PERMIS from his PC, is the simplest model for managing ACs, and the most efficient for decision making, since ACRLs are not needed.

As can be seen, the PERMIS infrastructure supports distributed authorisation management, in which different sites can run the PA and/or bulk loader tools and allocate ACs to their users and store them in their local LDAP directories. This will significantly ease the management of privileges in large distributed environments, such as GRID networks, Internet marketplaces etc, as the policy governing access to target resources only needs to tell the PERMIS API which LDAP directories to contact and which remote SOAs to trust.

We see that this mechanism can be extended to any type of attribute or role certification e.g. Microsoft Certified Engineer, BSc (Hons) University of Salford etc. and that these "roles" can easily be built into PERMIS via the authorisation policy. We have already used this mechanism in an electronic prescribing system that we built [9], to allow the Royal College of Pharmacy to allocate pharmacist roles to qualified pharmacists, and the General Medical Council to allocate doctor roles to qualified doctors.

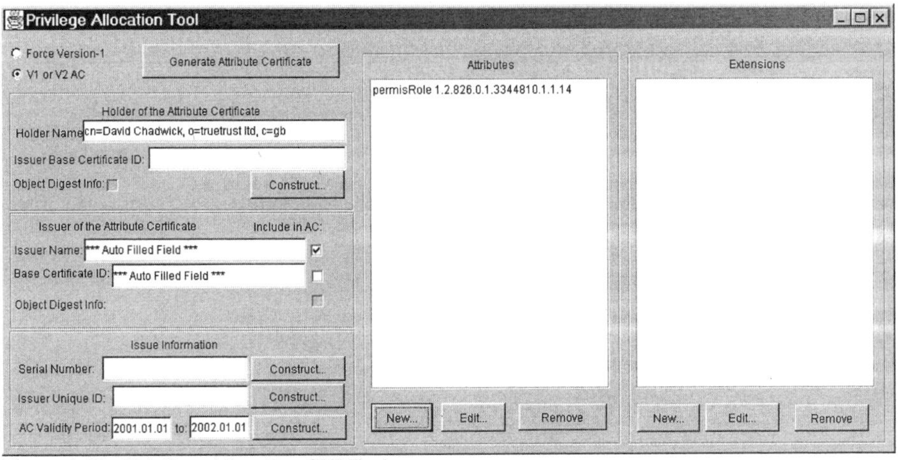

Figure 4. The Privilege Allocation GUI Tool

6. The PERMIS Decision Engine

An application gateway (see Figure 5) is responsible for authenticating and authorising remote users and providing access to targets. The ISO 10181-3 Access Control Framework [15], splits the functionality of the application gateway into two components: an application-specific component termed the Access Control Enforcement Function (AEF), and an application-independent component termed the Access Control Decision Function (ADF). In this way, all access controls decisions in a domain can be consistently enforced by the ADF independent of the application. The ADF makes its decisions based on the authorisation policy for the domain, on who is initiating a request, what action is being requested on which target, and environmental factors such as the time of day. The PERMIS decision engine is an implementation of an ADF.

The AEF and ADF can be interconnected via either a local application programmable interface (API) for local invocation, or via a communications protocol for remote invocation.

An API between the AEF and ADF has already been defined by the Open Group. It is called the AZN API [19], and is specified in the C language. A similar API is also being developed by the IETF, called the Generic Authorization and Access control (GAA) API [21]. PERMIS has drawn on the work of the Open Group in order to specify the PERMIS API in Java. This is described in the following section.

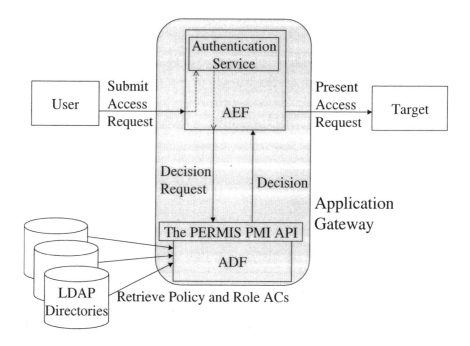

Figure 5. The PERMIS Application Gateway

The OASIS group has defined the SAML protocol [6] as a standard protocol for invoking authorisation decision requests from a remote ADF service. In 2003 we started to work with the Global Grid Forum to produce a profile of SAML for use by Grid applications. This profile [8] has in fact identified a number of deficiencies in the standard SAMLv1.1 protocol, and has defined a few extensions to it. The resulting protocol has now been implemented by PERMIS, and this will allow the PERMIS ADF to run as a stand-alone service. The protocol is also shortly to be incorporated into Globus Toolkit V3, thus allowing grid applications to invoke PERMIS to make authorisation decisions on its behalf.

6.1 User Authentication

In order to get through the application gateway, each user needs to be issued with an application specific authentication token acceptable to the gateway. If a PKI is being used, this will be a digitally signed public key certificate. If a conventional authentication system is being used it will be a username/password pair. Alternatively, the application gateway may support Kerberos authentication, one-time password authentication, biometric authentication or any other scheme. The PERMIS API has been designed to be authentication agnostic. PERMIS simply trusts the calling application gateway to have performed authentication of the user to its own satisfaction. All that PERMIS requires is that the application gateway pass to PERMIS the authenticated LDAP DN of the user. PERMIS will then use this to retrieve the user's X.509 ACs, on which to make its authorisation decisions.

To summarise, in the PERMIS model, a user accesses resources via an application gateway. The AEF authenticates the user in an application specific way, then asks the PERMIS ADF if the user is allowed to perform the requested action on the particular target resource. The PERMIS ADF accesses one or more LDAP directories to retrieve the policy AC and the role ACs for the user, and bases its decision on these. If the decision is grant, the AEF will access the target on behalf of the user. If the decision is deny, the AEF will refuse access to the user. The AEF talks to the PERMIS ADF via either the PERMIS Java API or the GGF SAML protocol.

7. The PERMIS Java API

The PERMIS Java API comprises 2 simple methods: GetCreds, and Decision, and a Constructor. The Constructor builds the PERMIS API Java object. For construction, the AEF passes the name of the SOA (the root of trust for target authorisation), the Object Identifier of the policy to be used, and a list of LDAP URIs from where the ADF can retrieve the policy AC and subsequently the role ACs. The policy AC is always retrieved from the SOA's entry in the LDAP directory pointed to by the first URI in the list. The Constructor is usually called just once, whilst the AEF starts up. After construction of the API has completed, the PERMIS ADF will have read in and validated the XML of the authorisation policy that will control all future decisions that it makes.

When a user initiates a call to the target, the AEF authenticates the user, then passes the LDAP DN [16] of the user to the PERMIS ADF through a call to GetCreds. In pilot services users have been authenticated in different ways. In an e-tendering application, the user sent an S/MIME email message to the AEF; in an e-planning application, the user opened an SSL connection using an X.509 client certificate.

In all cases the authentication yielded the user's LDAP DN. The PERMIS ADF uses this DN to retrieve all the role ACs of the user from the list of LDAP URIs passed at initialisation time (this is termed the "pull" model [10]). The role ACs are validated against the policy e.g. to check that the DN is within a valid subject domain, and to check that the ACs are within the validity time of the policy etc. Invalid role ACs are discarded, whilst the roles from the valid ACs are extracted and kept for the user, and returned to the AEF as a subject object. (The GetCreds interface also supports the "push" model [10] (called user-pull by Park et al [20]), whereby the AEF can push a set of ACs to the ADF, instead of the ADF pulling them from the LDAP directories, but since our ADF currently does not retrieve ACRLs, this mechanism is unused at present).

Once the user has been successfully authenticated he will attempt to perform certain actions on the target. At each attempt, the AEF passes the subject object, the target name, and the attempted action along with its parameters, to the PERMIS ADF via a call to Decision. Decision checks if the action is allowed for the roles that the user has, taking into account all the conditions specified in the TargetAccessPolicy. If the action is allowed, Decision returns Granted, if it is not allowed it returns Denied. The user may attempt an arbitrary number of actions on different targets, and Decision is called for each one. In order to stop the user keeping the connection open for an infinite amount of time (for example until after his ACs have expired), the PERMIS API supports the concept of a session time out. On the call to GetCreds the AEF can say how long the session may stay open before the credentials should be refreshed. If the session times out, then Decision will throw an exception, telling the AEF to either close the user's connection or call GetCreds again.

The AEF can stop using a particular ADF at any time, for example if circumstances dictate that the authorisation policy should be changed. If the AEF invokes a new PERMIS ADF constructor, standard Java garbage collection will delete the old ADF. This can happen, say, if the SOA wants to dynamically impose a new authorisation policy on the domain. The AEF can invoke a new Constructor call, and this will cause the ADF to read in the latest authorisation policy and be ready to make access control decisions again based on this.

8. The PERMIS Trust Model

The PERMIS trust model has a single trusted root of authority, from which all other trust is inherited. When the PERMIS ADF is initialised, it is passed the name of the SOA for the target (the root of trust), the unique OID of the policy to use, and a list of LDAP URIs to access. This allows the PERMIS ADF to fetch the policy AC from the SOA's entry stored in the LDAP directory pointed to by the first LDAP URI in the list. PERMIS checks the digital signature on this policy AC, and if it does not correspond to that of the SOA, then the policy is not to be trusted and it is discarded. If the policy AC has been signed by the SOA, then it is trusted, and its embedded unique OID is compared to that passed at initialisation time. If they are the same, this confirms that the correct policy is being used.

Inside the policy is the SOAPolicy. This gives a list of remote SOAs and AAs to be trusted to allocate role ACs to users. Further, the RoleAssignmentPolicy states which attributes/roles these SOAs and AAs are trusted to issue. Attributes not in this policy will be discarded by PERMIS at decision time. Also the RoleAssignmentPolicy says which subjects these attributes can be assigned to. This ensures that remote SOAs do not allocate roles to wrong groups of users. However, the remote SOAs are trusted to, and expected to, authenticate the subjects prior to issuing them with role ACs. In this way the PERMIS ADF can be assured that all the roles it uses in its decision making have been assigned according to the policy, and are trusted.

Finally, the policy AC says what access rights are given to each role. The PERMIS ADF makes decisions according to this, and the AEF trusts PERMIS to make the correct decisions.

9. Conclusion

We have shown how the standard X.509 PMI can be adapted to build an efficient role based trust management system, in which the role assignments can be widely distributed between organisations, and the local authorisation policy determines which roles are trusted and what privileges are to be given to them. The PERMIS authorisation policy governs all aspects of access to the targets in the local domain. The PERMIS authorisation policy is written in XML and the DTD has been published by XML.ORG. A user friendly policy management GUI is being built that will allow non-technical managers to easily create PERMIS policies.

PERMIS provides an authorisation decision engine which determines which users are allowed to perform which actions, based on the authorisation policy and the X.509 role ACs allocated to the users. Two tools are provided for allocating role ACs and storing them in LDAP directories: a graphical Privilege Allocator tool and a bulk loading tool.

A simple Java API and SAML interface are provided which allow applications to easily incorporate the PERMIS decision engine as either their local or remote authorisation decision making machine. A public release of PERMIS is available for educational and research use from our web site (http://sec.isi.salford.ac.uk/permis).

Acknowledgments

This initial PERMIS project was 50% funded by the EC ISIS programme, and partially funded by the EPSRC under grant number GR/M83483. The SAML interface and the GUI policy management tool are being funded by JISC. The authors would also like to thank Entrust Inc. for making their PKI security software available to the University on preferential terms.

References

[1] Adams, C., Lloyd, S. (1999). "Understanding Public-Key Infrastructure: Concepts, Standards, and Deployment Considerations". Macmillan Technical Publishing, 1999.

[2] Bertino, E., Castano, S., Farrari, E. "On specifying security policies for web documents with an XML-based language". Proceedings of the Sixth ACM Symposium on Access control models and technologies 2001, available from ACM digital library.

[3] Blaze, M., Feigenbaum, J., Ioannidis, J. "The KeyNote Trust-Management System Version 2", RFC 2704, September 1999.

[4] D.W.Chadwick, A. Otenko. "RBAC Policies in XML for X.509 Based Privilege Management" in Security in the Information Society: Visions and Perspectives: IFIP TC11 17th Int. Conf. On Information Security (SEC2002), May 7-9, 2002, Cairo, Egypt. Ed. by M. A. Ghonaimy, M. T. El-Hadidi, H.K.Aslan, Kluwer Academic Publishers, pp 39-53.

[5] D.W.Chadwick, A. Otenko. "The PERMIS X.509 Role Based Privilege Management Infrastructure", Proc 7th ACM Symposium On Access Control Models And Technologies (SACMAT 2002), Monterey, USA, June 2002. pp135-140.

[6] "OASIS eXtensible Access Control Markup Language (XACML)" v1.0, 12 Dec 2002, available from http://www.oasis-open.org/committees/xacml/.
OASIS. "Assertions and Protocol for the OASIS Security Assertion Markup Language (SAML)". 19 April 2002. See http://www.oasis-open.org/committees/security/.

[7] Damianou, N., Dulay, N., Lupu, E., Sloman, M. "The Ponder Policy Specification Language", Proc Policy 2001, Workshop on Policies for Distributed Systems and Networks, Bristol, UK 29-31 Jan 2001, Springer-Verlag LNCS 1995, pp 18-39.

[8] Von Welch, Frank Siebenlist, David Chadwick, Sam Meder, Laura Pearlman. "Use of SAML for OGSA Authorization", Jan 2004, Available from https://forge.gridforum.org/projects/ogsa-authz.

[9] D.W.Chadwick, D.Mundy. "Policy Based Electronic Transmission of Prescriptions". Proc of Fourth IEEE Int Workshop on Policies for Distributed Systems and Networks, Lake Como, Italy, 4-6 June 2003, p197-206.

[10] Farrell, S., Housley, R. "An Internet Attribute Certificate Profile for Authorization", RFC 3281, April 2002.

[11] Sandhu, R., Ferraiolo D., Kuhn, R. "The NIST Model for Role Based Access Control: Towards a Unified Standard". In proceedings of 5th ACM Workshop on Role-Based Access Control, pages 47-63. (Berlin, Germany, July 2000).

[12] Housley, R., Polk, T. "Planning for PKI: Best Practices Guide for Deploying Public Key Infrastructure". John Wiley and Son, ISBN: 0-471-39702-4, 2001.

[13] ITU-T Recommendation X.680 (1997) | ISO/IEC 8824-1:1998, Information Technology - Abstract Syntax Notation One (ASN.1): Specification of Basic Notation.

[14] ISO 9594-8/ITU-T Rec. X.509 (2001) The Directory: Public-key and attribute certificate frameworks.

[15] ITU-T Rec X.812 (1995) | ISO/IEC 10181-3:1996 "Security Frameworks for open systems: Access control framework".

[16] Wahl, M., Kille, S., Howes, T. "Lightweight Directory Access Protocol (v3): UTF-8 String Representation of Distinguished Names", RFC2253, December 1997.

[17] D.W.Chadwick, "The X.509 Privilege Management Infrastructure" in Proceedings of the NATO Advanced Networking Workshop on Advanced Security Technologies in Networking, Bled, Slovenia, June 2003.

[18] "OASIS eXtensible Access Control Markup Language (XACML)" v1.0, February 2003, available from http://www.oasis-open.org/committees/tc_home.php?wg_abbrev=xacml.

[19] The Open Group. "Authorization (AZN) API", January 2000, ISBN 1-85912-266-3

[20] Park, J.S., Sandhu, R., Ahn,G. "Role-Based Access Control on the Web", ACM Transactions on Information and Systems Security, Vol 4. No1, Feb 2001, pp 37-71.

[21] Ryutov, T., Neuman, C., Pearlman, L. "Generic Authorization and Access control Application Program Interface C-bindings" <draft-ietf-cat-gaa-cbind-05.txt>, November 2000. See http://www.isi.edu/gost/info/gaaapi/.

[22] Sandhu, R.S., Coyne, E.J., Feinstein, H.L., Youman, C.E. "Role Based Access Control Models". IEEE Computer 29, 2 (Feb 1996), p38-43.

[23] See http://www.educause.edu/eduperson/.

40

Security and Privacy in Advanced Networking Technologies
B. Jerman-Blažič et al. (Eds.)
IOS Press, 2004

Simplifying PKI Usage through a Client-Server Architecture and Dynamic Propagation of Certificate Paths and Repository Addresses[1]

Brian HUNTER

Fraunhofer Institute for Secure Telecooperation,
Dolivostraße 15, 64293 Darmstadt, Germany

Abstract. PKI deployment and use has not met its expectations. One reason that PKIX has not been fully accepted is due to the complexity of the system. Any application wishing to use PKI must implement complicated logic for certificate parsing, certificate path building and policy management. Certificate path building, in particular, is further complicated by the non-standardized method of certificate discovery and retrieval. Thus, many applications do not utilize or cannot utilize public key technology. We propose a new PKI Server which offers access to PKI services and only requires a simple Client API and a small Client library that enables even resource-limited clients to be supported. This can greatly reduce application development time and complexity and allow PKI usage to propagate into more applications. Furthermore, we introduce the concept of a PKI Server-to-Server Protocol which allows knowledge of certificate repositories and certificate paths to be shared among different PKI Servers. This technique will simplify the task of certificate retrieval and path building for individual PKI Servers.

Introduction

PKI is the model that was supposed to link together global security infrastructures and allow seamless secure communication between any two entities. This idea dates back to Diffie and Hellman who envisioned that the complexities of key distribution would be solved by publicly available public keys instead of shared secret keys. To some extent PKI has solved this problem, however PKI has also created separate islands of key distribution areas. This is caused by businesses and organizations setting up their own private PKIs to allow key management within their organization. Without a central root certificate authority (CA), these islands were not able to be interconnected and inter-organizational communication was hampered.

Several methods have been introduced to solve this lack of connectivity including cross-certification [7] and Bridge Certification Authorities [11]. These methods have helped to interconnect disparate PKIs, however they have introduced another layer to the PKI system and further complicated its use. We believe two main reasons why widespread PKI adoption has faltered are the disconnected nature of organizational PKIs and the complexity

---

of the system. The former reason is being alleviated by the trials and adoption of the aforementioned cross-certification and Bridge CAs. However, this has further compounded the complexity needed for a client or application to make use of PKI. Furthermore, with the introduction of cross-certification connectors, it further removes a user and the certificate she wants to use. It makes the problem of finding the repository containing the certificate she wants to use more difficult even when she knows the subject DN or issuer DN of the desired certificate. The question remains, how can one find the repository where a certificate is stored?

We propose that as the PKIX standard currently stands, it is not feasible for organizational clients to find and build arbitrary certificate paths. Once an organization grows beyond a closed communication circle including only specified partners, the task of configuring all clients with every new repository becomes prohibitive. Therefore, we have one goal to achieve, simplify PKIX by removing the arduous task of certificate discovery. We propose a PKI Server [2] which amalgamates the complexities of PKI away from the client. Although this does not solve the inherent difficulty of certificate discovery, it does simplify the administrative task of configuration since only one central server needs to be configured with all needed repositories instead of needing to configure every client application.

We have focused on the goal of simplifying the task of a client (or application) using a PKI. Currently, a client needs to be aware of several protocols, such as LDAP [3], OCSP [9], and be able to do complex path processing before it is able to retrieve a certificate or verify a signature. Our proposal has a simple Client API which accesses the services of the PKI Server (PKIS). Similar work has been proposed in draft papers in the PKIX working group including Delegated Path Discovery and Validation [10] and Simple Certificate Validation Protocol [8]. These drafts focus on the protocol, whereas we enhance the idea and create a service. We aim to reduce the cost of PKI security integration into any application, whether on a PC or mobile device. That is, our service will support a variety of clients, including clients with limited bandwidth, memory or computational power.

This paper is laid out in the following manner. The complexities of PKI are described in the following section, followed by the requirements of a validation server in section 2. Section 3 describes our proposed PKI Server, including a PKI Server-to-Server protocol. Finally, a brief conclusion is given in section 4.

1. Complexity of PKI

In today's PKI, it is the client that brings together information from separated repositories in order to search for or validate a certificate. In order to achieve this in an heterogeneous PKI, it is conceivable that a client must know a multitude of access protocols and repository addresses, possess certificate path building logic, be able to process validation and certificate policies and be able to parse PKIX X.509 certificates [7].

1.1 Certificate Searching

Another issue of using certificates is how does one initially obtain a certificate. For example, if one only knows the email address of the desired recipient or perhaps her name and knowledge of her company and work group, how does one obtain her certificate? Again, there are no standard methods of discovering this certificate. Even if the global DN structure was adhered to, there are no standard methods of discovering where each segment of the hierarchy is stored. As a counter example, consider the DNS system, and how one searches for a company web page. A user will probably initially try typing "www.thecompany.com". This is often successful and through the traversal within the DNS servers, the actual IP address is found. Similarly, it would be ideal if a client could search for certificates in a similar manner with say LDAP servers routing the request to the correct repository. For example, when one was looking for a certificate, they could try "Country=Germany, Organization=Fraunhofer, Name=Brian Hunter". Even though this quasi-DN name is not complete (it contains no organization unit), or possibly not unique, if LDAP servers could route to the Fraunhofer LDAP server and return a list of all Brian Hunters, this would greatly aid in finding a given certificate.

This is not new, the idea of the global DN structure is old, however, we are suggesting to push routing capabilities into PKISs, similar to DNS servers. In this manner, client certificate queries could be as transparent as DNS lookups are today.

This would help alleviate some usage pains of today's PKI. Therefore, we propose our central PKIS which will perform these routing and discovery tasks, making these services transparent to PKI clients.

1.2 Access Protocols

There are many repositories or services where certificates may be queried or searched for. LDAP provides a simplified repository based upon an X.500 DAP system. It allows the storage and retrieval of X.509 certificates based upon a distinguished name (DN) in the certificate. A feature in DNSSEC [4] has been introduced to allow the storage and retrieval of certificates from any DNS server. A DNS server stores all entries under domain names which are derived from entries in the subjectAltName in the certificate based upon a prioritised set of rules. Thus, the two systems not only use different access protocols but the stored certificates are also referenced differently.

A certificate must not only be retrieved but the validity of it must also be verified. The initial service defined for PKIs was certificate revocation lists (CRLs). There are two inherent problems with CRLs, their size and update timeliness. Hence, delta CRLs were introduced which are issued more frequently and only contain the certificates that were revoked since the last full CRL, hence they are smaller. CRLs may be retrieved from DNS servers and both CRLs and delta CRLs may be retrieved from LDAP servers.

Even though delta CRLs improved the timeliness of revocation dissemination, they do not provide real-time verification of revocation status. Online Certificate Status Protocol (OCSP) [9] was introduced to allow real-time verification of the status of a certificate. This protocol allows a single certificate to be queried and provides a response giving the current status and information regarding when this status was issued and when the next update will be. That is to say, an OCSP responder may be directly linked with the CA and have real-time status information or it may simply be retrieving CRLs and parsing them for the client.

A client must be able to use at least a subset of the above protocols and the application may need to be upgraded when a protocol changes or a new protocol is added.

1.3 Certificate Path Building

A client must be able to check that a received certificate has been issued by a trusted CA. That is, a client has a given set of trust anchors (CAs that it trusts) and it must find a certificate path from the received certificate to one of these trust anchors. If it cannot find such a path, it must assume that the certificate is invalid. In a strict tree hierarchy PKI, such as in the US Department of Defence, this task may be relatively simple since there is a unique path between any two clients. Furthermore, the root CA of the tree will likely be the trust anchor for the client and the path logic will only need to traverse from the certificate up to the root.

Certificate path building becomes more complicated in a non-hierarchical PKI and even more so when disjoint PKIs are connected through cross-certification and Bridge CAs (see Figure 1 for an example certificate path). In this case, there may be multiple paths between a trust anchor and a given certificate. The client must know how to start from the certificate and build forward to its issuing CA, then to the issuing CA of that CA and so on until it reaches a trust anchor. Instead of following an issuing CA, the client may follow a different path with a cross-certificate. The client must also verify the validity and status of each of these certificates in the path. Thus, path building can be very time consuming. [5] discusses the advantages of applying name and policy constraints during path construction.

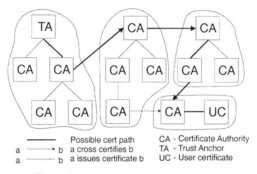

Figure 1. Interconnected PKI Architecture

Caching previous results can greatly improve the time needed for future paths. Even an old path that only partially overlaps the new requested path can save many repository queries and fruitless path branches. Depending on the elapsed time and user policy, the status of some or all of the certificates may need to be re- verified. Despite the benefit of a local cache, every client caching old paths is redundant and could be better served if common clients, that is, clients who build paths for similar certificates and similar trust anchors, could access a common cache. This would reduce the number of times the same path was built, cryptographically validated and possibly reduce the overall frequency of certificate status checking.

1.4 Certificate Parsing

A client must be able to parse and understand a PKIX X.509 certificate and related CRLs. This includes optional extensions to certificates and their criticality flag. The criticality flag causes unknown extensions to be ignored or the certificate abandoned. This technique may work well within limited organizations or single vendor implementations, but this method can hamper useful functionality contained in extensions to be consistently dropped. A centralized service could be more aware and extensible of non-mandatory but useful extensions.

2. PKI Server Goals

The PKIS is intended to simplify clients and reduce the complexity on the client side. The goal is to allow more applications to make use of PKI services, applications on PCs as well as on devices with limited resources. Because of the need to support devices with limited resources, such as PDAs, cellular phones or IPsec boxes, it is not sufficient to use a standard, multi-megabyte library. CML [1] is such a free library but is not suitable for small devices, as it is composed of several large libraries. Therefore, we decided to move computation and complexity to a server and allow the client access through a simple API and small client library. From our main goal of simplification, we derive many sub- goals.

2.1 Application Robustness and Longevity

Most applications wishing to make use of PKI services must have all the PKI logic built in or make use of some existing certificate library. Taking the complexity of PKI into account, it can be assumed that the more applications that develop their own security logic, the greater the chance that some implementations will contain security holes due to oversights made by implementers who are not familiar with security. It is also probable that lack of thorough testing will allow security holes to remain. These holes may be avoided, or at least reduced, by using a security library or PKIS that has been developed and thoroughly tested by security professionals.

Development cycles can be shortened when the client API is used because the API reduces the amount of code that needs to be written and tested. Furthermore, since no PKI protocols are contained on the client side, this relieves the need to patch or upgrade the client when access protocols change, such as LDAP. The PKIS can be patched and upgraded as need be without applications being aware of it. The application only depends on the PKI-Client-Server protocol which will remain static.

2.2 Centralized Policy Management

Within an organization, central management of certificate validation policies is desirable. If all applications contain their own certificate handling logic, all applications for every user must be configured with the correct validation policy. This is simplified when all applications query a given, or a given set of, PKIS in the organization. In this case, the administrator may define a set of validation policies that all users, or applications, must use when validating certificates and signatures. Then the administrator only needs to configure for each user the PKI Client API with a reference to the correct policy on the PKIS. Now the administrator can make policy changes for the whole organization in one centralized place.

2.3 Device Independence

The PKIS is implemented and runs on a server independent of any client. The client only directly uses the Client API and Client library. This has two consequences. The first is that the demand on client resources is diminished since most of the processing occurs on the PKIS. This allows the PKI Client API and library to be used by clients with limited resources, which may be the only way for them to access PKI services. Secondly, although the PKI Client API and library are not platform independent, the speed and ease of porting to new platforms is increased due to the small size and simplicity of the client side.

2.4 Response Time

There are two types of devices that will make use of the PKIS, those that cannot support such complex processing on their own and those that can. That is, the time and resources required for certificate path building for a small cellular phone may be prohibitively high and the phone must offload these computations. On the other hand, a powerful PC may have sufficient resources but still wish to offload such computations to reduce code complexity or to save computation time for other pending tasks. Also, the PKIS may be able to respond faster than a PC could validate a path itself because the PKIS has a cache of previous responses (from many clients). Using this cache for subsequent similar validations compared to initial validations may be significantly faster. In [6], they noted a 5-10 second response time for an initial signature validation and less than 1 second for subsequent validations when the certificate path is cached.

3. PKI Server

The PKIS is designed to provide PKI services to requesting clients. The intent of the PKIS is not to provide cryptographic functionality to clients. This can be obtained from cryptographic libraries. The services provided are: certificate validation, signature verification, certificate search, certificate path building and validation.

3.1 Varying PKI Services

Different levels of services are provided because clients may have varying trusts in PKISs and varying computation abilities. For example, a PC application may be able to perform path validation and simply need the PKIS to return the constructed path and the relevant CRLs. The PC application does not need to have any trust in the PKIS since it can verify itself the validity of all returned certificates and CRLs. On the other hand, a cellular phone application may not be able to even parse a certificate and relies on the PKIS to validate a received signature and return a simple 'valid', 'invalid' or 'unknown' answer. In this case, the application would completely trust the PKIS since it has no way of checking whether the PKIS deceived it or not. These different levels of trust arise from the type of PKIS accessed. A public PKIS will likely be less trusted than a private organizational PKIS.

Even though most information that a PKIS accesses is publicly accessible and self protected, we still require that all PKIS responses be authenticated. We want to ensure that a client can verify that the response is from the PKIS. This is achieved either through the use of a secure channel or by being signed or both. This is especially important when the client completely trusts the PKIS and only receives a 'valid' or 'invalid' response from the server. A modification by a man-in-the-middle of this response could be disastrous. Similarly, a client must know that a response answers its unmodified request. Therefore, we mandate that it must be possible to check the integrity of a request in the corresponding response. In this manner, the client can always be sure that the response came from the intended PKIS and it answers its original request. In an organization where records are kept of transactions, non- repudiation is important. A signed response which includes a record of the request provides non-repudiation of the client request. However, this is only valid for proving to a third-party who trusts the same PKIS. In order to prove to an arbitrary third-party, the client must request all validation material to be included in the server's response.

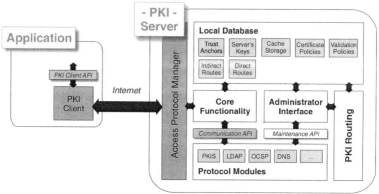

Figure 2. PKI Server and Client Architecture

3.2 Architecture

The NSI architecture can be seen in Figure 2. As can be seen, the whole architecture has been modularised to reduce the effects of an outside change, such as LDAP changing versions. Also, we have defined our own Client-Server protocol based on [10] draft protocol. As a requirement, we have specified that the Client-Server protocol will be transported over IP to remove any underlying network dependence. Therefore, the only requirement for a client to access our PKIS is connectivity with the Internet (or intranet). There is an administrator interface which not only supports maintenance and monitoring functions, but it also allows input of trust anchors. This is important since the trust anchors must be validated through offline methods and accepted by an administrator. Thus, they cannot be dynamically exchanged like repository addresses as discussed in section 3.4. The "Core Functionality" module is the central processing module of the server where path processing, certificate validation and cryptographic functions are performed on behalf of a client's request.

As mentioned above, the client contains two parts, the Client API and the Client library. The Client API is a simple interface allowing initialisation and configuration of the library before it can access the PKIS. The PKIS handles all repository accesses and maintains a cache of previously found results. However, even though the server can maintain a cache, there is no requirement for the server to maintain state of any client request. This is to simplify the server as well as prevent possible DoS attacks.

3.3 Scalability

The issue of scalability is always important in modern services. Recent service models have been developed, such as, peer-to-peer and distributed systems, which can distribute workloads across varying resources. This may be the optimal solution in general, however, the PKIS has a fundamental requirement, trust. Routing and data collection protocols may use unidentified resources, but validation services, signature and certificate, must be dependable, accountable and configurable. Our PKIS model provides these needs and allows for central configuration.

The main limiting factor of PKIS scalability is public key operations (PK ops). This is inherent to the services it provides and cannot be avoided. Since every response must be signed or protected in transport, the minimum PK ops for any request is one. Added to this total are the validations required during path construction. These certificate PK ops may optimally be reduced to zero if the complete path is cached, has been validated and is sufficiently fresh. The effectiveness of cached certificate paths depends on the correlation of client requests. Thus, the number of clients a PKIS can support depends on the client environment it is deployed in.

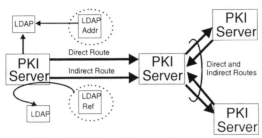

Figure 3. PKI-Server-Server route propagation

3.4 PKI-Server-Server Protocol

We also define the PKI-Server-Server Protocol (PSSP). The aim of this protocol is to allow servers to share information with each other, similar to how IP routers propagate routing information. This information regards certificate paths and certificate repositories and can be seen in the Direct/Indirect Routes (DR, IR) database block in Figure 2. Trust anchors are not shared since they need administrative confirmation of acceptance and thus cannot be dynamically shared. The need for route propagation arises because certificate path building is a complex task and not all servers will be configured with the same access to LDAP and other repositories. In this way, when a server finds a certain certificate path or certificate repository, it can advertise to neighbouring (cooperating) servers that it has path information about this certificate path, see Figure 3 for an example propagation. If the neighbouring servers do not have information regarding this path, they can store a pointer to the advertising server in their IRs, referencing the said path. In this manner, servers will cache DRs of certificate paths when they can contact the given repositories themselves. They will have IRs when they must query another PKIS for this repository access. The servers may decide to share repository addresses in which case the IR would be changed into a DR. This may not be possible or desirable for two reasons. First, the knowledgeable PKIS may have privileged access to this repository and the neighbouring PKIS could thus not make independent use of it. Secondly, the principle of centralised caching occurs again and it may be more efficient to simply query another PKIS for path information, also the querying server's cache storage is reduced since IRs may amalgamate several DRs.

The PSSP propagates path information similar to an IP router. That is, a PKIS may receive broadcasts from more than one neighbour advertising that it knows about a particular certificate path. However, one broadcast might be advertising the knowledge of an IR to this repository while the other advertises a DR. Thus, the PKIS can choose the most direct routing information, whether that be an actual DR or an IR. It should be noted that IRs may have more than one level of redirection and thus one IR may be less direct than another IR. This may occur for similar reasons as Direct Routing information not being shared, that is, administrative policies state not to share direct routing information or access rights to certain PKISs may be restricted. For example, an organization may have several PKISs but only allow one to be accessed by outside PKISs. This one PKIS would have a role similar to a firewall and help manage the release of publicly accessible organizational data and the protection of private organizational data.

The PSSP is important to aid in recovery of a crashed server or a newly online server. PSSP allows a new server to quickly establish (possibly indirect) routes to repositories. In the case of a recovered crashed server, if it propagated Direct Routing information before it crashed then it can re-obtain this direct information by querying its neighbours. However, if the server only propagated IRs and privately stored the DRs, these routes will have been lost and the server must recreate these routes itself. This also presents the problem of IRs being inaccessible due to PKIS failures. Therefore, an active polling must be undertaken to ensure that routes are still active. This may occur periodically, or when a new broadcast is received advertising knowledge of the same route, or when the actual route is needed for path construction, or a combination of all three.

4. Conclusions

We have discussed one of the current limiting factors of PKI usage, namely complexity of certificate retrieval and discovery. We have also revisited the global DN structure in light of allowing dynamic routing, similar to DNS systems, for certificate searches.

Along with the above ideas, we have the goal of providing a simplified PKI service for client applications, a flexible service that allows any client to access it. Thus, we introduced the PKI Server which allows the client to offload certificate searching, path construction and validation and policy handling to the server. We also discussed the idea of propagating certificate and repository information between PKI Servers, which is one step closer to the transparent interconnection and use of PKIs.

References

[1]   Certificate Management Library (CML). Getronics Government Solutions, Mar. 2002.
[2]   NSI – New Security Infrastructure: Analysis of Requirements. Fraunhofer Institute for Secure Telecooperation, www.sit.fhg.de, Jan. 2002.
[3]   S. Boeyen, T. Howes, P. Richard, "Internet X.509 Public Key Infrastructure Operational Protocols - LDAPv2", RFC 2559, Apr 1999.
[4]   D. Eastlake, O. Gudmundsson, "Storing Certificates in the Domain Name System (DNS)", RFC 2538, Mar 1999.
[5]   Y. Elley, A. Anderson, S. Hanna, S. Mullan, R. Perlman, S. Proctor, "Building Certification Paths: Forward vs. Reverse", Proceedings of NDSS 2000.
[6]   D. Fillingham, "DoD Bridge Certification Authority Technology Demonstration, Lessons Learned - Future Plans", Federal PKI Tech. Working Group, Apr 2000.
[7]   R. Housley, W. Ford, W. Polk, D. Solo, "X.509 Internet Public Key Infrastructure Certificate and CRL Profile", RFC 2459, Jan 1999.
[8]   A. Malpani, R. Housley, T. Freeman, "Simple Certificate Validation Protocol", Internet Draft (work in progress), <draft-ietf-pkix-scvp-07.txt>, Feb 2002.
[9]   M. Myers, R. Ankney, A. Malpani, S. Galperin, C. Adams, "X.509 Internet Public Key Infrastructure Online Certificate Status Protocol - OCSP", RFC 2560, Jun 1999.
[10]   D. Pinkas, "Delegated Path Validation and Delegated Path Discovery Protocols", Internet Draft (work in progress), <draft-ietf-pkix-dpv-dpd-00.txt>, Jul 2001.
[11]   W. Polk and N. Hastings. Bridge Certification Authorities: Connecting B2B Public Key Infrastructures. NIST PKI Projects. Sept. 2000.

Infrastructure Security

Security and Privacy in Advanced Networking Technologies
B. Jerman-Blažič et al. (Eds.)
IOS Press, 2004

On the security of 802.11 wireless networks

Marco Domenico AIME (*)   Antonio LIOY (*)   Daniele MAZZOCCHI (+)

m.aime@polito.it   *lioy@polito.it*   *mazzocchi@ismb.it*

(*) Politecnico di Torino, Dip. di Automatica e Informatica,
Corso Duca degli Abruzzi 24, Torino, Italy

(+) Istituto Superiore Mario Boella, Via P.C.Boggio 61, Torino, Italy

Abstract. This paper deals with the security issues of wireless networks implemented in IEEE 802.11 technology. The problems related to its use to build wireless LANs or ad-hoc networks are thoroughly investigated, resulting in a taxonomy of security features, vulnerabilities, and attacks. Starting from this taxonomy, the current and future solutions proposed to cope with the 802.11 security problems (that is WEP, 802.11i, TKIP, CCMP and 802.1X) are evaluated with respect to their robustness, performance and compatibility with a general security architecture.

1. Introduction

The term "wireless" is nowadays one of the most used and abused buzzwords in the Information Technology area. This is mainly related with the success of two different technologies that exploit wireless communication channels: cellular telephony and WLAN (Wireless Local Area Network). Moreover many other wireless technologies are emerging and have the potential to become mass market players: Bluetooth and ZigBee (IEEE 802.15.4) for PAN (Personal Area Network) and ad-hoc networking, UWB (ultra-wide-band) modulation, RFID (Radio Frequency Identifier) and DVB (Digital Video Broadcasting). All these technologies clearly demonstrate the importance of wireless communication techniques.

In particular, starting from the end of '90s, WLANs have gained increased popularity for two specific reasons:

- simple provisioning and reconfiguration of LAN connectivity in premises that exhibit problems to the deployment of traditional wired LAN (such as historical buildings);
- communication support of mobile users equipped with laptops and other portable devices (e.g. PDAs, smart phones). The commercial success of hot-spots installed in airports and railway stations is a clear evidence of the mobility demand from users.

Unfortunately this kind of convenience comes at a price: a wireless communication is clearly more vulnerable to security threats. As an example, eavesdropping is much simpler in wireless networks as there is no need to physically enter a building and access the cables to capture the packets. With a WLAN, packet sniffing can take place from the parking lot or the street below.

Although wireless technology can be used to create both structured connections and ad-hoc networks, in this paper we will focus mostly on the security aspects of structured wireless communications (i.e. WLAN). So far there have been three proposals for WLAN standards: the IEEE 802.11 project [1], the ETSI HIPERLAN/2 project and the Japanese HiSWANa proposal. Without discussing the respective technical merits, the market winner is clearly 802.11. It includes three different communication standards:

- 802.11b which operates at 2.4 GHz with a maximum bit rate of 11 Mbit/s;

- 802.11a which operates at 5 GHz with a maximum bit rate of 54 Mbit/s;
- 802.11g which operates at 2.4 GHz with a maximum bit rate of 54 Mbit/s.

These three standards have identical security characteristics and therefore we will not distinguish among them in our discussion. On the other hand, HIPERLAN/2 and HiSWANa have different security properties but, as they aren't widely deployed, the biggest research efforts have been dedicated to explore security aspects of 802.11 networks.

The story of 802.11 WLAN security goes back to 1997: the first 802.11 specification proposed the WEP protocol to prevent attacks and obtain a level of security equivalent to the wired LAN implementations. Starting from 1999 a lot of research [2, 3, 4, 5] has been done which demonstrated the insufficiency of WEP. Luckily, the new 802.11i specification [6] is being developed to define new protocols to provide a secure framework for WLAN deployment.

The rest of the paper is organized as follows: the rest of the introduction is devoted to a brief overview of the 802.11 standard. Section 2 presents a taxonomy of 802.11 security-related problems. Section 3 is an in-depth analysis of the security properties of 802.11 networks and the proposed protection architectures. Finally in section 4 we draw some conclusions about the overall security level of current WLAN networks.

1.1 A brief overview of the 802.11 standard

The IEEE 802.11 standard [1] defines 802 Local Area Networks (LANs) working on wireless media. The physical layer can be either based on a infrared or a radio shared channel.

The radio-based physical level is the one that has determined the wide spreading of 802.11 technology: at the moment, three different extensions exist to the original 802.11 standard that define three radio physical layers with different characteristics and performances, namely 802.11a, 802.11b and 802.11g.

All the 802.11 radio specifications exploit frequencies in the license-free ISM bands. 802.11b, the most widely used till now, defines a 802.11 physical layer working at 2.4 GHz: this is the 802.11 radio that has currently achieved the major market acceptance. It uses a modulation technique known as Direct-Sequence Spread Spectrum (DSSS) on a shared channel of nearly 22 MHz, reaching a throughput of 11 Mbps on the air. 802.11b divides the available bandwidth into up to 14 5-MHz channels[1]: due to 802.11b channel width, only three of the 14 channels are truly independent. 802.11a and 802.11g exploit the Orthogonal Frequency Division Multiplexing (OFDM) channel coding technique. They both use 20 MHz channels, achieving a throughput of 54 Mbps. 802.11a allocates 12 channels with central frequencies spaced by 20 MHz at 5 GHz[2], while 802.11g uses the same channel plan defined in 802.11b (thus, not all of the available channels are actually independent).

The 802.11 MAC layer is rather more complex than the one used in wired 802 LANs such as 802.3. The harsh transmission characteristics of the radio medium require the 802.11 MAC to include a series of additional features, such as frame acknowledgment, channel reservation mechanisms and fragmentation. A direct consequence is that the MAC layer overhead is considerable: the 802.11 higher layer throughput is not much greater than 5 Mbps, while 802.11g and 802.11a reach 22 and 32 Mbps respectively. Moreover, in association with the peculiar characteristics of the wireless medium, the 802.11 MAC is also more vulnerable to malicious behaviour, as it will be analysed in details in the rest of this chapter.

---

[1] The actual number of available channels depend on country-specific regulations.
[2] More precisely, this is just a channellization plan compliant with USA regulations as defined in the 802.11a specifications: the position and number of channels actually available depend on country-specific regulations.

An *802.11 station* (named STA in 802.11 standard) is any device equipped with a network interface with the physical and the MAC layers compliant with the 802.11 specifications. Two or more 802.11 stations can form an 802.11 cell, or a Basic Service Set (BSS) in 802.11 terminology. A BSS can work in two different modes.

A BSS in *ad-hoc mode* (or Independent Basic Service Set, IBSS) is built by cooperating peer stations: in this mode, 802.11 targets networks dynamically created for a specific use and for a limited range of time. Remarkably, a node in a 802.11 IBSS is not required to forward traffic for other nodes: IP routing capability is required to support communication between nodes placed outside their respective radio coverage. In a IBSS, all 802.11 MAC-level features are implemented in a fully distributed way.

802.11 also specifies an *infrastructure mode,* where a single node – named Access Point (AP) – is responsible of BSS management. All communication among stations in a BSS transit through the AP. Notably, when 802.11-level security is in place, all stations establish security associations with the AP: thus the AP is involved in station authentication and network access control and it solves the key management problem in a infrastructure BSS. The AP can provide access to the *Distribution System* (DS), that is a backbone able to connect multiple BSSes together and/or with the rest of the network (including a global IP network as the Internet). In current WLANs, the DS is commonly an 802.3 network, but 802.11 can exploit any 802 network: in particular, the 802.11 MAC itself includes specific functionalities to implement a wireless DS. 802.11 identifies as *Extended Service Set* (ESS) a set of APs (at limit just one) connected through a DS and building a single WLAN segment.

Besides traffic forwarding and security mechanisms, the AP has also a key role in handoff procedures and station power management. Wireless connectivity enables node mobility features not available in traditional wired LANs. In an infrastructure BSS, 802.11 stations can switch the AP they are attached to while they move through the connectivity ranges of multiple APs: when the network connectivity is preserved this procedure is commonly called *handoff*. 802.11 includes specific features to support transitions among different APs, however the exact mechanisms required to enable efficient and smooth handoff procedures are left out of scope [3].

802.11 stations are battery-powered to support seamless mobility: the scarcity of energy resources is a key characteristic of any network technology for mobile terminals. 802.11 includes power management mechanisms that nodes can use to safely enter a sleep state to reduce power consumption [4]. The AP can buffer traffic directed towards sleeping stations in the BSS, while in a IBSS each transmitter is required to buffer traffic for its destination when they are known to be asleep.

For additional details regarding the 802.11 physical and MAC layers, the key reference is indeed the 802.11 specifications and, in particular, the 1999 core standard document [1], publicly available at the IEEE's web site through the "Get IEEE 802" program.

2. A taxonomy of 802.11 security issues

Security cannot be achieved unless threats are fully understood. Therefore, it is vital to build a threat model of 802.11 networks. In the this section we first look at peculiar vulnerabilities of 802.11 networks, understand their origin and then we outline practical attacks that exploit these vulnerabilities.

---

[3] Actually, solutions to handoff-related issues have been investigated by IEEE as an extension to the core 802.11 specification, currently frozen in draft status, and are currently evolving inside the IETF community.
[4] We will indifferently use the terms "sleep", "stand-by" or "power-save" mode to address the power saving status defined in the 802.11 specifications.

As a preliminary step, let us clarify the target network scenarios. 802.11 can be used in a wide variety of scenarios with very different security threats: from wireless local loop for public Internet access to networks of micro sensors, from peer-to-peer gaming to C4 (Command, Control, Communications, and Computer Systems) battlefield networks. To cope with this heterogeneity, our model abstracts from specific applications and starts by analysing the major characteristics of 802.11 relevant for security issues. Based on these characteristics, a set of reference scenarios will be outlined to focus on causes and consequences of different vulnerabilities and attacks.

2.1 Security-related features

With reference to the scenarios previously outlined, we have identified a set of features of 802.11 networks that directly or indirectly affect their security. They are listed below.

(C1) Radio transmission. This is indeed the main feature of 802.11, also for security analysis. Radio communication is physically unbounded with generally mutable and unknown boundaries: within the coverage area all transmitted information is accessible to any device equipped with the proper radio.

(C2) Network architecture. 802.11 supports two different architectures:

(C2a) Cellular architecture. Multiple BSSes operate in 802.11 Infrastructure mode: the APs are the core elements that control all BSSes in the network. All traffic exchanged in a BSS transits through the AP: this includes the traffic that enters/exits the BSS and even the data exchanged between two stations attached to the same BSS. The BSS are connected through a LAN acting as a DS among all the APs [5].

(C2b) Mesh architecture. This is a peer-to-peer scenario where no network infrastructure is present and all members' nodes have the same capabilities and the same rights; all the stations operate in 802.11 Ad-hoc mode.

(C3) Internetworking. 802.11 networks can typically exchange data with external IP networks through one or more logical elements called Portals. In cellular architectures (C2a) only APs can act as Portals.

(C4) Shared medium. A single radio channel is shared among different devices. This differs from 2G/3G cellular networks that support channels dedicated to a single device. Moreover, a unique channel can be shared by multiple independent 802.11 networks: for example, an IBSS can coexist in the same area and on the same channel of an ESS cell. A mechanism is needed to coordinate the access to the shared medium: actually, this is the very purpose of the 802.11 MAC protocol. 802.11-1999 defines two algorithms for medium access control:

(C4a) CSMA/CA (Carrier Sense Multiple Access with Collision Avoidance). This is a distributed coordination mechanism fit for best effort data traffic. Support of CSMA/CA is mandatory and it is the only medium access algorithm typically available in current 802.11 implementations.

(C4b) Polling. This is an optional medium access mode, available only in Infrastructure networks (C2a). The AP is responsible to cycle through associated stations and grants the right to transmit pending traffic. The traffic transmitted in polling mode is given a higher priority when accessing the medium: C4a traffic is confined within time windows when the polling access is disabled, under a best-effort policy. The polling management is based on two specific 802.11 control frames (e.g.., CF-End) and specially-tagged Data frames (e.g., Data+CF-Poll).

---

[5] In 802.11 terminology, this is named an *Extended Service Set* (ESS)

(C5) Cryptography. Some cryptographic mechanisms can be present. The model assumes that, if a security measure is active in a particular scenario, any possible compromise of any security property must be considered a relevant security threat. In particular, three different security frameworks are considered:

> **(C5a) Open.** No cryptographic system at the 802.11 level is used to achieve confidentiality and integrity of transmitted information. The access to network resources is open and no authentication mechanism is in place to identify nodes accessing those resources.
>
> **(C5b) WEP.** The network uses the protection mechanisms specified in 802.11-1999, that is member nodes exploit the WEP algorithm for data confidentiality and integrity and authenticate other nodes through the Shared Key Authentication procedure.
>
> **(C5c) 802.11i.** In this case, the 802.11i security framework is in place to protect all network communications. In particular, the CCMP algorithm is used for data integrity and confidentiality and 802.11i key management mechanisms are exploited [6]. Moreover, the 802.1X authentication architecture [7] is in place in scenarios where this is applicable (C2a).

(C6) Mobility. 802.11 stations are typically mobile and this has two major consequences:

> **(C6a) Network Topology Changing.** Due to the limited range of 802.11 radio, mobility of nodes directly translates into frequent changes of network topology: in a ESS stations can roam from a BSS to another (C2a), while, in ad-hoc scenarios (C2b) the neighbours of a node can frequently change.
>
> **(C6a) Limited energy resources.** To support mobility beyond nomadism, 802.11 nodes are usually battery-powered; the exceptions are the APs in C2a scenarios that are supposed to be attached to an inexhaustible power supply.

(C7) Node association. For security (C5) and mobility (C6) reasons, nodes need to actively maintain associations among themselves: this depends on the particular network architecture (C2) in place. In C2a scenarios all stations in a BSS are associated to the AP. Otherwise, in C2b scenarios a node maintains associations with any other node that is within its radio range and that it wants to exchange data with. The 802.11 MAC makes use of specific frames to manage the association state among nodes: these are known as *Management frames* (e.g., (De)Authentication, (Re)Association and Disassociation, Beacon and Probe Response). Some security frameworks (e.g., C5c) can add special frames and specific procedures to setup and manage data-link layer security associations among 802.11 nodes.

(C8) Power save mode. To save battery power, 802.11 devices can enter a power save (or standby) state. In this state a node cannot transmit nor receive 802.11 frames: periodically, it can wake up and request pending traffic. Nodes must implement buffering mechanisms to support this feature. In particular, the AP buffers traffic directed to attached stations that are known to be in standby mode. In peer-to-peer scenarios (C2b) every transmitting node must buffer frames directed to standby stations it is associated to. The 802.11 standard includes specific control frames (PS-Poll) to let a node request its buffered traffic. A station becomes aware of pending traffic by periodically listening to traffic indication information published in Beacon by the AP or to special management frames (ATIMs) in a IBSS.

(C9) Logical channel sensing. To cope with the well known hidden terminal problem[7], 802.11 makes use of the Duration header field and specific control frames (RTS and CTS) to implement a logical channel sensing function.

---

[6] The use of TKIP is not considered here because it is just a migration path to CCMP.

[7] See [1] for a detailed explanation of the hidden terminal problem related to the 802.11 MAC.

(C10) Retransmission. Due to the coarse conditions of radio transmission, the 802.11 MAC layer includes retransmission capabilities. This is based on the use of ACK control frames and proper retransmission timers. Note that this feature is available only for unicast traffic.

(C11) Fragmentation. 802.11 frames can be fragmented to enhance the chance of correct delivery over the air. Every node must support the required buffering mechanisms to handle defragmentation.

The previous characteristics leaded us to define a set of five reference scenarios, distinguished in terms of the underlying network structure and the security measures in place.

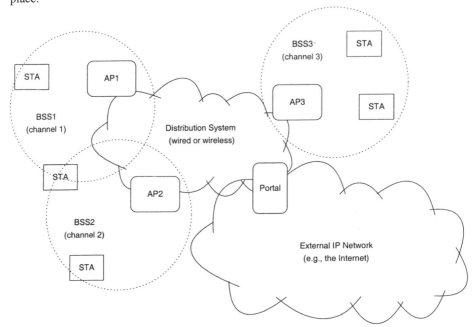

Figure 1: The ESS scenario

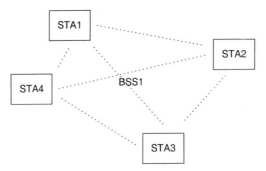

Figure 2: The IBSS scenario

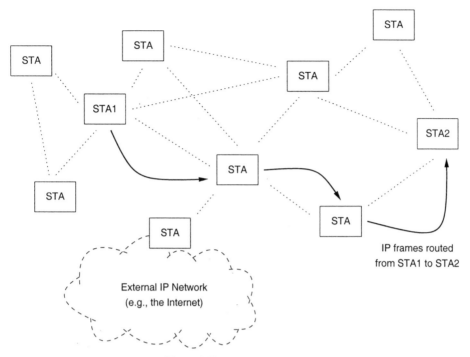

Figure 3: The MANET scenario

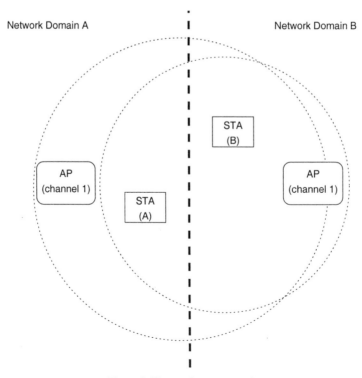

Figure 4: The coexistence scenario

(S1) Open ESS. As shown in Figure 1, this is a cellular scenario (C2a) where no security mechanism is setup at the 802.11 layer (C5a) The DS can be either wired (typically an 802.3 network) or wireless (802.11) [8]; the DS is supposed to be attached to a global IP network, such as the Internet. This can be the typical scenario of a public hot-spot with free access.

(S2) 802.11i ESS. This case is similar to S1, but the 802.11i security framework (C5c) is supposed to be fully in place; this will probably be the typical scenario of future corporate wireless LANs.

(S3) IBSS. This scenario includes a single 802.11 Independent BSS in which stations communicates directly one to each other within the 802.11 radio range (Figure 2); the IBSS is not interconnected with other networks and no 802.11-level security is exploited (C5a). This represents the common scenario of an ad-hoc meeting or gaming network.

(S4) Mobile Ad-Hoc Networks (MANET). This is the case of a wide area 802.11 network that operates in ad-hoc mode (Figure 3 shows an example). Stations typically move and are required to cooperate for routing IP traffic to enable communication beyond the direct 802.11 radio range. For completeness, the MANET is supposed to be attached (through one or multiple member nodes) to a global IP network [9].

(S5) Coexistent BSSes. In all previous scenarios a single wireless network is present, subject to single authority (this can apply to all scenarios) or to no authority at all (this is possible just in S3 and S4). Instead, this fifth scenario considers two or more networks that coexist in a single area and are subject to completely independent authorities: this is exemplified in Figure 4.

2.2 Vulnerabilities

Based on the network scenarios and the basic 802.11 characteristics described before, the following vulnerabilities have been identified.

(V1) Channel jamming. This is a consequence of characteristic C1: radio transmission is inherently subjected to jamming at the physical layer.

(V2) AP compromise. In infrastructure networks (C2a), a successful attack against an AP blocks the whole controlled BSS. Possible attacks include subversion of the current AP, denial of service attacks directed against it and spoofing of the AP identity.

(V3) Data confidentiality and integrity. Due to C1, 802.11 data frames can be read and injected by any node in the transmission range. Thus, without dedicated security mechanisms in place, no data origin authentication and no data confidentiality is granted.

> **(V3a) Unprotected networks.** In the Open network scenarios (C5a), data frame confidentiality and integrity are not guaranteed at all.
>
> **(V3a) WEP protected networks.** Due to WEP flaws (discussed in section 3.2.1), the effective protection achievable in C5b networks is almost null: the model considers C5a and C5b scenarios as equivalent in terms of security guarantees.
>
> **(V3c) CCMP protected networks.** In C5c, this model supposes that there are no significant flaws in CCMP cryptographic primitives. Moreover, when the 802.1X architecture is used (scenarios S1 and S2), the EAP authentication

---

[8] The mode in which the wireless DS operates (e.g., a single Independent BSS or an upper-layer Infrastructure BSS) is irrelevant.

[9] Even though the connectivity to external networks is generally helpful when building security frameworks (mainly to support trust models), in the mere contest of security vulnerabilities this augments attack chances and diversity.

algorithms provide strong security. Note that, even in this scenario, it is not possible to prevent nodes from accepting unprotected frames. In fact, as explained in C4, many different independent networks can coexist on the same radio channel, with completely different security policies and trust models in place.

(V4) Unprotected Management frames. In all the security-related scenarios (C5), 802.11 Management frames (C7) have no integrity and no data origin authenticity protection.

(V5) Unprotected Control frames. In all the security related scenarios (C5), 802.11 control frames have no integrity and no data origin authenticity protection: these includes frames for polling management (C4b), standby related frames (C8) and transmission control frames (C9 and C10).

(V6) Power save mode. The AP stores frames for stations known to be in standby mode (C8). Without appropriate authentication and integrity properties in place (see C5), an attacker can make this traffic to be transmitted when the legitimate receiver is not awake. Symmetrically, an attacker can force an AP to buffer traffic for an awake node: for example, to delay time-sensitive traffic.

(V7) Battery exhaustion. Battery energy (C6 and C8) is a scarce and precious resource: battery-powered nodes are subject to attacks that aim to exhaust their batteries. These can include sleep deprivation attacks (i.e., attacks that prevent a station to enter power save mode) and attacks that make nodes waste resources in useless processing (e.g., by invoking cryptographic operations over fake data).

(V8) MAC fairness. 802.11 MAC requires stations to work fairly (C4 and C9). The major threats may arise from violating the medium access time intervals and the backoff mechanism [10] to control an unfair share of transmission resources. Note that the 802.11 extensions for QoS support (under definition by 802.11 WG, TG E) allow a station to assign frames to priority classes defined in terms of different SIFS and backoff intervals.

(V9) Logical channel sensing. Wrong values in the Duration MAC header field can be used to disrupt the logical channel sensing function (C9). Note that the Duration field is not integrity protected with any security suite (C5), because it can change during retransmissions (C10) due to a data rate fallback. Moreover, in S5 scenario the Duration field must be accessible to all stations, even if belonging to independent network domains.

(V10) Frame buffering. Without proper counter-measures, attacks can be mounted against buffering mechanisms required to handle frame retransmission (C10) and fragment reassembly (C11).

> **(V10a) Retransmission buffering.** AP and stations keep buffers to support frame retransmission (C9). Without appropriate aging functions, violation of ACK sending rules can exhaust buffering resources.

> **(V10b) Fragmentation buffering.** Without appropriate aging functions, also defragmentation buffers can be exhausted. The effect depends on the particular implementation, but should influence only fragmented traffic.

(V11) Upper layer vulnerabilities. A station participating in a BSS is vulnerable to all attacks based on higher level protocols (e.g., TCP/IP protocol suite). Moreover, in all scenarios but S3, the nodes can exchange data with a global external IP network, such as the Internet (C3).

---

[10] For a detailed description of the 802.11 MAC access mechanisms see [1].

2.3 Attacks

Given the features and vulnerabilities described in the previous sections, the following attacks are possible.

(A1) Passive attacks. Passive attacks are particularly scary since they cannot be revealed by any security monitor mechanism (e.g., Intrusion Detection Systems). The V2 vulnerability enables two main classes of passive attacks: those against confidentiality of transmitted data and those against privacy:

(A1a) Confidentiality attacks. These include frame sniffing with analysis on traffic patterns and eavesdropping of data traffic. In Open networks (C5a), a traffic sniffing software is the only requirement. In WEP-enabled networks (C5b), a certain amount of traffic must be captured to recover the, static, shared secret; then it falls back to C5a case. In C5c scenarios, this model supposes that 802.11i security guarantees hold: only traffic analysis is possible with protected frames, while it is equivalent to C5a with all those messages (e.g.. 802.11 management frames) not covered by CCMP protection [11].

(A1b) Privacy attacks. As long as 802.11 nodes move (C6), the current location of a particular node can become a sensitive information. Even with the 802.11i security framework in place (C5c), 802.11 header information is covered by integrity protection but is transmitted in clear. This means that at least 802.11-level identifiers (i.e., MAC addresses) can be used to track node's movements. When the 802.1X architecture is used (S1 and S2), identity tracking based on EAP credentials depends on the particular EAP authentication mechanisms that are enabled.

(A2) Physical level jamming. This directly derives from the vulnerability V1. The 802.11 systems use spread-spectrum transmissions: this gives some resistance against narrowband interferences. Thus, physical jamming requires power emission on a consistent subset of the whole transmission band: an attack of this kind is then power-consuming and easy to localize, but also easy to realize with dedicated hardware.

(A3) MAC level jamming. Common to this class of attacks is to aim to block an entire BSS (or, more precisely, all the station in the transmission range of the attacker radio) by disrupting MAC specific logics. However, an acceptable result can be just to slow the BSS down enough to prevent normal network operations. Jamming attacks at the MAC level are generally less power-consuming and more hidden than physical ones. Note that, mainly due to mobility features (C9), also malicious devices can be battery-powered. Moreover, their presence and location is indeed a key information that any security monitoring system aims to pursue. These attacks are generally based on violation of channel access mechanisms (V7 and V8). An extensive study of their effects in 802.11 networks was firstly presented in [8] and another interesting analysis can be found in [9].

(A3a) Backoff time attack. This exploits the violation of backoff times (V8) and requires the attacker to transmit a packet/signal every SIFS interval (20? s). This attack is still very expensive since it requires to send approximately $50K$ signals per second. Typically, off-the-shelf hardware does not support modification of backoff timing. However, diffusion of devices supporting 802.11 QoS extensions and programmable 802.11 hardware (e.g., for research and testing) is going to change this.

(A3b) Duration field attack. This is similar to A3a. However, this attacks the logical sensing instead of the physical one and is much cheaper. It basically consists in sending spoofed frames with very large Duration field values. With

---

[11] See section   for a detailed discussion on the CCMP protection scope.

a Duration value of 32767ms, the attacker needs only to inject 30 frames per second: the attacker can even shut down the radio modem (to save power) among injected packets. A workaround, suggested in [8], could be to reject Duration values grater than a reasonable threshold: legitimate Duration values are relatively small (few milliseconds).

(A3c) Frame trashing attack. In this case, the attacker transmits signals only when another station is already transmitting. This aims to corrupt subset of the legitimate frame and make the receiver discard it (due to FCS verification error). This is less expensive than A3a. The attack is detectable only by looking for unusual high error rates on the channel. Note that, by trashing just the physical-level CRC, the attacker is even able to eavesdrop packets that he is jamming: this can be used to mount man-in-the-middle attacks in which the attacker disrupts the direct channel between two legitimate nodes to force all the traffic to pass through itself.

(A4) Bandwidth exhaustion (unfairness). Mainly through simulations, the research community has shown how the 802.11 MAC can cause serious unfairness among correlated TCP flows. In scenarios such as S5, this can represent a serious security treat: a coexistent network can easily capture the whole available bandwidth, even without exposing any malicious behaviour. In particular, this can happen in multi-hop ad-hoc networks (see S4), where nodes are easily subject to the hidden and exposed node problems. The 802.11 binary exponential backoff mechanism favours nodes that experience less collisions: this interacts with TCP congestion control leading to the complete starvation of penalized flows. The same effects may also arise from the interaction among TCP flows and rate-unlimited UDP ones.

(A5) Attacks against buffering. These attacks exploit the V9 vulnerability.

(A5a) Attacks against retransmission. Attack against retransmission buffers becomes a potential threat when frame forwarding is enable either in the 802.11 layer (e.g., at APs) or in upper layers (e.g., MANET nodes in scenario S4). Without, proper buffer management, deliberate missing of ACK-sending can exhaust buffers available to handle retransmission of legitimate frames. On the contrary, when associated to jamming techniques against the receiver, the injection of fake ACKs defeats retransmission techniques. However, it is necessary to remember that 802.11 does not guarantee data delivery.

(A5b) Attacks against fragmentation. This is a sort of level-two SYN flood: an attacker sends incomplete fragmented packets to exhaust node ability to accept further fragmented traffic.

(A6) Attacks against association status. The target of these attacks is association status kept by 802.11 nodes. These exploit vulnerabilities related to 802.11 associations (V2 and V4).

(A6a) Disassociation attacks. Due to V4, in all cryptographic scenarios (C5), an attacker can inject spoofed Disassociation frames. In Infrastructure mode scenarios (S1 and S2), this deletes the association among stations and the current AP and thus prevents stations to legitimately access the network (C7). Moreover, when 802.11i security framework is in place (C5c), this results in existing security associations to be deleted. In particular, a Disassociation message sent with a spoofed station address makes the AP deletes association status for the given target. Similarly, a spoofed message sent with the AP address, makes the target believe to be disassociated. Moreover, a single message broadcasted spoofing the AP address can deassociate all current stations. In all cases, every deassociated station needs to repeat the association procedures. This is particularly negative when security associations must be recreated; for example, through lengthy and expensive key agreement procedures.

(A6b) Deauthentication attacks. This is almost identical to A3a, but it works also with nodes in ad-hoc mode (e.g., in scenarios S3 and S4). Spoofed Deauthentication frames are used instead of Disassociation ones. Being authenticated and re-authenticating is a very suspicious behaviour easily detectable by a security monitor system like an IDS. A workaround for both Disassociation and Deauthentication attacks has been suggested in [8]: since legitimate nodes do not transmit data after deauthenticating, a disassociation/deauthentication request can be deferred for some seconds and discarded if a valid frame is received during this window.

(A7) Attacks against the DS. ESS scenarios (S1 and S2) involve the presence of a DS, which can itself become the target of two major classes of attacks.

(A7a) Reassociation attacks. This consists in the attacker attempt to reassociate/associate a spoofed station in a different BSS than the one the station is currently attached to (without any disassociation in the former BSS). The aim is to disrupt the bridging function in the DS: for instance, in S1, this would aim to confuse the Spanning Tree algorithm in the switched Ethernet acting as the DS. Strong security (C5c) can prevent this attack since the AP is expected to update node location information in the DS only after having fully authenticated the station.

(A7b) DoS Attacks. The key principle is that every disrupting attack available against a single BSS can equally target the wireless DS. Moreover, directed against the DS, an attack can achieve broader effects since it may affect not only a single BSS but every BSS connected to the DS. This includes jamming attacks (A2 and A3), bandwidth exhaustion attacks (A4) or deassociation attacks (A6).

(A8) Hidden AP (AP spoofing). A Hidden AP is malicious node setup on the same are and channel of a legitimate AP: it transmits only some key frames, not respecting any protocol. More generally, it includes attacks that involve spoofing frames which can be only sent by an AP. Presumably, the legitimate AP will ignore these spoofed frames, but they are a perfect target for intrusion detection systems.

(A8a) Beacon spoofing. A Beacon frame contains key information like timestamp, indication of pending traffic [12] and capabilities. A spoofed Beacon frame can cause the lost of synchronization of station timers in the BSS, which is critical for Frequency hopping systems: a successful attack will prevent stations to communicate with the legitimate AP, thus blocking the whole BSS. A spoofed Beacon that signals the start of a new polling period [13] makes receiving stations believe that the medium is accessed in polling mode. Every station will than wait for CF-Poll frames which will never arrive, so all transmissions are blocked. Fake pending traffic information can be used to prevent stations to enter sleep mode, as discussed in further details in A9.

(A8b) CF-Poll spoofing. This attack aims to disrupt polling access mode and requires the BSS to be already in a contention-free period: spoofed CF-Poll frames make stations transmit when it is not their turn. In 802.11i scenario (C5c) CF-Poll frames are authenticated and this makes the attack impossible.

(A8c) Probe Response spoofing. A fake Probe Response frame targets BSS joining. The Probe Response frame contains key information like timestamp, capabilities, including transmission rates and security suites. A station with

---

[12] This is included in the (D)TIM fields as specified in [1].

[13] That is, as specified in [1], a Beacon that carries a DTIM(CF) field.

such wrong information will likely be unable to join or properly transmit. It is a matter of policy implemented on the station, if an 802.11 node can be forced to choose a weak cipher such as WEP: in any case, this requires also the spoofing of beacon frames (see A8a). To be noted is that the true packet also reaches the joining station that will presumably consider the first received.

(A9) Battery exhaustion. These attacks are mounted against energy resources (V7): these can be divided into two main classes.

> **(A9a) Useless invoking of cryptographic operations.** An attacker can flood stations that are not in power save mode, with bogus encrypted traffic: the aim is to consume energy resources by invoking expensive cryptographic operations. This attack is effective only in scenarios where cryptography is required (C5b and C5c). In Open networks (C5a), station configuration (i.e., WEP-related MIB values) leads to discard every protected frame. Wasted resources are bigger when the cryptographic primitives invoked are more complex. For instance, CCMP anti-reply, integrity checks and decryption can be performed in parallel: the actual sequence followed by an application can directly affect the amount of resources lost to detect malicious replicas of encrypted packets.

> **(A9b) Sleep deprivation attacks.** In an Infrastructure BSS, an attacker can send spoofed Beacon frames carrying a TIM (Traffic Indication Map) that signals presence of pending traffic for a given station. The station will send a PS-Poll frame to retrieve the buffered frame and will stay awake for the entire Beacon interval if a response is not received. The attacker can then repeat the process and be able to prevent the target station to exploit power management features. These attacks can simultaneously target multiple stations by properly constructing the traffic indication map. Even without Beacon spoofing, an attacker can send bogus packets towards a station to prevent it to start or continue sleeping. In networks with global IP connectivity, a similar attack can become particularly treating since it can be mounted from an external network. Once the station has awaked the first time, every PS-Poll frame will get the answer that there is more buffered traffic: the station can be tempted to stay awake to fetch it. However, it is not possible to force the station to remain in active state after the first frame has been polled [14]. Bogus traffic can instead achieve worst effects in an IBSS, where stations are expected to be awake in the first part of every Beacon interval and fake ATIMs (Announcement Traffic Indication messages) transmitted in these windows can prevent a station to enter power save mode.

(A10) Attacks against the power save mode. These attacks exploit vulnerabilities related to power save mode management (V6 and V5).

> **(A10a) Traffic stealing attacks.** This consists in the request of buffered traffic of a station in power save mode: the sleeping station will never receive that traffic. Due to (V4), PS-Poll frames are not authenticated so this attack works also in C5c scenarios.

> **(A10b) Traffic freezing attacks.** An attacker can send spoofed frames making the AP incorrectly believe that the target is in power save mode. This can be exploited even under 802.11i security (C5c), since the Power Management bit

---

[14] At least is not possible to keep it awake for more than a single Beacon period per each Listen Interval, as defined in [1].

is included also in the unprotected Management frames [15]. Any successive frame transmitted by the victim re-establishes correct status information. Meanwhile, this can delay time sensitive traffic (e.g., RTP multimedia traffic).

3. Protection of 802.11 networks

Despite its short life, the security suite for 802.11 networks has already an instructive history.

The first edition of the 802.11 core specification appeared in 1997, followed, in 1999, by the current version. In contrast with other IEEE 802 MAC standards, the 802.11 one natively includes a security framework. This security suite has explicitly a limited scope: to grant a level of security just equivalent to the one provided by wired IEEE 802 networks, as also suggested by the name of its main building block, the *Wired Equivalent Privacy* algorithm, or simply *WEP*.

Nevertheless, soon after its publication, it was discovered that WEP is unable to provide an acceptable level of security.

As a consequence, IEEE has started to work on the next generation 802.11 security framework that is known as *802.11i*. This has gradually expanded from a mere replacement of the defective WEP cryptographic mechanisms up to a comprehensive redesign and evolution of the security architecture.

Future 802.11 networks will be to some extent much more secure than current switched wired networks, but this will come at the cost of replacement of today hardware equipment. As a migration path, a subsection of the 802.11i framework implementable on current hardware has already been released under the commercial name of *Wi-Fi Protected Access*, or *WPA*.

In the following sections, we examine the 802.11-1999 security suite, outline its known problems and finally discuss the new 802.11i framework.

3.1 The Wireless Equivalent Privacy (WEP)

The 802.11 security framework is based on a single building block: the *Wireless Equivalent Privacy* algorithm (WEP). The scope of WEP, and thus of the whole security architecture, is:

1. to provide data confidentiality at the 802.11 link layer (note that, in the 802.11 specification, the "privacy" term is somehow misleadingly used with the sense of "confidentiality") ;
2. to provide data integrity at the 802.11 link layer ;
3. to provide authentication for network access control purposes.

WEP is a fairly simple protocol based on RC4. Designed in 1987, RC4 is currently the stream cipher most widely used in the Internet (prior to WEP, the main application of RC4 was in the SSL and TLS protocols). WEP is applied over the payload of 802.11 frames, while the header information is not affected nor protected. Actually, WEP protects only Data and Authentication frames and leaves unprotected Control (e.g., ACK, RTS/CTS or PS-Poll) and Management (e.g., Beacon, Re/Association, Deauthentication and Disassociation) ones.

Actually, WEP has a completely different semantics when protecting Data or Authentication frames. WEP main purpose is to provide confidentiality and integrity of

---

[15] Actually, 802.11i does not include the Power Management bit in the CCMP AAD construction: thus, this information is not protected even in Data frames. Simply, Management frames can be easily spoofed/replayed unlike Data ones.

802.11 Data frames, while Authentication frames exploit WEP to implement a challenge-based authentication mechanism for network access control.

802.11 compliant stations (included the APs) can operate under three different protection policies:

- No Confidentiality (confidentiality and integrity features are not used at all)
- Restricted System (all data frames are encrypted according to the WEP protocol; unencrypted data frames are discarded by stations)
- Open System (stations always sends encrypted Data frames, but accepts both encrypted and plain data frames)

3.1.1 WEP for confidentiality and integrity

The will to send and receive WEP encapsulated frames can be signalled in Beacon, Probe Response and (Re)Association Response frames. Figure 5 presents the WEP protocol encapsulation, while Figure 6 outlines the encapsulation procedure.

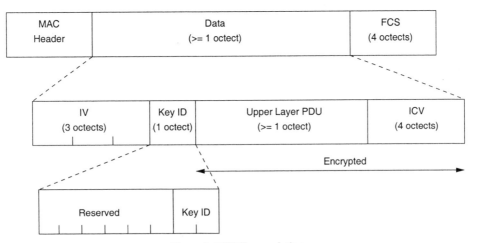

Figure 5: WEP Encapsulation

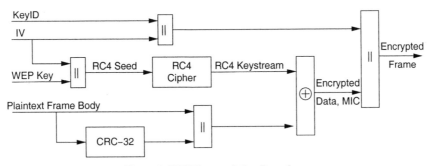

Figure 6: WEP Encapsulation Procedure

Verbally:

1. First, the proper *shared secret* K_{WEP} must be selected for the current frame body M. This differs based on the nature of the receiver address in the frame. When this is a group address, the shared secret is selected within an array of four possible *default*

keys. On the contrary, when it is a unicast address, if a specific shared secret for the current transmitter/receiver pair is available, it will be used; otherwise a default key will be selected. The used secret is signalled in the *Key Identifier* field K_{ID} of each frame: this is the index into the default key array, or 0 when a pairwise key is used.

2. A 32-bit *CRC* is computed over the current frame body. This CRC is appended to the plain payload to provide integrity protection and it is unrelated to the CRC carried in the FCS field of each 802.11 frame. Thus, the current frame data is changed into $M_{CRC} = M \mid crc32(M)$

3. A 24-bit *Initialisation Vector IV* is selected for the current frame and concatenated to the shared secret *KWEP* to produce the *per-frame RC4 key*, $K_{RC4} = K \mid IV$

4. K_{RC4} is fed into the RC4 cipher algorithm to produce the *keystream KS* of length equal to M_{CRC}. Thus $KS = first(len(M_{CRC}), rc4(K_{RC4}))$

5. The ciphertext M_{enc} is computed by xor-ing M_{CRC} and *KS*; $M_{enc} = M_{crc} \oplus KS$

6. Finally, M_{WEP} (the data actually encapsulated in the 802.11 frame sent over the air) is computed as the concatenation of the *IV*, the K_{ID} and the encrypted data; $M_{WEP} = IV \mid K_{ID} \mid M_{enc}$

3.1.2 WEP for network access control

In the context of network access control and node authentication, 802.11 allows a station to follow two different policies. **Open System Authentication** is a null authentication policy that grants access to any station requesting it. This is the 802.11 default authentication policy, while **Shared Key Authentication** is a challenge-based authentication mechanism that exploits the WEP protocol.

The current authentication policy is defined in the configuration of each station: 802.11 does not specify any explicit mechanism (e.g., in Beacon and Association frames) to signal the required authentication policy.

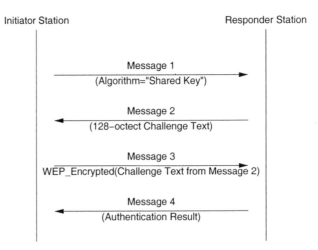

Figure 7: Shared Key Authentication

Figure 7 shows how the WEP protocol is exploited by the 802.11 Shared Key Authentication mechanism for network access control. In Infrastructure BSSes:

1. The station wishing to authenticate sends to the AP an Authentication frame that requests the use of Shared Key Authentication

2. The AP challenges the initiator station with an Authentication frame that contains a random nonce of 128 octets
3. The station sends back the challenge nonce in a third Authentication frame that must be WEP-encrypted with the secret shared between the station and the AP
4. The fourth and last frame signals commit the final result of the authentication attempt to the initiator station

In a IBSS, each of the two stations willing to authenticate independently initiates a Shared Key Authentication procedure: thus, mutual authentication can be achieved.

3.1.3 WEP properties

The 802.11 standard outlines the properties of WEP as: to be reasonably strong, to be self synchronizing, to be efficient and to be optional.

Actually, when considering the whole 802.11 security architecture, a different set of aspects must be taken into consideration for a comprehensive security analysis. Unfortunately, most of these properties directly translate into serious vulnerabilities.

The next paragraphs describe the properties that do determine WEP security guarantees, while the next section will discuss the resulting vulnerabilities.

Absence of any access control and key management infrastructure

802.11 authentication solution is completely distributed and thus equally applies to infrastructure BSSes and to ad-hoc IBSS.

Actually, this nice characteristic is simply the result of having defined no mechanism for key management. In other words, 802.11 does not specify any way to populate the shared key array or the transmitter/receiver pairwise key array.

In general, neither an access control model is outlined in the standard nor an underneath trust model. In particular, it is interesting to note that, whether Shared Key Authentication mechanism provides mutual authentication in a IBSS, in an Infrastructure BSS the AP cannot be challenged by stations.

Scope of WEP security associations

WEP confidentiality and integrity apply exclusively to the Frame Body field of Data frames. Thus, despite WEP being a link-layer security solution, no link-layer information is in fact protected. Moreover, neither Management nor Control frames are protected by WEP.

On the other side, WEP security associations are, by definition, single hop: i.e., WEP cannot secure communications between stations without direct radio connectivity. In particular, a frame flowing between two stations attached to two distinct APs can incur in three encryption/decryption steps if 802.11 is used for communications among APs (or, in other words, for the Distribution System).

Per-frame re-initialisation

A well-known cryptographic principle explains that the keystream produced by a Vernam cipher (such as RC4) cannot be reused without compromising the cipher strength. By combining the shared secret and the IV, WEP generates a new RC4 key per each encrypted frame: this enable per-frame encryption and still avoid keystream re-utilization. However, WEP does not guarantee the same IV is not reused for multiple different frames. Actually, 802.11 suggests, but does not mandate, to change the IV for each transmitted frame.

CRC algorithm provided integrity

This choice heavily contrasts with common cryptographic practice that relies on keyed-digests based on strong hash functions such as MD5 or SHA1. On the contrary, WEP tries to minimize the message overhead and to maximize functional block reuse (a CRC function is already needed for the FCS field in every 802.11 frame).

3.2 The need for further attempts: WEP flaws

WEP is the best example of how the lack of open review in security-related standards is particularly risky today. Soon after 802.11-1999 was published, the security research community started to point out a number of critic WEP design flaws. These flaws have been shown to be easily exploited in practical attacks able to subvert any security achievable through WEP.

The next subsections will firstly discuss the main vulnerabilities known in literature and, subsequently, present the major attack classes that have been shown effective against WEP.

3.2.1 WEP vulnerabilities

The following is a list of the major known vulnerabilities of the whole 802.11 security framework.

IV length

When IVs are changed per each frame, the limited IV space is rapidly exhausted: only $2^{24} \approx 17M$ different IVs are possible. Without any key management mechanism in place to support frequent key refreshment, this leads to keystream reuse in a finite time (just dependent on the network traffic rate). A busy AP that continuously sends 1500-byte packets at 5 Mbps will exhaust IV space in $(1500*8)/(5*10^6)*2^{24} \approx 40000\,sec$, or 11 hours.

Some 802.11 implementations select IVs as random numbers: this is even a worse choice due to the Birthday Paradox. If we apply the Birthday Paradox to WEP IV space, the collision chance exceeds the 99% after 12,430 frames (few seconds at 5 Mbps traffic).

Some other implementations use instead sequentially incremented IVs, but they set the counter to 0 each time the station is reinitialized (e.g., at power-up).

In practice, the effectiveness of attacks based on IV reuse is heavily dependent on the specific 802.11 implementation being attacked.

Absence of any key management architecture

This prevents to setup policies for automated key refreshing. Additionally, most installations use a single secret for all stations in a BSS or even for an entire ESS. This violates any principle of correct secret sharing since it allows any authorized station to impersonate any other station.

Note that attacks based on IV collisions are made easier since collisions can now happen in communications among any station in the network.

Absence of mutual authentication in Infrastructure BSSes

In an Infrastructure BSS, the Shared Key Authentication challenge only allows the AP to authenticate associating stations. On the contrary, no authentication of the AP takes place. In other words, there is no mechanism, at association time, to recognize a rogue AP.

CRC algorithm provided integrity

The CRC algorithm is a poor choice for a Message Integrity Code (MIC): it was designed to efficiently detect random errors, but it is not resilient against intentional malicious modifications. This mainly depends on two facts. Firstly, CRC computation does not depend on a shared secret: thus, knowledge of the plaintext is sufficient to build the corresponding CRC digest. This means that, once a sufficient portion of the keystream associated to a particular IV is known, it is possible to create new valid WEP-protected messages without ever knowing the shared secret. Moreover, CRC is linear: in other words, a property of CRC checksums is $crc(M_1 \oplus M_2) = crc(M_1) \oplus crc(M_2)$. Therefore, flipping an arbitrary bit in the original plaintext results in a deterministic set of bits in the CRC to be flipped to produce a correct checksum on the modified plaintext.

CRC's linearity becomes particularly scary when associated to Vernam ciphers. With a stream cipher, to flip a bit in the ciphertext corresponds, upon decryption, into flipping the correspondent bit in the plaintext: therefore, it is possible to selectively modify the original message even not being able to cipher/decipher it. Consequently, in WEP, it is possible to flip arbitrary bits in a protected message and correctly adjust the CRC checksum (again by simply flipping the correspondent encrypted bits) so that the resulting modified message still appears valid. In other words, the frame $M_\Delta = (M, crc(M)) \oplus rc4(K) \oplus (\Delta, crc(\Delta))$ is still valid provided that M is a valid message.

RC4 key scheduling weaknesses

In 2001, two main weaknesses in the key scheduling algorithm of RC4 were presented in [10] that have devastating effects on WEP construction.

The first weakness is relative to the existence of a large class of weak keys for which a small subset of key bits determine a large subset of the resulting keystream. This can be exploited in cryptanalysis over a large set of collected WEP frames that aims to recover the shared key.

A second vulnerability exists when a subset of the key is public (as with the IV part in WEP). In practice, when the same secret part is associated to numerous different public parts to form RC4 keys, it is possible to reconstruct the secret part by analysing the first word in a sufficient number of keystream samples. Actually, the number of required samples depends on the concatenation order and the length of the public part. In WEP the initial keystream word can often be derived by knowledge of a highly predictable plaintext (e.g., upper layer protocol header). In WEP, if IVs are chosen incrementally, an average of 1 or 4 million samples (dependent on the counter being big or little endian) have to be collected in order to recovery the whole WEP 104-bit shared secret.

Some WEP implementations have soon been updated to avoid RC4 weak keys. As outlined in [10], the previous key scheduling related vulnerabilities could be eliminated by discarding the first N words of each keystream (with $N=2^n$ where n is the RC4 word bit length; typically N is equal to 256).

3.2.2 Practical attacks against WEP

The flaws discussed in the previous section lead to a series of practical attacks: in the following, they are presented roughly divided into three main classes.

Key recovery attacks

The best demonstration of how serious WEP vulnerabilities are is to test open source programs such as WEPCracker [16] or AirSnort [17] that exploit the RC4 key scheduling weaknesses to perform WEP key recovery. As already outlined, the average time required for a successful breaking depends on the particular vendor implementation being tested, but in some cases these tools can recover a WEP shared secret in amazingly short time.

---

[16] http://airsnort.shmoo.com/
[17] http://sourceforge.net/projects/wepcrack

Data decryption attacks

Even without whole key recovery, the keystream reutilization allows to launch known-plaintext and chosen-ciphertext attacks that are able to recover part of or the whole confidential content of WEP-protected frames. All these attacks manage to recover partial sections of the keystream associated to a particular IV and then use them to infer the content of subsequent frames that use the same IV.

For example, an attacker can use an host somewhere on the Internet to send packets directed to a monitored station. The content of those packets will be known to the attacker so that, after intercepting their correspondent encrypted version, he will be able to recover the used keystream.

A passive eavesdropper can perform statistical analysis on messages encrypted with the same IV to infer increasingly larger parts of plaintext. A lot of information carried in IP packets is fixed or easily predictable: this allows the attacker to immediately recover partial keystream for every captured frame. Each newly gathered information on traffic patterns can then provide insight to reconstruct the content of variable fields.

For instance, by starting from the XOR of two plaintext messages (with a Vernam cipher this is just the XOR of two frames encrypted with the same keystream), an attacker can exploit pattern recognition techniques to infer part of the contents of the two messages (e.g., simple programs can be found on the Internet that are able to handle this problem in case of two English texts).

Multiple IV collisions quickly increase the success rate of statistical analysis. Over time, due to the limited IV space, it is even possible to build a database for real-time decryption of captured packets. This decryption table lists IVs and corresponding keystream and requires a fairly small amount of storage: for example, with 1500 bytes keystream blocks it requires just $1500*2^{24} \approx 23.5$ GB.

Traffic injection attacks

As already mentioned, the knowledge of a keystream portion of sufficient length associated to a single IV allows the injection of virtually any packet in the 802.11 network.

For instance, a particular attack can be mounted against the 802.11 Shared Key Authentication mechanism. A part from the challenge text, the content of Authentication frames is fixed or predictable and the challenge itself is transmitted in clear in the first Authentication message. By recording a single challenge/response exchange, an attacker can thus recover the whole keystream used in the third frame: the attacker is now able to reuse this keystream to correctly authenticate against any subsequent challenge that uses the same shared secret.

However, even without knowledge of any segment of the keystream, new fake packets can be injected just by flipping arbitrary bits in a message and then successfully adjusting the encrypted CRC as described in the previous section. For example, this could be exploited to alter shell commands sent over a telnet session. Another interesting attack is related to packet diversion by successfully altering the destination address of 802.11 encapsulated IP frames. An attacker able to guess the IP destination of a transmitted frame can modify it (again through ciphertext bit-flipping and CRC fixing) and redirect the IP packet to a machine under his control somewhere in the Internet. The AP will decrypt the modified frame, forward it unencrypted towards the attacker's machine and thus reveal both plaintext and keystream. In practice, to effectively implement this attack some further tricks are needed to adjust the IP header checksum to avoid the modified IP packet is simply dropped before forwarding.

A different attack, that does not require Internet connectivity, can be performed against TCP traffic by using the receiver as an oracle to unknowingly decrypt the packets. The attacker flips bits at position *I* and *I*+16 in the TCP payload and wait for the ACK packet back from the destination (TCP ACK packets can be easily identified by their size). The TCP checksum field remains unchanged (and thus valid) only if $bit(I) \oplus bit(I+16)=1$ holds (with $bit(I)$ the value of the bit at position I in the original packet). Thus, if the checksum has remained valid, the forged TCP packet gets accepted by the receiver and a TCP ACK is sent back; otherwise, the packet is dropped silently.

Denial of service attacks

The absence of any integrity feature on frames of type Management can be exploited to easily mount DoS attacks in Infrastructure networks.

Actually, an attacker can disassociate any authorized station by sending a single Disassociation or Deauthentication frame with a spoofed MAC address. By spoofing the AP MAC address it is even possible to disassociate all stations in a BSS by sending a single broadcast Disassociation or Deauthentication frame.

3.3 The 802.11i security framework

To react to WEP flaws, the 802.11 WG has charged the Task Group I to define and standardize a completely new security framework for 802.11 networks. At the moment, the future IEEE 802.11i standard is a working draft [18].

802.11i outlines Authentication and Confidentiality as the main primitives required to build a robust and secure 802.11 network. Since the wireless medium does not guarantee any physical control over network access, a logical function is needed to authenticate 802.11 nodes and take decisions about network access. Moreover, since the access to transmitted frames depends only on the sensibility of the radio receiver, a mechanism is required to limit disclosure of sensitive data to a closed group of nodes (from two nodes to an entire BSS).

To avoid WEP mistakes, 802.11i also includes mechanisms to glue the two previous functions together in accordance with the best cryptographic theory and practice. Thus, a consistent key management architecture is specified to build and maintain robust and secure associations among 802.11 nodes, or the *Robust Security Network Associations* (RSNAs) as they are referenced in 802.11i.

The following sections will analyse the concept of RSNA and the solutions in terms of node authentication, data confidentiality and integrity and security association management.

3.3.1 The Robust Security Network Association (RSNA)

The RSNA concept synthesizes the whole 802.11i security architecture. More specifically, it includes:

- enhanced solutions for node authentication;
- algorithms to derive and manage per-session shared secrets;
- new security protocols to encapsulate transmitted frames.

802.11i replaces the WEP algorithm with two alternative protocols, the *Counter-Mode/CBC-MAC Protocol* (CCMP) and the *Temporal Key Integrity Protocol* (TKIP). CCMP is the mandatory choice, while TKIP is provided as a migration path to be implemented by current WEP-capable devices.

802.11i relies on the IEEE *Port-based Network Access Control* standard (or 802.1X) for node authentication and key management. As the name suggests, 802.1X specifies a

---

[18] The final release is expected in the first part of 2004, even if its publication has already been delayed multiple times. This paper references the draft version D7.0 of October 2003.

framework to manage the access to network resources by controlling the ports (physical or logical) the nodes can attach to. Additionally, 802.11i extends some of the protocols and mechanisms defined in 802.1X to build a complete key management solution: the core part of this extension is known as *4-Way Handshake*.

An 802.11 association is an RSNA when the new session key derivation and confirmation procedures take place and CCM or TKIP are used for data encapsulation.

802.11i includes mechanisms to ensure backward compatibility with *pre-RSNA* devices, i.e. 802.11-1999 WEP-enabled devices. However, a strong security policy can be applied only when all associations are RSNA ones: in this case, the network can be referenced as a *Robust Security Network* (RSN). A network that includes both RSNA-capable and pre-RSNA nodes is referenced as a *Transition Security Network* (TSN): a TSN is subject to almost all the security vulnerabilities and attacks discussed previously for WEP.

RSNA selection

Before an RSNA can be established, 802.11i-enabled nodes need to announce their RSNA capabilities by including a special data structure, named *RSN Information Element* (RSN IE), into all frames of type Beacon, Probe Response, (Re)Association Request and Response.

Element ID	Length	Version	Group Key Cipher Suite	Pairwise Key Cipher Suite Count	Pairwise Key Cipher Suite List	Authentication and Key Management Count	Authentication and Key Management List	RSN Capabilities	PMKID Count	PMKID List
Octects 1	1	2	4	2	4*m	2	4*n	2	2	(16*s)

Figure 8: The RSN Information Element

The mere presence of the RSN IE (illustrated in Figure 8) signals that the station is able to establish RSNAs. However, it can optionally include information about supported ciphersuites, extensions to 802.11i basic features and cached session keys.

Table 1: RSNA ciphers

Cipher Suite	Group Key, IBSS	Group Key, ESS	Pairwise Key
Use Group Key	No	No	Yes
WEP-40	Yes	Yes	No
WEP-104	Yes	Yes	No
TKIP	Yes	Yes	Yes
CCMP	Yes	Yes	Yes

An RSN IE can convey information about one ciphersuite to be used to protect the multicast traffic, one or more ciphersuites that can be chosen for unicast traffic and the mechanisms available for node authentication and key management. Table 1 summarizes the cipher algorithms supported by 802.11i: their applicability depends on the type of traffic and the BSS structure.

The supported authentication protocols are 802.1X or a basic shared secret mechanism named Pre-Shared Key.

If two stations cannot agree on a common set of algorithms they will not establish an RSNA: it is then a matter of policy installed on the two stations if they will anyway be able to communicate in insecure mode or not. Similarly, a station is free to choose whether establish a session with a node that does not includes an RSNA IE in its Beacon or Probe Response frames.

802.11i authentication procedures

802.11i abandoned the Authentication facilities included in the 802.11 MAC and exploited by 802.11-1999. In particular, the Shared Key Authentication procedure is no more supported in RSNAs, while the Open System Authentication is retained for compatibility with 802.11-1999 state machine. 802.11i authentication exchanges use normal Data frames instead of Management ones and, in Infrastructure BSSes, take place after the association phase.

For what concerns specific authentication algorithms, 802.11i can use static shared secrets or any mechanism supported by the IETF *Extensible Authentication Protocol* (EAP) as specified by 802.1X. Section analyses the whole 802.1X architecture and its use in 802.11 networks.

Either from the static shared secret or during the EAP authentication exchange, a shared master secret is derived for the current RSNA: 802.11i references this as the *Pairwise Master Key* (PMK).

The key management mechanisms

802.11i distinguishes between two classes of symmetric keys for data integrity and confidentiality: the *Pairwise Transient Keys* (PTKs) for unicast traffic and the *Group Transient Keys* (GTKs) for broadcast an multicast traffic. Each station needs one PTK for each other station it want to communicate with and at least one GTK for sending/receiving broadcast traffic.

802.11i defines also the mechanisms able to derive these keys: the *4-Way Handshake* and the *Group Key Handshake*. In particular, the 4-Way Handshake aims both to confirm the correctness of PMK and to agree on the current PTK: in this way, the dependencies are ensured between node authentication and data confidentiality mechanisms. During the 4-Way Handshake it is also possible to distribute a GTK, otherwise the Group Key Handshake can be used to distribute it. In any case, the GTK is sent protected by the PTK: thus, the Group Key Handshake can take place only after the 4-Way Handshake has been successfully completed. The purpose of the Group Key Handshake is to enable fast refreshing of GTKs: since a GTK is secret shared among a group of entities, the best cryptographic theory and practice mandate it is changed any time the composition of the group changes[19].

The key management procedures slightly differ when considering an Infrastructure BSS or an IBSS. In an Infrastructure BSS, each client station establishes only an RSNA with the AP. This means, that a 4-Way Handshake takes place between each station and the AP to derive a $PTK_{STA-to-AP}$ used to protect station-to-AP and AP-to-station unicast traffic. The AP selects and distributes a GTK_{AP} to all associated nodes to secure broadcast traffic in the BSS. This process is outlined in Figure 9.

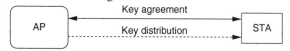

Figure 9: Key management in an Infrastructure BSS

---

[19] In this way a new node is unable to decrypt traffic transmitted before and after its association to the group, traffic that it is not necessarily entitled to access.

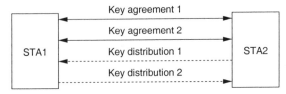

Figure 10: Key management in an Independent BSS

In a IBSS, each station must agree on a PTK with each other station it is willing to communicate with. In particular, for each pair of stations two 4-Way Handshake sequences take place that derive two PTK keys: actually, the one selected in the handshake initiated by the station with the greater MAC address will be used to protect the traffic in the two directions[20]. Each station also distribute its GTK_{STA} to all other nodes in the IBSS. This process is outlined in Figure 10: $N*(N-1)$ 4-Way Handshake procedures must be completed in an IBSS with N participating stations. Moreover, a new node joining the IBSS may cause as much as $2*N$ 4-Way Handshake procedures to be accomplished. This heavily contrasts with the concept of a *group key* as traditionally accepted in applied cryptography literature. The 802.11i GTK is more correctly described as a *broadcast key*: its aim is not to represent the group as a single entity but just to protect the broadcast traffic directed from a member of the group to all other members.

The confidentiality and integrity algorithms

The presence in 802.11i of two alternatives for data encryption is the compromise between the need for strong security in next generation 802.11 networks and the requirements for short-term fixes to WEP critic vulnerabilities.

The mandatory algorithm, CCMP, is based on the *Advanced Encryption Standard* (AES). The use of AES will require the replacement of current 802.11 hardware: in particular, common APs do not have sufficient processing resources to handle the change from WEP to CCMP. On the contrary, TKIP is an enhancement of WEP and can be made available as a firmware upgrade for current WEP-enabled devices.

Actually, in May 2003, the Wi-Fi Alliance started to certify the first 802.11 devices compliant to the *Wireless Protected Access* (WPA) security specifications. Under the name of WPA, some vendors are releasing early draft versions of the 802.11i security solutions. In particular, two levels of WPA compliance are defined: WPA 1.0, that includes the support of 802.1X and TKIP, and WPA 2.0, that includes 802.1X and CCMP. The products currently certified are conformant to WPA 1.0.

RSNA life cycle

This section summarizes the different phases an RSNA can traverse from its establishment to its permanent deletion. As illustrated by Figure 11, the overall sequence of actions that an 802.11i station follows to establish an RSNA is:

1. The station discovers the 802.11 networks (either Infrastructure or Independent) present in its area: this is further analysed in section 3.3.4
2. Based on the capabilities announced by the different BSSes, the station select the one to associate to
3. The Open System Authentication exchange is performed for 802.11-1999 compatibility
4. If the selected BSS works in Infrastructure mode, the 802.11 association procedure takes place

---

[20] The double handshake is needed to adhere to the 802.1X port control logic.

5. A full 802.1X authentication exchange takes place or, alternatively, a static shared secret is selected to derive a PMK for the current RSNA [21] ; in an Infrastructure BSS this can involve communication with a remote Authentication server
6. Whatever authentication mechanism has been performed in the previous step, the 802.11i key management procedures are performed to derive a PTK and a GTK for the current RSNA

After the previous steps, the RSNA is setup and can be used by the station to securely access and provide services on the wireless network. The security mechanisms used to protect this traffic are detailed in section 3.3.2.

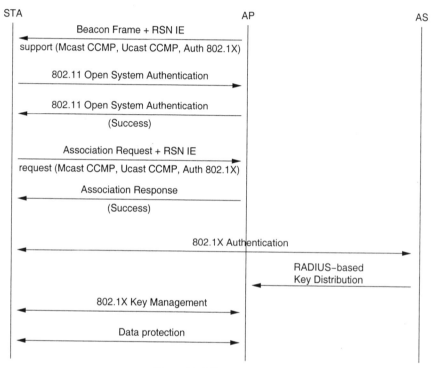

Figure 11: RSNA life cycle

The topology of a wireless network may be subject to frequent changes: for instance, a station can perform *handoff* procedures to move among different APs in a ESS. In these situations, existent RSNAs must be updated or deleted and new RSNAs must be created. 802.11i includes a set of mechanisms that aim to make these operations as efficient and fast as possible: these are analysed in section 3.3.5.

When an RSNA is removed (e.g., when a Deauthentication or a Disassociation message is received, or, in general, when the radio connectivity between the two stations sharing the RSNA breaks), some security associations that are part of the RSNA must be deleted: this is further discussed in section 3.3.4.

---

[21] A third case occurs when the two associating nodes already possess a shared secret derived during a previous RSNA established between them; this is investigated in detail in section 3.3.5

3.3.2 Confidentiality and integrity

The two following paragraphs will analyse the cryptographic primitives and the encapsulation procedures in TKIP and CCMP respectively.

The Temporal Key Integrity Protocol (TKIP)

TKIP tries to overcome WEP vulnerabilities by introducing a set of extensions to the basic WEP algorithm.

Firstly, a cryptographic Message Integrity Code (MIC) is added for integrity protections. This MIC uses a specifically designed algorithm known as *Michael* and it is computed over the source address *SA*, the destination address *DA*, the frame priority and the plaintext of the message. The TKIP MIC is appended to the original MSDU data prior to fragmentation: the result is than encrypted with WEP.

The WEP 24-bit IV is replaced by the 48-bit *TKIP Sequence Counter* (TSC). The 48-bit length extends the life of encryption keys that need to be refreshed less frequently to prevent IV reuse. With 100-byte packets and 5 Mbps traffic the TSC space is exhausted in $(100*8)/(5*10^6)*2^{48} \approx 1428$ years.

The TSC provides also anti-reply protection. As its name suggests, it is interpreted as a true frame sequence counter: frames with an out-of-sequence TSC are discarded by the receiving station.

To neutralize RC4 key scheduling vulnerabilities, TKIP adds a *Mixing Function* that combines the current TKIP encryption key, the transmitter address and the TSC into the RC4 seed. In major details, the mixing function includes two phases. The first step combines the encryption key, the transmitter address and the 32 most significant bits of the TSC into a temporary key. The second one combines the result of the first phase, the TKIP encryption key and the 16 least significant bits of TSC into the per-packet key. These last key is used as the RC4 key to run the basic WEP algorithm. The two-step construction of TKIP mixing function allows caching the result of the first phase for 2^{16} consecutive frames.

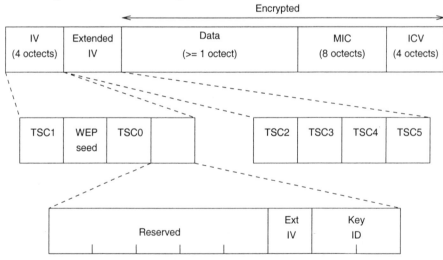

Figure 12: TKIP encapsulation

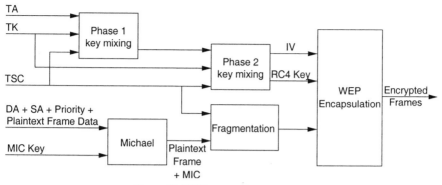

Figure 13: TKIP encapsulation process

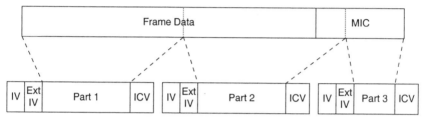

Figure 14: Fragmentation of TKIP-encapsulated MSDUs

Figure 12 and Figure 13 illustrate respectively the TKIP encapsulation schema and encapsulation process:

1. Michael is used to compute the MIC over the original frame body M, the source address SA, the destination address DA and the optional priority field; M and the MIC are then concatenated as $M_{MIC} = M \mid michael_{K_{MIC}}(SA, DA, M)$

2. If necessary, the M_{MIC} is fragmented in a series of fragments M_{frag}: this is shown in Figure 14

3. For each transmitted frame, the TSC is incremented and a new WEP seed $KWEP$ is computed through the Mixing Function phases [22]

4. Each M_{frag} is encrypted with WEP: $M_{enc} = wep(M_{frag})$

5. Finally, the proper TSC is inserted into each $Menc$ to enable correct decryption at the receiver

Michael produces a 64-bit MIC, but has been demonstrated that its effective strength is limited to 30 bits [11]. The choice of Michael can be exclusively explained by considering that TKIP targets devices with so scarce processing resources that even the use of plain WEP turn out to be an heavy task. As outlined in [12], Michael is an invertible algorithm: the knowledge of the plain message and the related MIC value is sufficient to recover the integrity key. For this very reason, it is essential that the Michael output is encrypted before transmission. This also means that the same RC4 keystream cannot be used to encrypt two TKIP messages of different length, otherwise the MIC value in the shortest one is disclosed and the integrity key compromised. Fortunately, TKIP anti-reply mechanisms can effectively prevent keystream reuse.

---

[22] More specifically, the first phase is performed at most once per encrypted MSDU, while the second phase once per MPDU.

Michael remains too weak against active attacks: a 2^{30} attack just requires $(100*8)$ / $(5*10^6)*2^{30} \approx 48$ hours, at a rate of 5 Mbps and with 100-bytes packets. In order to make this class of attacks impractical, TKIP specify a set of *counter-measures* that a station must implement when an active attack is actually detected. Both the Supplicant and the Authenticator of TKIP-protected session collaborate to monitor the Michael verification failure rate. If the current MIC error rate exceeds the threshold of 2 errors per 60 seconds, a station must renegotiate all TKIP security associations. In particular, the node deauthenticates (i.e., by a 802.11 Deauthentication frame) all other nodes it shares a TKIP security association with and stop transmitting/receiving TKIP-protected frames for the next 60 seconds. Moreover, in the same period, the node blocks all new security associations that use TKIP. In a BSS working in Infrastructure mode, this means that the AP disassociates all TKIP stations and disallows associations requesting TKIP for 60 seconds. After this period, normal operations are restored.

TKIP counter-measures aim to make active attacks impractical by limiting the rate an attacker can inject forged frames. However, an attacker must be prevented to exploit them to force continuous key renegotiation with related bandwidth under-utilization and processing resource waste. TKIP MIC verification occurs after the FCS, ICV, and TSC have been checked. The FCS and ICV avoid unnecessary MIC failure events due to noise on the transmission channel, while the TSC check effectively makes DoS attacks more expensive. The attacker is in fact required to capture a legitimate packet while preventing the recipient to receive it: as recognized in [11], this can be achieved by jamming the physical layer CRC of the transmitted frame. In fact, the same results can be achieved with less cost by mounting a man-in-the-middle attack. The attacker stands between the Authenticator and the Supplicant forwarding frames until the TKIP session is fully established: after the first TKIP-protected frame is sent, the attacker can launch the DoS attack. Note that, to mount the man-in-the-middle attack, the attacker is not required to effectively use a single node placed in the range of both the station and the AP: two probes can instead be placed in the proximity of the two attacked entities. These probes can tunnel the whole authentication procedure and the subsequent traffic exchanged between the legitimate nodes and are able to mount the DoS attack at any time: a similar attack is known ad the *wormhole* attack (see [13] for a detailed description) in literature on ad-hoc network security.

In general, the previous considerations leads to affirm that as long as an attacker is able to interpose between the AP and one of the legitimate stations, it can prevent a BSS using TKIP to work.

The Counter-mode/CBC-MAC Protocol (CCMP)

This is the mandatory solution for data confidentiality and integrity, data origin authentication and anti-replay protection in 802.11i networks.

CCMP uses the *Advanced Encryption Algorithm* (AES, [14]) with a key-length of 128 bits. In further details, CCMP use AES in *Counter-mode with CBC-MAC* (CCM). This is a recent symmetric block cipher mode specifically designed with the 802.11i application in mind and then published in the Informational RFC3610. A key feature of CCM is that it unifies confidentiality and integrity protection in a single cryptographic primitive (see in the following of this section for a discussion on this topic).

CCMP exploits CCM to provide the following security features to 802.11 data frames:

- confidentiality of the whole frame body;
- integrity of both the frame body and a subset of the MAC header field;
- data origin authentication since the transmitter MAC address is integrity protected.

Figure 15 and Figure 16 illustrate the CCMP encapsulation process:

1. The proper CCMP key KCCMP is selected for the current frame

2. The 48-bit packet number *PN* associated to the current K_{CCMP} is recollected and incremented. In order to maintain CCM strength, the same K_{CCMP} - *PN* pair should not be used for two different frames

3. The CCM *Additional Authentication Data AAD* is constructed from a subset of the MAC header information; this will be covered by integrity protection

4. The CCM *Nonce* is built from the *PN*, the packet priority[23] and the transmitter address *TA*

5. The CCM primitive is invoked with K_{CCMP}, *Nonce*, *AAD* and *M* inputs; the result the encrypted MSDU M_{enc}[24]

6. The CCMP header *HDR* is built from the *PN* and then prefixed to the encrypted data to allow anti-reply protection and proper decryption at the receiver

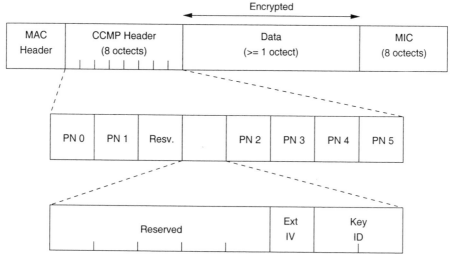

Figure 15: CCMP frame format

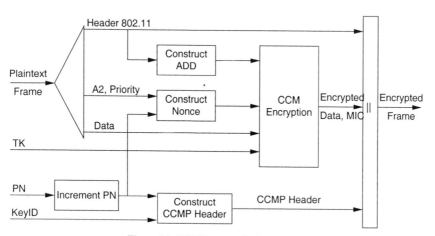

Figure 16: CCMP encapsulation process

---

[23] This new optional header field has been proposed by the 802.11 quality of service extensions [15].

[24] This is the concatenation of the Counter mode encrypted frame body and the 8-bytes truncated CBC-MAC computed over *M* and *AAD*.

The receiver of a CCMP frame performs two main functions (Figure 17): the security de-encapsulation through the CCM primitive (including MAC verification), and the anti-reply checking by making a comparison between the extracted PN and the PN' buffered from the last correctly received packet.

The scope of CCMP integrity protection directly affects the damages that still an attacker can pose to the MAC level logics. In particular, CCMP integrity protection does not cover header information that can change during 802.11 normal operations, mainly across retransmissions.

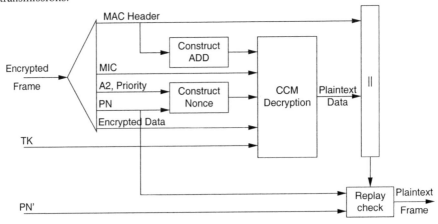

Figure 17: CCMP de-encapsulation process

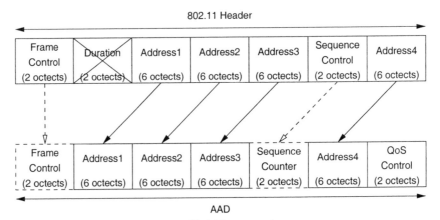

Figure 18: AAD construction

More precisely, Figure 18 illustrates the AAD construction process. The major information left unprotected is outlined below:

- the Duration header field since it changes value when a different transmission rate is selected during a retransmission;
- in the Frame Control field, the Subtype, Retry, PowerManagement and MoreData subfields;
- the SequenceNumber in the Sequence Control field.

Section 2 includes considerations about vulnerabilities introduced by leaving the previous fields unprotected. In general, the replay of a protected packet with modified versions of these fields is not straightforward since the packet would be discarded by the anti-reply mechanisms. The attacker is instead required to also prevent the receiver to get the original copy of the frame, either by jamming the CRC part during transmission or by previously mounting a man-in-the middle attacks. Typically, attacks based on the forging of the previous fields are easily mountable by using unprotect able frames such as Management or Control ones.

Some thoughts on cryptographic primitives

CCMP choice in terms of cryptographic primitives is fairly innovative: the single primitive used is AES in CCM.

CCM is a block cipher implementation mode proposed by Whiting, Housley and Ferguson in the early 2000 [16]. The main feature distinguishing it from other more classic block cipher implementation modes, like for instance ECB, CBC or CTR mode, is that, along with providing confidentiality of the message, it also provides message integrity.

The research on this kind of block cipher modes started in the year 1999 with an authenticated-encryption scheme called PCBC proposed by Gligor and Donescu [17]. That mode was wrong, as pointed out by Jutla in [18], but it contributed to the development of following research. In the year 2000 Jutla proposed two new block cipher implementation modes to achieve authenticated encryption supported by claim of provable security. On these schemes IBM has filed a U.S. patent.

At present, CCM is one of most important block cipher implementation modes to achieve authenticated encryption, together with OCB, which refines one of the Jutla's schemes [19]. Proposed by Rogaway, Bellare, Black and Krovetz, OCB was submitted to NIST (National Institute of Standards and Technology) in the year 2001.

CCM can be applied to any block cipher working with message blocks of 128 bit length, therefore it allows the use of the algorithm AES ([14]). Proposed by Vincent Rijmen and Joan Daemen with the name Rijndael, it was chosen from NIST between fifteen candidates as the new Advanced Encryption Standard. It is suited to be implemented efficiently on a wide range of processors and in dedicated hardware. It works with message blocks of 128 bit length and keys of 128, 192 or 256 bit length, which makes infeasible an exhaustive search attack. Moreover, AES has been designed to provide a strong level of security against differential, linear cryptanalysis and other among most known attacks. It does not have weak keys.

Encryption is achieved using AES in Counter (CTR) mode, i.e. the message is xor-ed with a keystream obtained by chaining the blocks S_i, where:

$$S_i = E(K, A_i) \quad \text{for } i = 0, 1, 2, \ldots$$

where the blocks A_i's contain a counter i encoded in some way. They are also depending on a Nonce.

Let us notice that both encryption and decryption operations require only the block cipher encryption function. As we will see below, also for the computation of the authentication field, CCM requires only the block encryption function. This represents an advantage especially in the case of using AES as block cipher. Indeed the cipher AES and its own inverse have some significant differences: the inverse uses different transformations and therefore a circuit implementing the cipher does not support automatically the computation of its inverse. With respect to the cipher, performance degradation is observed on 8-bit processors and the key expansion for the inverse cipher is slower on 32-bit processors. As a consequence, the use of only the encrypt function can lead to a significant saving in code size or hardware size.

In addition, Counter mode allows the pre-computation of the keystream for both sending and receiver. Once the keystream is computed, both encryption and decryption become very fast because they are reduced to a XOR.

This mode does not have propagation error, i.e. if there is a wrong bit in a packet, it compromises only the decryption of that bit in that packet, but does not affect any one else, while it affects, as it is expected, the authentication field, so that authentication fails.

Integrity is ensured by adding to the message an authentication field (a MAC) which is computed using CBC-MAC, in the following way:

$$X_1 = E(K, B_0)$$

$$X_{i+1} = E(K, Xi \oplus B_i) \text{ for } i=1,2,\ldots n$$

where B_0 is an initialisation block depending on a Nonce and the other B_i's are message blocks, where the last one has been padded with zeroes if necessary. Between B_0 and the message blocks, it is optional to insert some additional data, called authentication data, which have to be transmitted in clear to the receiver and are used for the MAC computation. The MAC is given from the first m bytes of the last block X_{n+1} (where m is the fixed authentication field size), xor-ed with S_0, i.e. the encryption of the first counter.

In order to check integrity, the receiver cannot pre-compute anything but the first block of the keystream, S_0 used for encrypting the MAC. The receiver must wait for the message, decrypt it and use the plaintext for computing the MAC. However, let us notice that it is not necessary to wait for the encryption of the whole message in order to start computing the MAC. Both operations are parallelizable: given a message block, it is possible to decrypt it and in the same step to compute the corresponding CBC-block to be used for the MAC. CCM does not require to keep these blocks: to save memory, it is convenient to keep only the last one until the next step, in which it will be used for computing the next CBC-block.

The main requirement for the Nonce is that, within the scope of a single key, the it is unique for each message. A common strategy is to use sequential numbers as the Nonce. However, this kind of Nonce exposes CCM, as well all other block cipher modes, to the pre-computation attack: an attacker generates a table with $2^{n/2}$ pairs (K, S_1) with the same value of the Nonce and waits for messages sent with that Nonce. Then for each message, she computes S_1 (it is simple under the hypothesis that first 16 bytes of the plaintext are known) and looks on her table for a pair with a matching value of S_1. Other component of the pair is the secret key. She can expect a match after $2^{n/2}$ messages. Therefore, if the bit key length is 128 the requested steps for the attacker are only 2^{64} instead of 2^{128}. Suggested ways of avoiding this attack are either to use keys with a larger bit key length (256), which forces the attacker to compute 2^{128} pairs, which is infeasible, or to introduce in the Nonce a random bit, or to make the Nonce depending on the IP address of the sender. In that way the attacker's table does not work for every one: the attacker should expect $2^{n/2}$ messages from the same sender and the attack would become infeasible. CCMP uses 128-bit keys, but specifies that the transmitting address must be part of the Nonce. Combined with a sequential number, it allows the recipient to detect replay attacks and message reordering. CCM has been criticized in [20].

3.3.3 The 802.1X authentication framework

Standardized in 2001 by IEEE, the *Port-Based Network Access Control* (802.1X) architecture is not specific for 802.11 networks, but it was designed as an access control solution for any IEEE 802 network. The main target during its specification was indeed 802.3 networks: 802.1X can be implemented on 802.3 switches to authenticate devices that attach to their ports.

However, 802.1X features have quickly become an essential requirement of 802.11 networks, although no physical port exists and any access control semantic must be provided by the association logic among nodes.

As its name suggests, 802.1X solutions are based on the concept of *port*: through a port, a device may both request and provide services to the network. A 802.1X-enabled node has a logical module (named *Port Access Entity*, PAE) dedicated to control its network ports, either physical ones (e.g., a 802.3 network interface) or logical ones (e.g., a 802.11 association with another node). 802.1X defines both the control logic applied by this module (that is the access control enforcement mechanism) and a protocol that two nodes can use to affect the state and behaviour of each other control module (that is the authorization mechanism). The primary requirement of such a protocol is to allow the authentication of each other node, the corner stone to implement any authorization decision.

An 802.1X PAE can impersonate two distinct roles:

- **Authenticator** - the module controlling the port that is granting the network access, after enforcing authentication, adopts the Authenticator role

- **Supplicant** - the module willing to access the services offered by the Authenticator adopts the Supplicant role

Beyond Authenticators and Supplicants, 802.1X architecture includes a third class of logical entities, the *Authentication Server* (or AS). The Authenticator demands authentication and authorization decisions to the AS that is supposed to understand the authentication procedures and credentials that can be used by the Supplicant. The AS can be either co-located with the Authenticator or a remote node accessible through the network. In this second case, the Authenticator and the AS a specific network protocol is needed to allow the Authenticator and the AS exchange authentication and authorization requests/responses.

Actually, 802.1X network access control was designed to easily integrate into well established AAA (Authentication, Authorization and Accounting) architectures. In particular, 802.1X uses the *Extensible Authentication Protocol* (EAP) (designed by IETF in [21]) to encapsulate authentication exchanges. Moreover, 802.1X suggests to exploit the *RADIUS* protocol [22, 23] for communications between the Authenticator and a remote AS.

Figure 19 depicts the relationships among 802.1X entities.

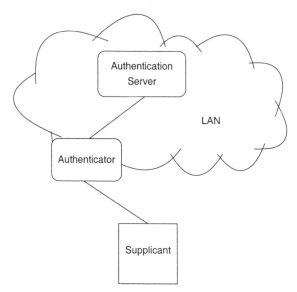

Figure 19: The 802.1X entities

802.1X operations

Figure 20 illustrates the management operations an 802.1X-controlled port is subject to.

If the Supplicant has not been authorized yet, the port at the Authenticator is blocked, or in the Unauthorized state in 802.1X terminology. In this state, the Authenticator filters all the inbound/outbound traffic relative to the specific Supplicant. Symmetrically, the Supplicant block all traffic to/from the Authenticator. Note that, in case of logical 802.1X ports, the block can be actually implemented by filtering on the data-link layer identifier of the involved nodes.

The Supplicant needs to initiate a new authentication procedure to gain access to the network. Actually, every 802.1X port is in fact a pair of logical ports: the *Controlled port* and the *Uncontrolled port*. The first is the port that does provide the access to network resources. The second one is the path, through the Authenticator, that the Supplicant can use for the authentication exchange against the AS.

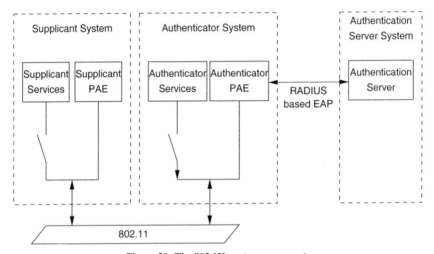

Figure 20: The 802.1X port management

Only after the authentication phase succeeds, the Authenticator switches the Controlled port in the *Authorized state* and the Supplicant is granted access to the network.

As already mentioned, EAP is leveraged in the 802.1X authentication procedures. In particular, 802.1X defines a new protocol, named *EAPoL* (EAP over LAN), that encapsulates EAP messages within 802 MAC layer frames exchanged between the Supplicant and the Authenticator. The Authenticator receives the EAPoL frames through the Uncontrolled port, de-encapsulates them and then forwards them to the AS entity. The last step may involve the re-encapsulation of the EAP messages inside AAA packets, such as RADIUS one.

From the previous description, it should be evident that all the three 802.1X roles (the Supplicant, the Authenticator and the AS) are necessary to complete an authentication exchange. However, a given network node may cover one or more of these roles. As already cited, the Authenticator and AS entities can be co-located within the same node; this allows that node to perform the whole authentication and authorization functions without contacting any remote server. Additionally, the same port can managed under both the Supplicant and the Authenticator logic in different authentication exchanges.

Generally, in a 802.1X ESS, the AP covers the role of the Authenticator while the stations willing to access the ESS acts as Supplicants. The AS, as already mentioned, can be implemented as a RADIUS server accessible by the AP. However, this cannot apply to the ad-hoc mode: in a IBSS, each member station impersonates all the three roles at different times. In particular, each node is required to perform a 802.1X authentication exchange with all other members in the IBSS.

The following sections will analyse in further details the protocols and mechanisms involved in 802.1X access control procedure.

The EAP Protocol

The use of EAP is a key feature that boosts 802.1X flexibility: the Authenticator is not supposed to understand any particular authentication logic, but only to recognize and pass through EAP packets between the Supplicant and the AS. This means that the Authenticator logic can be left as simple as possible to reduce per-port costs on devices such as Ethernet switches or APs: in particular, this allows the hardware implementation of EAPoL protocol processing. Moreover, new authentication mechanisms can be plugged into the architecture without any change in the Authenticator logic: again, this is an important feature when considering network devices such as switches or APs [25].

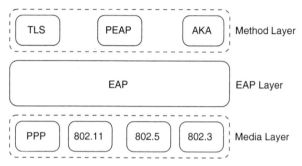

Figure 21: The EAP layer

Figure 21 explains the scope of the EAP layer, and its ability to provide independence between the transport level and the authentication modes.

Code	Identifier	Length	Type	EAP Data
(1 octect)	(1 octect)	(2 octects)	(1 octect)	(n octects)

Figure 22: The EAP frame format

The format of an EAP message is depicted in Figure 22. The *Code* header field selects among four classes of EAP packets: EAP Requests, EAP Responses, EAP Success and EAP Failure. The first two types encapsulate authentication related messages: *EAP Requests* carry the messages from the AS to the Supplicant (e.g., the authentication puzzle), while *EAP Responses* convey Supplicant responses to the AS (e.g., the puzzle solution). *EAP Success* and *EAP Failure* frames are used by the AS to indicate the final result of the authentication attempt.

In EAP Requests and Responses, the *Type* field indicates the contents of the message and is used for authentication management. In general this field indicates which particular authentication mechanism this frame belongs to. However, messages of type *Identity* can optionally be used as the first messages in the authentication session to convey the user identity: this allows the AS to select the proper authentication mechanism on a per-user

---

[25] The Supplicant and the AS must instead be upgraded to support any new authentication mechanism.

basis. *NAK* are instead sent by the Supplicant to reject the authentication method chosen by the AS and to notify an alternative.

The number of messages in a authentication session varies based on the authentication mechanism being used: Figure 23 illustrates an example of a generic authentication exchange.

Note that the EAP encapsulation does not provide any confidentiality or integrity guarantee on the authentication exchange: if required, these must be provided directly by the specific authentication mechanism itself. For instance, the original EAP specifications included the support to three simple authentication methods: an MD5 challenge scheme and two mechanisms based on one-time passwords.

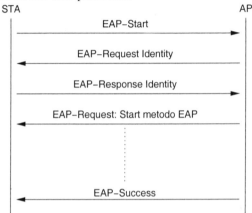

Figure 23: Generic EAP exchange

In 1999 [24] proposed a new EAP method based on a TLS exchange [25]. *EAP-TLS* provides a set of strong security properties. It forces the use of the TLS client authentication option and thus allows to use the X.509 digital certificates ([26]) as user credentials: this avoids the error-prone management of a large set of pairwise shared secrets and supports the use of tamper-resistant cryptographic tokens such as the smart-cards. Moreover, EAP-TLS provides mutual authentication: the Supplicant can now authenticate the AS (again based on X.509 certificates) and thus, in some extent, the network it is attaching to. Finally, the two participants derive a fresh session key that can be used to protect the traffic exchanged between the Supplicant and the network after the authentication phase concluded.

Recently, some EAP methods has been proposed that try to achieve strong security properties as with EAP-TLS without necessarily incurring in the complex task of digital certificate deployment and management.

The *TTLS* (Tunnelled TLS) method has been proposed in [27] by Funk, a leading vendor of Radius authentication architectures. It includes two phases: in the first step a TLS channel is created with server-side authentication, while, in the second, the Supplicant is authenticated through a weak scheme (e.g., a digest based on a shared secret) under the protection of the TLS channel. This avoids to manage a large set of client-side certificates and integrates with legacy user authentication mechanisms already in place.

PEAP (Protected EAP) has been proposed by Microsoft, Cisco and RSA in [28]. This method is almost equal to TTLS. The only difference is that TTLS can use any authentication method in the second phase, while PEAP allows only EAP methods.

A part from the flexible choice for client authentication mechanisms, an interesting feature that distinguishes the tunnelled methods from EAP-TLS is the ability to protect the identity of the authenticating client from eavesdroppers on the wireless link [26].

Since they are all based on a TLS exchange, EAP-TLS, TTLS and PEAP can in theory exploit the Session ID option and thus support a fast mechanism to establish new security associations between the same AS-Supplicant pair. This feature is particular interesting to limit the delay imposed by the 802.1X authentication phase during an 802.11 handoff. The previous participation in a full authentication exchange is proven and a new session key is derived to protect the traffic at the new network attachment point, but the authentication phase itself can be skipped. The EAP-TLS specification does not explicitly include the use of this opportunity, that is instead reintroduced in TTLS and PEAP proposals.

EAP-AKA ([29]) exploits authentication and session key distribution mechanisms used in mobile telephony networks. In particular, it supports the 3G AKA (Authentication and Key Agreement) algorithm, but also includes backward compatibility to GSM authentication. AKA is based on a symmetric secret stored at the AS and at the Supplicant in a tamper-resistant cryptographic module, the Subscriber Identity Module (SIM). The key differences between AKA and the GSM authentication are the support to longer session keys and mutual authentication. These methods can be used to provide a unique authentication mechanism to a device able to indifferently attach both 802.11 and 3G/2.5G networks.

A serious vulnerability was recently discovered that applies to tunnelled authentication mechanisms such as EAP-TTLS and PEAP. Firstly presented in [30], this vulnerability leads to a practical man-in-the-middle attack that allows an attacker to overcome the 802.1X authentication and gain access to the network. The key problem is related to the absence of any binding between the authentication mechanisms in the external protocol (that is the TLS tunnel) and the internal client authentication protocol. In particular, the man-in-the-middle opportunity is evident when considering that a node can potentially reuse the internal authentication mechanism in a context different from 802.11 authentication (e.g., not protected by an external secure tunnel) and that the session key depends solely by the external protocol (which is not client-authenticated).

This vulnerability is not limited to EAP methods, but, in general, applies to a wide set of protocols defined in IETF that rely on an external TLS tunnel. Basically, a solution has to be found in a suitable mechanism able to provide a binding between the two authentication protocols: a first proposal, under investigation at IETF, can be found in [31].

The EAP over LAN (EAPoL) protocol

802.1X defines the EAPoL protocol to transport EAP packets between the Supplicant and the Authenticator. The EAPoL layer provides independence from the specific data-link layer been used: this allows to deploy 802.1X architecture on any IEEE LAN technology. Figure 24 illustrates the EAPoL packet format and its encapsulation in the data-link layer frame.

---

[26] In EAP-TLS the identity of the client is included in the X.509 certificate transmitted during the TLS handshake.

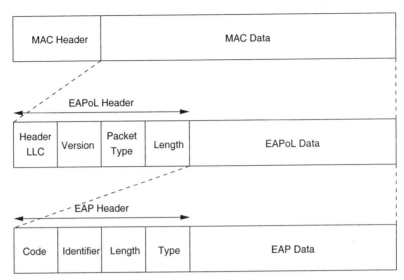

Figure 24: EAPoL packet format

The MAC level header carries the physical address of the Supplicant and the Authenticator in the medium specific format. The *Type* field selects among five different classes of EAPoL packets:

EAP-Packet, used to relay EAP frames between the Supplicant and the AS;

EAP-start can be used by the Supplicant to solicit the beginning of the 802.1X authentication phase; normally the Authenticator is responsible to initiate the authentication procedure after detecting the Supplicant has attached (either physically or virtually) to the 802.1X port;

EAPoL-Logoff is an explicit disassociation notification that the Supplicant can use to remove authentication status at the Authenticator [27];

EAPoL-Key is an optional packet that can be used at the end of the authentication phase to distribute keys or other cryptographic material for the session;

EAPoL-Encapsulated-ASF-Alert can be used to forward alert messages (e.g., SNMP traps) through a Port that is in the Unauthorized state.

Note that, the EAPoL protocol does not provide any confidentiality or integrity mechanism. Only the EAPoL-Key message includes a *Key Signature* field to carry information to proof the authenticity of the session key being distributed. However, 802.1X does not specify any particular mechanism to populate this field, as well as it does not suggest any specific mechanism to encrypt the session key itself.

802.1X and 802.11 coupling

As already mentioned, 802.1X was not specifically designed for 802.11 networks. Actually, the integration of the 802.1X authentication into the 802.11 framework has critical security implications.

First of all, the characteristics of 802.11 medium pose precise characteristics on the EAP methods that can be used. In particular, a suitable method must provide mutual authentication and session key agreement between the Supplicant and the AS. Moreover, the association state at the Supplicant must depend directly on the result of the mutual authentication phase. In general, both the Supplicant and the Authenticator should be forced

---

[27] In general, the Authenticator can remove the authentication state (practically, it resets the 802.1X port in the unauthorized state) either after receiving an EAPoL-Logoff messages, after detecting MAC level disconnection or after a configurable re-authentication timeout.

to accept not-EAPoL packets only if protected by an integrity key derived during the authentication phase.

If the previous requirements are not met, the resulting architecture is easily vulnerable to man-in-the-middle (MITM) and session hijacking attacks, as firstly demonstrated in [32].

Figure 25 depicts the man in the middle attack. The attacker disguises itself as the legitimate AP and forces all the 802.11 station traffic to pass through it. Despite of the EAP authentication mechanism used, this can be achieved just by having the attacker to send an EAP-Success message. This is possible since the EAP-Success messages are not protected by any authentication feature and the Supplicant state machine, as defined in 802.1X specification, requires a transition to the Authenticated state as soon as an EAP-Success messages is received.

This attacks can be easily extended to a full man-in-the-middle attack by having the attacker to forward authentication messages from the Supplicant to the legitimate AP: this allows the attacker to impersonate the client station and inject traffic in the victim network.

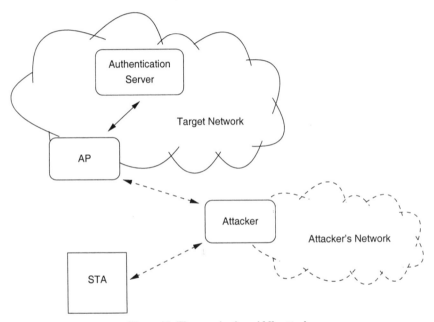

Figure 25: The man-in-the-middle attack

An even simpler attack is available when the attacker's aim is just to inject traffic into the target network. This is illustrated in Figure 26. After a normal authentication phase has been performed between the legitimate station and AP, the attacker sends an 802.11 Deauthentication or Disassociation message and starts to inject traffic by spoofing the station's MAC address. As already noted, 802.11 management frames are not integrity protected under any 802.11 security framework, 802.11i included.

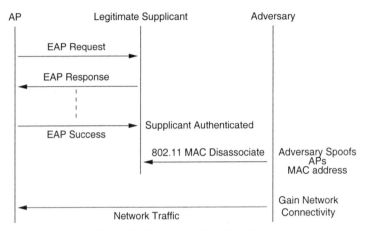

Figure 26: The session hijacking attack

While defining the 802.1X usage, 802.11i has ensured that the establishment of an RSNA meets the requirements needed to prevent the previous attacks. In particular, it allows only EAP methods that do provide mutual authentication and session key establishment. Moreover, as discussed in further details in section 3.3.4, it extends the 802.1X with a key confirmation exchange between the Supplicant and the Authenticator to make the 802.1X port state dependent on the security association established between them.

Even with strong security mechanism in place, the 802.1X authentication can still become the target of a series of DoS (Denial of Service) attacks.

As the 802.11-level Deauthentication and Disassociation messages, some 802.1X specific packets can be forged by an attacker to disrupt association state between 802.11 nodes. For example, the EAPoL-Logoff message, not protected by any authentication, can be easily sent by spoofing the Supplicant address and have the AP to remove current association state. An attacker can also spoof the AP address and send a fake EAP Failure message sent to the Supplicant while it is waiting for authentication result. Due to the Supplicant state machine, this forces the Supplicant to abort the current authentication attempt and wait a configurable amount of time before starting a new attempt.

A last DoS attacks can be mounted that tries to exhaust the number of pending authentication sessions that an AP can support. Even if the memory resources at the AP can handle a large set of 802.11-level associations waiting for 802.1X authentication to be completed, the 8-bit EAP Identifier field allows only 255 authentication sessions to be pending at the same AP. An attacker can continuously start 802.1X authentication attempts with different MAC addresses and thus prevent any other station to join the network.

3.3.4 Key management

802.11i extends the 802.1X EAPOL protocol to implement a complete key agreement and distribution system based on two procedures: the *4-Way Handshake* and the *Group Key Handshake*.

The 4-Way Handshake is overloaded with at least four aims:

1. To let the Authenticator select the ciphersuite to use for unicast and, optionally, multicast traffic
2. To verify that the Authenticator and the Supplicant share a secret, the *Pairwise Master Secret* (PMK), valid for the current session

3. To let the Authenticator and the Supplicant derive a shared session key (or PTK, *Pairwise Transient Key*) from the PMK; this will be used to protect unicast frames exchanged between them
4. To optionally let the Authenticator distribute a group key (or GTK, *Group Transient Key*) to the Supplicant for reception of multicast encrypted traffic sent by the Authenticator itself
5. To activate the pairwise and optionally the group security associations with the proper ciphersuites and keys

The Group Key Handshake can be used by an Authenticator to distribute/refresh a GTK without incurring in a whole 4-Way Handshake procedure.

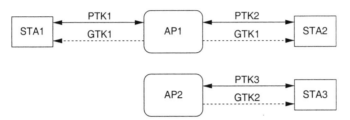

Figure 27: Key derivation in a ESS

In an Infrastructure BSS, the AP always plays the role of the Authenticator, while stations act as Supplicants. As shown in Figure 27, a 4-Way Handshake procedure is performed between the AP and each associated station to derive a unique PTK per each AP-station pair. A single GTK is distributed by the AP to all associated station: all nodes in the BSS will use this key to decrypt broadcast traffic. Note that a station need to send its broadcast frames firstly to the AP that will then diffuse them within the whole ESS, the originating BSS included.

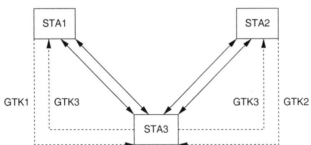

Figure 28: Key derivation in a IBSS

In an Independent BSS, each member station plays both the roles of Authenticator and Supplicant [28]. This means that two distinct 4-Way Handshake procedures are carried out per each station pair (see also Figure 28). The PTK that is actually used to protect the traffic between the two stations is the one derived during the 4-Way Handshake initiated by the station with the grater MAC address. Each station possesses a single GTK that it uses to encrypt broadcast traffic. Through a 4-Way or a Group Key Handshake procedure, every station must distribute its own GTK to all other stations, as well as, it must receive the GTK from all other stations.

---

[28] Actually, to some extent, it acts also as the Authentication Server since the authentication decisions are taken locally without the involvement of any remote server.

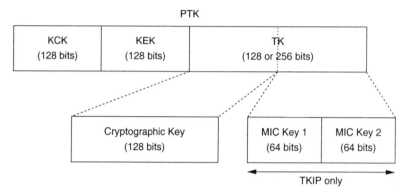

Figure 29: PTK structure

A secure key agreement protocol needs entity authentication as well as message integrity, while key distribution requires confidentiality. A shown in Figure 29, the PTK is actually a set of three shared keys instead of a single one: a 128-bit *Key Confirmation Key* (KEK) for the authentication of 4-Way and Group Handshake messages, a 128-bit *Key Encryption Key* (KEK) for key distribution confidentiality and a 128/256-bit *Temporal key* (TK) that is effectively used for bulk data traffic protection. The length of the TK changes based on the encryption protocol that will be used: CCMP needs just a 128-bit CCM key, while TKIP uses a 128-bit key for the mixing function and two 128-bit for MIC computation over frames exchanged in the two directions.

All key derivation procedures in 802.11i exploit the same pseudo random function based on the HMAC-SHA-1 algorithm (see [33] for HMAC specification).

Descriptor Type (1 octect)	
Key Information (2 octects)	Key Length (2 octects)
Key Replay Counter (8 octects)	
Key Nonce (32 octects)	
EAPoL–Key IV (16 octects)	
Key RSC (8 octects)	
Reserved (8 octects)	
Key MIC (16 octects)	
Key Data Length (2 octects)	Key Data (n octects)

Figure 30: EAPoL-Key frame format

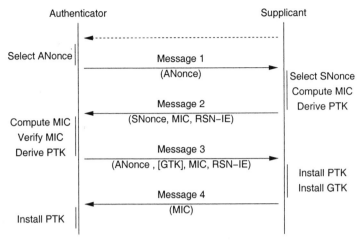

Figure 31: The 4-Way Handshake

The key management procedures use EAPoL-Key messages. Figure 30 illustrates the EAPoL-Key format as defined in 802.11i [29], while Figure 31 outlines the sequence of messages exchanged during the 4-Way Handshake:

1. The Authenticator selects a *ANonce* and send it to the Supplicant into the *Key Nonce* field in the first message; the identifier of the PMK to be used during the exchange is signalled within the *Key Data* field [30]

2. The Supplicant selects the *SNonce* and derives the PTK from the PMK, the *ANonce*, the *SNonce*, its MAC address $MAC_{Supplicant}$ and the address of the Authenticator $MAC_{Authenticator}$; more precisely the PTK is computed as

$$PRF(PMK,"Pairwisekey \exp ansion" |$$

$$\min(MAC_{Authenticator}, MAC_{Supplicant}) |$$

$$\max(MAC_{Authenticator}, MAC_{Supplicant}) |$$

$$\min(ANonce, SNonce) | \min(ANonce, SNonce) |$$

$$)$$

3. The Supplicant responds with the second frame that includes the SNonce and the supported ciphersuites in an RSN IE; this message is integrity-protected by a MIC carried in the *Key MIC* field and computed with the KCK through the HMAC-MD5 or the HMAC-SHA1-128 algorithms[31]

4. After receiving the SNonce in the second message, the Authenticator can derive the PMK and verify the MIC; it also verifies that the RSN IE is identical to the one received from the Supplicant in the 802.11 association (otherwise the message is discarded and the Supplicant disassociated)

5. The Authenticator sends, protected by a MIC, the third message that includes the ANonce, one or two RSN IEs and an optional encrypted GTK. The first, mandatory, RSN IE contains the ciphersuites supported by the Authenticator and the second, optional, one the particular ciphersuites that will be used for this association. When included, the GTK is encrypted through the KEK, either by the WEP algorithm if it is a TKIP key or by the AES key wrap algorithm [34] when it is a CCMP key; the

---

[29] 802.11i slightly modifies the EAPoL-Key frame format originally specified in 802.1X.

[30] The Key Data field in the EAPoL-Key frame format is a variable-length field used to transport any additional data not included in the fixed fields: e.g., RSN IEs, encrypted GTKs and PMK identifiers.

[31] The algorithm actually used is selected in the *Key Information* EAPoL-Key field.

EAPoL-Key IV field in the EAPoL-Key frame is used to convey the IV required by the previous key wrapping algorithms, while the *Key RSC* field carries the current frame sequence number for the GTK being installed to let the receiver initialise the TKIP/CCMP anti-reply mechanisms

6. The Supplicant verifies the first RSN IE to be equal to the one received by the Authenticator during the 802.11 association (otherwise the Supplicant disassociates) and stores the value of the last Reply Counter for anti-reply protection; after this message the Supplicant starts using the new PTK and GTK

7. The fourth message ends the process by making the Authenticator activate the new PTK and updating the Reply Counter value

The nonce values (ANonce and SNonce) should be not-predictable values: they grant that, starting from the same PMK, a fresh PTK is generated by each new 4-Way Handshake procedure. Indirectly, they also provide anti-replay protection to the messages exchanged since the MIC is computed with part of the PTK itself.

For completeness, Figure 32 depicts the Group Key Handshake procedure. The EAPoL-Key *Key Replay Counter* field is used for anti-replay protection: the Supplicant verifies that the value included in the received frames is grater than the last one saved for the current PMK and discards the message otherwise.

Once PTK and GTK security associations are successfully established, the 4-Way and Group Key Handshake can be re-run to refresh these keys. Both the 4-Way and Group Key Handshake procedures are always initiated by the Authenticator, but the Supplicant can request the Authenticator to start a new exchange through an EAPOL-Key frame carrying a properly formatted *Key Information* field.

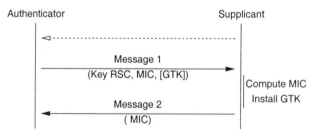

Figure 32: The Group Key Handshake

In case the association between two stations breaks, 802.11i specifies that each station deletes the shared PTK and the GTK received from the other station. in other words, a station A, when disassociated from a station B, must delete the $PTK_{A\text{-}to\text{-}B}$ and the GTK_B. Note that, while the deletion of PTK does not pose any particular concern, the removal of GTK does not ensure any security guarantee: a malicious station can decide not to remove the GTK and use it in the future to access traffic that it is no more entitled to receive. Even if not clearly stated in 802.11i, to preserve security properties, B should use the Group Key Handshake to distribute a new GTK GTK'_B to all stations other than A.

Apart from the 4-way and Group Key handshakes, 802.11i specifies a third, optional, key management exchange, the *STAKey Handshake* depicted in Figure 33. This can be used by an AP to distribute an ad-hoc generated *station-to-station key* to two associated nodes willing to communicate directly, still remaining associated to the AP[32].

---

[32] The opportunity to establish direct connections among stations associated to an AP has been firstly introduced in 802.11e [15].

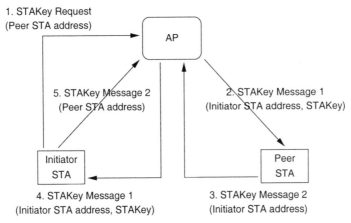

Figure 33: The STAKey Handshake

3.3.5 Handoff

Due to mobility, associations among 802.11 nodes change frequently: this can happen either in an ESS, where a station can switch AP, or in a ad-hoc scenarios where the sets of directly connected nodes may continuously change members.

RSNAs makes no exception, but cryptographic mechanisms involved in RSNA establishment can heavily affect handoff performance, both in time and computing resources. As RSNAs become more dynamic, it is vital to define solutions that accelerate RSNA refreshment: these are commonly known as fast handoff mechanisms.

802.11i supports three native methods for RSNA handoff. Moreover, the 802.11f specification ([35], an ongoing work at the IEEE 802.11 WG) targets the definition of an inter-AP communication protocol that supports the transfer of association contexts, including security related information. For an in-depth analysis of the IEEE 802.11 MAC see [36].

802.11i basic association

In case no special fast handoff solution is in place or they have failed, the whole RSNA establishment procedure must be followed as previously described. After the 802.11 level (re)association, the 802.1X takes place and the 4-Way Handshake exchange is run.

PMK Caching

802.11i nodes can cache PMKs they have agreed upon after the 802.1X or Pre-Shared Key authentication. This means that PMK security associations can survives across handoffs, while PTK and GTK security associations must be removed.

To each cached PMK is assigned an identifier, named *PMKID*, that can be included in the RSN-IE carried by (Re)Association Request frames. In this manner, if the association request is accepted, the 802.1X phase will be skipped and only the 4-Way Handshake exchange is performed.

The major limitation of this solution is clearly that it does work only for associations among nodes that have met in a recent period of time: the validity of a cached PMK cannot be very long without incurring in serious vulnerability breaches.

The Pre-Authentication

This optional 802.11i mechanism extends the previous one by defining a solution to compute a PMK with another node prior to the association time.

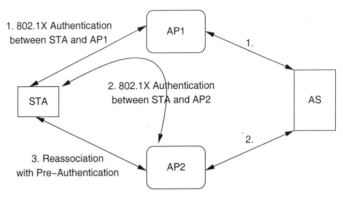

Figure 34: The Pre-Authentication mechanism

In particular, as shown in Figure 34, a station can initiate an 802.1X authentication phase with a new access point AP_{new} while still attached to AP_{old}. All 802.1X messages are exchanged through the current AP and a fresh PMK is derived. When the station decides to roam to AP_{new}, it requires the use of the PMK Caching mechanism to skip the 802.1X phase.

Before initiating this procedure a station needs to discover the target AP and that it does support pre-authentication. An AP can signal its ability to handle this method in the RSN-IE in Beacon messages, but this requires the station to be in the area covered by both AP_{old} and AP_{new}. With a fast moving station, this heavily limits the time window available to complete the 802.1X exchange.

Even with a sort of AP advertising mechanism, this solution is not able to scale to very high speeds, since it must be completed during the time a station is in the previous AP range. For an in-depth analysis of pre-authentication see [37, 38]

The 802.11f standard and its extensions

802.11f defines the so called *Inter Access Point Protocol* (IAPP) that APs can use to communicate to each other during the handoff phase, as well as mechanisms to secure this transfer. With IAPP, AP_{old} (the AP the station has initially associated to) transfers the association *context* to AP_{new} (the AP where the station has just associated).

802.11f does not define what information is actually included in the context, but only the manner to transfer it. For instance, the context can include security information, like session keys, or frames that AP_{old} has buffered for the station. The SEAMOBY WG at IETF has proposed a data format to encapsulate various classes of context information [39].

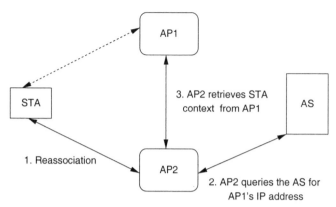

Figure 35: Reassociation with IAPP

After receiving a re-association request, an IAPP-enabled AP establishes a TCP session with the previous AP to request the transfer of the context relative to the associating station. This requires AP_{new} to know the IP address of AP_{old}. The 802.11 Reassociation Request frames include a field to convey the MAC address of the previous AP. The translation from MAC to IP addresses can be implemented with a static lookup table or with the help of a central server, such as a Radius server. This process is illustrated in Figure 35.

Since the context includes sensitive information, the Radius server may also distribute encryption keys to the involved APs to protect the transfer (this feature is optional if the DS is considered trusted). In this case, the Radius server acts as key-distribution server in a Needham-Schroeder system and, consequently, it also need to authenticate all served APs to exclude rogue ones to participate in the IAPP process [40].

The 802.11f proposal avoids that costly and lengthy cryptographic operations are performed during handoff. However, the whole context transfer procedure must now be completed before the station can access the network: this may introduce consistent delay, in particular in case of retransmissions due to errors on the DS.

To overcome these limits, IAPP can be extended with support for proactive distribution schemes in which an AP transfers in advance the context related to attached stations to the other APs in the network. To limit traffic, each AP can build a neighbourhood graph and then transfer the context only to the closer APs[33].

In particular, a solution of this kind, named *Proactive Key Distribution* [41, 42], has been proposed that specifically targets the transfer of security associations.

As shown in Figure 36, with Proactive Key Distribution in place, after the 802.11i RSNA has been established, the AP AP_A notifies the Radius server AS that a station STA_A has successfully authenticated. The AS warns the other APs that can request the AS to send them the PMK to be used to authenticate STA_A in case it moves within their range. The AS send a different PMK to each AP: these are derived as

$$PMK_{AP_B-to-STA_A} = TLS - PRF(MK, PMK_{AP_A-to-STA_A}, MAC_{AP_B}, MAC_{STA_A}),$$

where MK is the master key shared between STA_A and AS after the 802.1X authentication phase, and MAC_X is the MAC address of the given node.

By making the new PMK to depend on the old one, the previous schema supports key epochs that help to ensure the freshness of the used PMK. At re-association time, the AP can signal the epoch of the PMK it possesses for the associating station and the station can decide if this is sufficiently recent or not.

---

[33] AP neighbourhood relationships can be easily built by tracking over time the roaming patterns of stations through their associations.

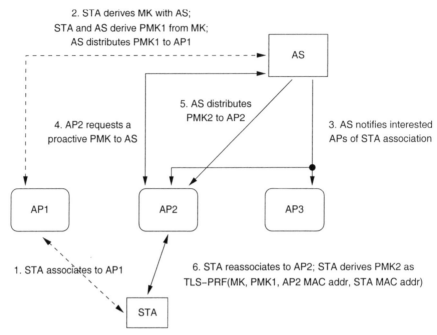

Figure 36: Reassociation with the Proactive Key Distribution scheme

4. Conclusions

Although IEEE 802.11 wireless LANs are already of common use in several places, we have shown that there are still several security problems that need to be solved before they can be declared safe for general use and appropriate also for highly sensitive environments.

By learning from the previous mistakes (i.e. WEP) the IEEE community has recently developed better solutions to some existing problems: they will hopefully appear as the 802.11i standard and should greatly improve the basic level of security of 802.11 wireless networks. As 802.11i will be integrated with the 802.1X authentication framework, better coordination between the wireless and wired security solutions will also be possible.

Despite these attempts to improve the security of the 802.11 standard, we have shown in our taxonomy that there are some vulnerabilities that simply can't be coped with by using only technical security measures. Therefore a mixture of protection, management and surveillance techniques will still be needed also when 802.11i will be in place, due to the inherently basic insecurity of wireless networks.

Acknowledgments

We are in debt with many researchers at the Politecnico di Torino and the Istituto Superiore Mario Boella for helpful discussions on these topics. In particular, we want to express special thanks to Daniele Brevi, Giorgio Calandriello, Stefano Campanella, Daniele Poma and Lucia Tamburino.

References

[1] IEEE Std 802.11-1999, Part 11: Wireless LAN Medium Access Control (MAC) and Physical Layer (PHY) Specifications, 1999.

[2] N. Cam-Winget, R. Housley, D. Wagner, J. Walker, "Security flaws in 802.11 data link protocols", Communications of the ACM (CAMC), vol. 46, no. 5, pages 35-39, 2003.

[3] A. Stubblefield, J. Ioannidis, A. Rubin, "Using the Fluhrer, Mantin, and Shamir Attack to Break WEP", 9th Annual Symposium on Network and Distributed System Security (NDSS), 2002.

[4] N. Borisov, I. Goldberg, D. Wagner, "Intercepting mobile communications: the insecurity of 802.11", Proceedings of the 7th annual international conference on Mobile computing and networking (MOBICOM), pages 180-189, 2001.

[5] W. A. Arbaugh, N. Shankar, Y.C. J. Wan, "Your 802.11 Wireless Network has No Clothes", IEEE Wireless Communications, Vol. 9, Is. 6, pages 44-51, Dec. 2002.

[6] IEEE Std 802.11i/D7.0, Part 11: Wireless Medium Access Control (MAC) and physical layer (PHY) specifications: Medium Access Control (MAC) Security Enhancements, October 2003.

[7] IEEE Std 802.1X-2001, Port-Based Network Access Control, 2001.

[8] J. Bellardo, S. Savage, "802.11 Denial-of-Service Attacks: Real Vulnerabilities and Practical Solutions", Proceedings of the 11th USENIX Security Symposium, Aug 2003.

[9] V. Gupta, S. Krishnamurthy, M. Faloutsos, "Denial of Service Attacks at the MAC Layer in Wireless Ad Hoc Networks", IEEE Military Communications Conference (MILCOM) 2002.

[10] S. Fluhrer, I. Mantin, A. Shamir, "Weaknesses in the Key Scheduling Algorithm of RC4", Proceedings of the 8th Annual Workshop on Selected Areas in Cryptography, Lecture Notes in Computer Science, LNCS 2259, 2001.

[11] N. Ferugson, "Michael: an improved MIC for 802.11 WEP", Submission to IEEE 802.11 WG, doc.: IEEE 802.11-02/020r0, 2002.

[12] A. Wool, A Note on the Fragility of the "Michael" Message Integrity Code, Technical Report EES2003-2, Dept. Electrical Engineering Systems, Tel Aviv University, 2003.

[13] Y. Hu, A. Perrig, D. B. Johnson, "Wormhole Detection in Wireless Ad Hoc Networks", 2002.

[14] J. Daemen, V. Rijmen, AES Proposal: Rijndael. Approved as FIPS-197, Specification for the Advanced Encryption Standard (AES) by US National Institute of Standards (NIST), November, 26, 2001.

[15] IEEE Std 802.11e/D5.0, Part 11: Wireless Medium Access Control (MAC) and physical layer (PHY) specifications: Medium Access Control (MAC) Enhancements for Quality of Service (QoS), July 2003.

[16] R. Housley, D. Whiting, N. Ferguson, Counter with CBC-MAC, Submission to NIST, June 3, 2002.
http://csrc.nist.gov/CryptoToolkit/modes/proposedmodes/ccm/ccm.pdf.

[17] V.D. Gligor, P. Donescu, "Integrity-Aware PCBC Encryption Schemes", Proceedings of the 7th International Workshop on Security Protocols, pages 153-171, Springer-Verlag, 2000.

[18] C. S. Jutla, "Encryption Modes with Almost Free Message Integrity", Proceedings of the International Conference on the Theory and Application of Cryptographic Techniques, pages 529-544, Springer-Verlag, 2001.

[19] P. Rogaway, M. Bellare, J. Black, "OCB: A block-cipher mode of operation for efficient authenticated encryption", ACM Transactions on Information and System Security (TISSEC), vol. 6, no. 3, pages 365-403, 2003.

[20] P. Rogaway, D. Wagner, "A critique of CCM", IACR ePrint Archive, Research Report 2003/070.

[21] L. Blunk, J. Vollbrecht, RFC 2284, "PPP Extensible Authentication Protocol (EAP)", 1998.

[22] C. Rigney, S. Willens, A. Rubens, W. Simpson, RFC 2865, "Remote Authentication Dial In User Service (RADIUS)", 2000.

[23] P. Congdon, B. Aboba, A. Smith, G. Zorn, J. Roese, RFC 3580, "IEEE 802.1X Remote Authentication Dial In User Service (RADIUS) Usage Guidelines", 2003.

[24] B. Aboba, D. Simon, RFC 2716, "PPP EAP TLS Authentication Protocol", 1999.

[25] T. Dierks, C. Allen, RFC 2246, The TLS Protocol Version 1, 1999.

[26] R. Housley, W. Polk, W. Ford, D. Solo, RFC 3280, Internet X.509 Public Key Infrastructure Certificate and Certificate Revocation List (CRL) Profile, 2002.

[27] P. Funk, S. Blake-Wilson, EAP Tunnelled TLS authentication Protocol (EAP-TLS), IETF Internet Draft, draft-ietf-pppext-eap-ttls-03.txt, 2003.

[28] A. Palekar, D. Simon, G. Zorn, J. Salowey, H. Zhou, S. Josefsson, "Protected EAP Protocol (PEAP) Version 2", IETF Internet Draft, draft-josefsson-pppext-eap-tls-eap-07.txt, 2003.

[29] J. Arkko, H. Haverinen, "EAP AKA Authentication", IETF Internet Draft, draft-arkko-pppext-eap-aka-11.txt, 2003.

[30] N. Asokan, V. Niemi, K. Nyberg, "Man-in-the-Middle in Tunnelled Authentication Protocols", IACR ePrint Archive, Research Report 2002/163.

[31] J. Puthenkulam, V. Lortz, A. Palekar, D. Simon, "The Compound Authentication Binding Problem", IETF Internet Draft, draft-puthenkulam-eap-binding-04.txt, 2003.

[32] W. A. Arbaugh, A. Mishra, "An Initial Security Analysis of the IEEE 802.1X Standard", Tech. Rep. CS-TR-4328, University of Maryland, College Park, February 2002.

[33] H. Krawczyk, M. Bellare, R. Canetti, RFC 2104, "HMAC: Keyed-Hashing for Message Authentication", 1997.

[34] J. Schaad, R. Housley, RFC 3394, "Advanced Encryption Standard (AES) Key Wrap Algorithm", 2002.

[35] IEEE P802.11f/D5, "Recommended Practice for Multi-Vendor Access Point Interoperability via an Inter-Access Point Protocol Across Distribution Systems Supporting IEEE 802.11 Operation", January 2003.

[36] A. Mishra, M. Shin, W. A. Arbaugh, "An Empirical Analysis of the IEEE 802.11 MAC Layer Handoff Process", ACM SIGCOMM Computer Communication Review, Vol. 33 , Is. 2, pages 93-102, April 2003.

[37] S. Pack, Y. Choi, "Pre-Authenticated Fast Handoff in a Public Wireless LAN Based on IEEE 802.1x Model", Mobile and Wireless Communications, IFIP TC6/WG6.8 Working Conference on Personal Wireless Communications (PWC'2002), October 23-25, 2002, Singapore, Kluwer, pages 175-182.

[38] S. Pack, Y. Choi, "Fast Inter-AP Handoff using Predictive-Authentication Scheme in a Public Wireless LAN", Networks 2002 (Joint ICN 2002 and ICWLHN 2002), Aug. 2002.

[39] J. Loughney, M. Nakhjiri, C. Perkins, R. Koodli, "Context Transfer Protocol", IETF Internet Draft, draft-ietf-seamoby-ctp-06.txt, 2003.

[40] R. Moskowitz, A. DeKok, "RADIUS Client Kickstart", IETF Internet Draft, draft-moskowitz-radius-client-kickstart-01.txt, 2003.

[41] A. Mishra, M. Shin, W. A. Arbaugh, "Proactive Key Distribution to support fast and secure roaming", submission to the IEEE 802.11 WG, doc. IEEE 802.11-03/084r0, 2003.

[42] A. Mishra, M. Shin, W. A. Arbaugh, "Pro-active Key Distribution using Neighbor Graphs", to appear in IEEE Wireless Communications,

http://www.cs.umd.edu/ mhshin/paper/Proactive_Key_Dist_NG.pdf.

Security and Privacy in Advanced Networking Technologies
B. Jerman-Blažič et al. (Eds.)
IOS Press, 2004

Security in Exotic Wireless Networks

Stephen FARRELL (1), Jean-Marc SEIGNEUR (1), Christian D. JENSEN (2)

(1) Distributed Systems Group, Computer Science Department,
Trinity College, Dublin 2, Ireland
stephen.farrell@cs.tcd.ie,
jean-marc.seigneur@cs.tcd.ie

(2) Informatics & Mathematical Modelling,
Technical University of Denmark,
DK-2800 Lyngby, Denmark
christian.jensen@imm.dt0075.dk

Abstract. In this chapter we review some exotic types of network such as ad-hoc networks or sensor networks, and the security requirements which apply in such contexts. We then examine whether and how those requirements can be met whilst at the same time, as far as possible, using standard security services and mechanisms. We finally note some areas where new types of security service may be required and give the example of how entity recognition may be more appropriate than normal user and host authentication in some circumstances.

Introduction

The most popular types of wireless networks (GSM [1], WAP [2], IEEE 802.11 [3], Bluetooth [4]) all have well known, albeit sometimes broken, security models (one of which, 802.11, is reviewed elsewhere in this book [5]). One thing that all of those security models have in common however, is that they all assume that there is some kind of infrastructure provider, be it an Internet service provider, an enterprise or a mobile network operator, who can take on a special, usually more trusted, role in the security model. For example, in GSM, the network operators trust one another implicitly when a user roams from one network to another. Another example is with 802.11 enterprise networks where generally the enterprise's systems administrators will (or should!) carefully allocate IP addresses and run firewalls and IPSec gateways in order to prevent the wireless segment of the enterprise creating a gaping hole in the enterprise security policy.

In contrast to those cases, there are networking scenarios where there is no suitable infrastructure provider (or indeed, where there is no real infrastructure!) who can play this trusted role in the security model. As might be expected, we will see that the lack of a mutually trusted party makes it quite hard (sometimes very hard) to get the benefits expected from the use of the standard security services and mechanisms that are used in more typical networking environments. We will argue that for some of those cases, it may be better to fall back to an apparently less "secure" set of services, which though providing less, may well do a better job overall. More importantly, we believe that making the weaker security model explicit is preferable to failing to implement a stronger security model. .

The remainder of the chapter is structured as follows: in the next section we review the types of exotic wireless networks with which we're concerned, then we examine the usual set of network security requirements and see that there are some new requirements in this context, next we consider ways to meet those requirements with security services and which are most important requirements to meet for which type(s) of exotic network; we then review existing work on security in this area and propose some new security technology areas that might be investigated in order to meet those new or modified requirements and we examine one such technology (entity recognition) in more detail; finally we draw some conclusions.

1. Exotic Wireless Networks

In this section we briefly outline three types of exotic network and their security-relevant characteristics. While we are presenting these independently of one another, it is important to note that a single exotic network may well fit into all of these categories at once! For example, the planned SeNDT network [6] is an ad hoc, delay tolerant, (sparse) sensor network.

1.1 Ad Hoc Networks

The notion of an ad hoc network is a new paradigm that allows hosts (called *nodes*) to communicate without relying on a predefined infrastructure to keep the network connected. Most nodes are assumed to be mobile and communication is generally assumed to be wireless. This means that traditional routing protocols are inadequate for ad hoc networks and a number of new routing protocols have been proposed for such networks [7, 8, 9, 10]. Ad hoc networks are collaborative in the sense that each node is assumed to relay packet for other nodes that will in turn relay their packets[1]. Thus, all nodes in an ad hoc network form part of the network's routing infrastructure. The mobility of nodes in an ad hoc network, means that both the population and the topology of the network can be highly dynamic.

In traditional networks, such as the Internet, routers within the central parts of the networks are owned and managed by a few well-known operators. These operators are generally assumed to be trustworthy, and this assumption is mostly justified since their entire business hinges on the preservation of this image of trustworthiness. However, this assumption no longer holds in ad hoc network, where all nodes may belong to users from different organizations and where all nodes may be called upon to route packets for other nodes. Malfunctioning or malicious nodes may disrupt the routing protocol by distributing false routing information to other nodes or by not performing the routing correctly themselves, thereby disrupting service in an area of the ad hoc network.

Sending packets in an ad hoc network, where the majority of routers may be unknown, entails a certain element of risk and requires the sending node to trust those routers to deliver the packet to the final destination. Since nodes may initially know nothing about any other router, this challenge is not unlike the challenge faced by human beings confronted with unexpected or unknown interactions with each other. Human society has developed the mechanism of trust to overcome initial suspicion and gradually evolve privileges. Trust has enabled collaboration amongst humans for thousands of years, so modeling route selection on the notion of trust may offer an approach to addressing the security requirements faced by secure routing in ad hoc networks.

---

[1] As most nodes also function as routers, the two terms are used interchangeably in this chapter.

Another challenging issue with wireless ad hoc networks is that the nodes are often quite power constrained which can affect routing and security – were any node to take on a "master" relationship with many "slave" nodes (say the winner of an election, or the first node in the area), then that node is likely to consume more power than others since it will be involved in more interactions. Ultimately, the ad hoc network is likely to partition when such a node has to drop out due to a lack of power. Solving this issue is not simple, since a naïve solution like using the node claiming the best power reserves allows an attacker to gain control of the network simply by claiming to have bigger batteries!

1.2 Sensor Networks

Sensor networks are another class of exotic network which are attracting much attention [11]. The purpose of many sensor networks is to collect some environmental data and to route that information back to some sink node which is usually connected to a more traditional network (e.g. the Internet). Sensor networks have many military applications (e.g. detecting the presence of various types of entity) as well as environmental applications (e.g. monitoring pollutants).

Sensor networks are generally considered to be self-deploying, that is, nodes may be scattered more or less carelessly and must then form a network using some of the ad hoc techniques described above - so many of the issues applying to ad hoc networks also apply to sensor networks, though once established, most sensor networks do not involve autonomously moving nodes.

However, there are also classes of sensor network where the traditional concepts of node addresses and packet routing have been abandoned! For example, in one such model [12] data queries are inserted into the sensor network and are forwarded to adjacent nodes (or not) on the basis of an algorithm which aims to answer the question whilst also minimizing the amount of traffic in the overall network (and other criteria). Say if the query was to find the average value of a pollutant, then the query from node 1 to node 2 will be of the form "send average foo value" and the result will be "average foo=bar", but where the "bar" value is calculated over all of the sub-network accessible via node 2. We can see that in such cases, node 1 never sees "addresses" for anything except its immediately adjacent peers.

Generally, the nodes in sensor networks are considered to be identical, with the possible exception of some special nodes which are often responsible for connecting the sensor network back to sink nodes on the Internet. Such special nodes are sometimes called "mules" because they may act like a mule train [13], occasionally picking up sensor data and bringing it back home.

One can see that there is a potential continuum of sensor networks, from extremely small, simple, pervasive "motes" [14] to more complex, capable, sparsely distributed sensor nodes [6]. From the security point of view, it may be useful to regard the former as "dense" sensor networks, and the latter as "sparse" sensor networks.

1.3 Delay Tolerant Networks

There is currently an Internet Research Task Force (IRTF) research group [15] developing the delay tolerant networking (DTN) [16] architecture [17] and the associated protocols [18]. That group is investigating how the DTN architecture can be used in an interplanetary network (IPN) [19] and associated projects [6] are working on sensor networking using the same technology.

The DTN architecture defines an overlay network which can layer upon various other networks, for example, the Internet or a set of CCSDS [20] compliant links. At the DTN "layer" information is organised into so-called "bundles" which can be sent between DTN nodes. The main difference between a bundle and a lower layer packet (e.g. a UDP packet) is that the bundle includes all the information necessary for routing through the DTN at the "highest" layer.

Bundles are sent between DTN nodes during "contacts", which are communications opportunities. For example, in a sensor network where nodes need to conserve power, the radios might only be turned on for 10 minutes per day – two nodes that wish to communicate therefore both need to know which 10 minute period is to be used – that information defines the contact. Of course, in some networks (e.g. with two DTN nodes which are both connected to the Internet), contacts are available "on demand", whilst in other contexts, contacts may be quite unreliable, in terms of there being no DTN node-node connection established, or perhaps due to large bit error rates. In the current reference DTN implementation [21], each DTN node follows a locally defined schedule of contacts.

DTN techniques span quite a range of applications, from animal movement monitoring [22] to lake water quality applications [6]. But there are also two more radical types of DTN which we will now briefly consider: acoustic networking and an interplanetary Internet.

Radio frequency (RF) communication is used for wireless communications in all of the above networks. However, RF cannot be used in some environments, in particular, under water. However, acoustic networking (i.e. encoding data in sound waves) is possible in this environment and networks using this mechanism have been developed for submarine detection [23] and environmental monitoring [24]. Acoustic networks differ from others in that the data rates are tiny compared to RF (hundreds of bps), signals are subject to new types of interference (e.g. due to passing boats), as well as more traditional types (multipath). Sound waves also clearly travel slowly enough for the inherent communications latency to cause such networks to require delay tolerant networking techniques to be applied.

Currently there are not enough space craft in deep (interplanetary) space to constitute a network. However, with some (currently unknown [25]) increase in the numbers of spacecraft, the communications required for deep space can form what has been called an interplanetary Internet [19]. This type of network differs from other delay tolerant networks in that: a) the delays involved are deterministic and governed by gravitation (and so can be calculated for some time in advance, given accurate enough information); b) the devices are truly extreme in terms of mass, power consumption and the amount of these scarce resources which are devoted to communications - each of these limitations are essentially caused by the difficulties of launching, and finally, c) from the security perspective, there is a huge imbalance in requirements depending on whether we're handling some uplinked commands, or some downlinked telemetry or science data - there are strong data integrity requirements for the former (which may be met simply enough if the transmitter requires a 70m antenna!) and arguably weak confidentiality requirements for the latter (whatever else happens, we don't want to loose science data).

2. Security Requirements

Here we review a traditional list of security requirements and briefly discuss how they are affected in the context of such exotic networks. Note that there will be exotic networks where the traditional security requirements apply as usual, but here we are only discussing the differences.

- Some exotic networks do require **confidentiality**, but not always using "strong" mechanisms, which could defeat the purpose of the network itself – the example of science data in space networks has been given already, others include "alarm" type sensor networks where confidentiality can only be provided if the existence of the signals is hidden (e.g. using spread spectrum), since the total information transmitted is the presence/absence of the signal. In the IPN case, there may be explicit requirements for weak-by-design cryptographic confidentiality, which may turn out to require different mechanisms compared to previous cases where export controls and law enforcement agencies attempted to force the use of weaker [26] or LEAF-enabled [27] encryption.

- **Data integrity** can take on a new meaning when a sensor network is calculating an average value as described above – in some sense there is no possible way to provide end to end data integrity (using standard cryptographic techniques) since no single set of bytes travels from one "endpoint" to another (indeed the concept of endpoint can become tenuous).

- **Authentication** in typical networks tends to require more or less long lasting identities, which we have seen may not exist in exotic networks (e.g. no node addresses). Even in ad hoc networks, nodes may be in such transient contact that the overheads associated with traditional authentication schemes are far too cumbersome to allow for their "set-up" phase.

- **Access Control** schemes usually assume a policy enforcement point (PEP) and policy decision point (PDP) model [28] where rules ("policy") are present somewhere in the network and are evaluated at run-time. Most of the exotic networks considered here cannot make use of such an infrastructure and we therefore have to consider how to control access to resources in a much more distributed, localised way.

- **Authorization** (more broadly considered than access control) also has some new aspects, in particular when we consider how to control which nodes are authorized to make use of the probably sparse resources on a network. In contrast to traditional networks, resources like power and data storage are more in need of protection here.

- **Accountability** will still be required, especially in ad hoc networks where people are the users – instead of an audit/logging approach; confidence/evidence based approaches may need to be considered [29]. Even if an auditing/logging approach is taken, synchronising and collating the logs in a meaningful sense may be challenging since the nodes which were logging may no longer be available. One must also avoid cases where the collation of logging events swamps the useful data which the network can transfer.

- **Routing security** is a much bigger issue in most of these networks since routers can not only see data, which is less likely to be protected (in the SSL-pipe sense), and given that those routers are almost certainly totally unknown to both source and destination nodes. There may however, be information flow topologies which transcend the routing topology (assuming nodes move about) which could be used to improve the confidence with which data can be routed.

- **Host security** in terms of firewalls and the use of NAT [30] to hide sub-network structure will also differ in these exotic networks (and it may even be too early to say how these network security aspects might best be handled).

- **Privacy** issues can also differ since ad hoc networks both increase the potential for surveillance whilst at the same time allowing many more opportunities for use of pseudonymity and similar privacy enhancing techniques. There are for example, possibilities to create routing schemes which inherently limit the set of nodes which will see a packet [31] – this would be similar to a topology aware "time-to-live" (TTL) field.

We can also list some requirements which rarely arise in more traditional networks, but which become important in this context:

- **Signal Stealth** is more of an issue in exotic networks, since as seen above the existence of a signal may be all that's needed to determine the signal's content – this also has implications for the ease with which a node may be spoofed.
- **Topology awareness** is normally not an issue, but in these exotic networks nodes may have to be somewhat aware of the network topology in order to be able to evaluate some security related metric. For example, this might ultimately require that packets be labelled using integrity protected "via" fields.
- **Perfect Forward Secrecy** (PFS) [32] is a security characteristic which means that even if an attacker is able to crack all of the cryptographic mechanisms used in a single transaction/session, then that attacker has as much work to do again in order to attack any subsequent (or preceding) transaction or session. It is an open issue as to whether PFS is desirable, or possible in most exotic networks, though clearly, given that we may be using inherently more "attackable" mechanisms (see section 5.1 below), forward secrecy (if not PFS) may become a more important requirement than heretofore.
- **Availability (Anti-Denial of XXX)**: there will be new possibilities to deny the use of resources to nodes, for example, one could attempt to starve a node of bandwidth (by using a higher power radio) or of power (by having it perform a lot of networking or computation). Availability (as a security requirement) will have arguably a quite different flavour from current networks where the main threats are the various forms of denial of service (DoS).
- **Secure Auto-configuration** will be required to be the norm in exotic networks whereas the opposite applies in standard networks (especially standard wireless networks). Whether secure auto-configuration is actually possible at any significant strength is an open question.

3. Using Existing Security Services

There are some standard security services and mechanisms which could be usable in many of these exotic networks. In this section we mention some of the more obvious security services and briefly discuss how to determine whether they may be usable in a given (exotic) networking context. For reasons of space, we omit discussion of security mechanisms but it is worth noting in passing that some of the more computationally intensive (e.g. asymmetric private key operations), bandwidth-hungry (e.g. ASN.1 encoding) and "chatty" round-trip (e.g. zero-knowledge protocols) mechanisms will face difficulties in many exotic networks.

3.1 Public Key Infrastructure

Public Key Infrastructure (PKI) [33] is a piece of security infrastructure which supports the binding of public keys (used in other services/mechanisms) to identities of various sorts[2]. PKI also supports the related revocation of such bindings which is an aspect that will often

---

[2] Here we are considering PKI in general, not just X.509 based PKIs, so the discussion also applies to SPKI, PGP etc.

preclude its use in exotic networks. However, there is an earlier barrier – the registration phases of use of PKI generally cannot be carried out at run-time in these networks, so nodes effectively must be able to connect to a more standard network at some stage (perhaps during manufacture!). If these registration stages can be handled then the use of PKI without revocation is generally fine. Revocation typically, however cannot be supported in exotic networks.

Aside however from the networking aspects of supporting PKI, there is also the fact that PKI requires a network of trusted third parties and so far as is known to the authors, there is no scalable way to build such a network on top of these exotic environments. However, there is no need for the PKI trust hierarchy (or trust topology, for non-hierarchical PKIs) to use the same networking technology as the run-time applications, so if the PKI can be built and maintained using say the Internet, then it may be able to support exotic networks.

The way that the wireless applications protocol (WAP) PKI [34] handled using X.509 based PKI [35] to support mobile phones is a case in point. In that case the PKI is based on the Internet, but with the handset manufacturers and (mainly GSM) network operators taking on special roles in order to ensure that the correct PKI data (root information, public key certificates) was in the right place at the right time.

3.2 Kerberos

Kerberos [36] is a widely used authentication and key distribution scheme which at first glance seems entirely unsuitable for these types of network given the requirement for communicating peers to both contact a local, trusted, key distribution service in order to set-up a secure connection between the peers. As it turns out, that first glance is mostly correct and schemes like Kerberos cannot be used in these exotic networks. It is however, instructive to break this down a bit more in order to see where Kerberos fails in such environments.

The first stage in using Kerberos is for a client to contact its trusted authentication service (AS), with which it plays out a protocol resulting in the client ending up with a ticket granting ticket. With the standard Kerberos protocol, it is possible for any host between the client and the AS to mount a dictionary attack on the TGT as it is returned to the client – a vulnerability which may be acceptable in some standard networking environments, but which is probably much less acceptable in exotic networks[3] where the routers are not trusted. For this reason, it may be that TGT acquisition is a stage (like PKI registration) which would generally have to take place when the node is connected to a standard network. Unlike PKI credentials however, Kerberos TGTs normally have a roughly working-day lifetime, which may further restrict where Kerberos can be practically applied.

When a Kerberos client wishes to set up a secure session with a peer, it first asks its ticket granting service (TGS, often the same as the AS) for a ticket for the peer, using its (the client's) TGT to authenticate the request. This use of the stored TGT in order to make the TGS stateless is actually quite a nice trick to apply in exotic networking! Unfortunately, we also see here an issue which arises in data-centric networks [12] – a Kerberos TGS request message includes the name (or IP address) of the peer. In data-centric networking it is entirely unclear what analogous information could be used – how then can one ask a question of the network but where only some hosts/nodes on the network can understand the question? (Or, where that subset of hosts is able to check data integrity for the query.)

---

[3] There is a pre-authenticated data option which can be used to ameliorate this vulnerability and which should work fine in most exotic networks.

Finally, Kerberos includes a data protection service, which is generally fine for use in exotic networks, but which is essentially suited for application layer field level protection of integrity and confidentiality. For more general traffic protection we must turn to other mechanisms.

3.3 IP Layer Security

IPSec [37] provides data confidentiality and integrity services at the IP layer, essentially allowing either integrity protection of the data (using the AH mechanism) or else encapsulation of the payload (the ESP mechanism) which provides some level of confidentiality as well as integrity. IPSec can also operate in tunnel mode where traffic is protected whilst in transit between two nodes which may not be the origin and/or destination nodes. This is how most VPNs work, with the remote access client being the origin and one tunnel endpoint, and some corporate host (say your IMAP server) being the destination node, but where the other IPSec tunnel endpoint is usually a specialised host in the corporate DMZ. An alternative mode is transport mode, where the IP packet's origin and destination are the IPSec endpoints. IPSec has an associated set of (overly complex) specifications for key management, generally termed Internet key exchange (IKE) [38], whose purpose is to establish (in a secure way) the cryptographic keys and other settings (e.g. algorithm choices) required to support the AH and/or ESP mechanisms.

The basic AH and ESP mechanisms ought to be quite usable for many exotic networks which are based on IP, so long as the intermediate nodes in the network are not expected to modify the packets in transit (e.g. by adding "via" type fields), since that would break the cryptography used in data integrity and encapsulation. However, one could fairly easily imagine how to modify AH and ESP so that such "via" fields would be allowed, even with each field having its own application of AH and/or ESP! The main argument against such a modified IPSec would probably be complexity and data expansion which may well be too much for many exotic networks.

In contrast to AH and ESP, the use of IKE is probably impossible for all but a small class of exotic network. This is largely due to the fact that IKE is overly complex, but also due to the requirement that IKE provide perfect forward secrecy (PFS), which leads to requiring a large number of roundtrips. Even IKEv2 [39], which simplifies a number of the problems with the current IKE standard requires either four or six roundtrips. Requiring any roundtrips prior to data transfer is simply impossible in some environments (e.g. IPN) which have large inherent delays. In other environments where round trip times (RTTs) may be acceptable, there may still be issues with communicating that many times with the same node (say in some putative Formula-1 ad hoc network with very high-velocity nodes, where a route between two peers may only exist for 3-4 RTTs at a time).

3.4 Transport Layer Security

The case with TLS [40] is similar to IPSec in that the application layer "protocol" of TLS defines a way to encapsulate data which is probably quite usable for exotic networks. One difference between TLS and IPSec is that TLS's handing of packet fragmentation is probably somewhat more suited for exotic networks, where presumably one should expect more fragmentation to be required (if bit rates vary substantially on different hops).

But just like with IPSec's IKE, the TLS handshake layer requires too many roundtrips (at least four) to be usable in some exotic networks. TLS does however have a feature allowing a peer to "resume" a session in fewer roundtrips (two) which should therefore be more usable. Unfortunately, this still doesn't meet the "no extra roundtrips" requirement which some exotic networks will impose.

4. Existing Work on Exotic Network Security

While there has been great activity in general area of wireless ad hoc networks, particularly in the design of routing protocols for ad hoc networks, so far little attention has been paid to the particular security characteristics of routing protocols in mobile ad hoc networks - most of the effort has focused on the extension of existing identification and authentication based security models to the infrastructure-less environment of mobile ad-hoc networks (MANETs).

Zhou and Haas [41] have proposed a PKI mechanism for ad-hoc networks installed and run for the benefit of a single organisation, e.g., by an army in a battlefield. Their PKI mechanism relies on threshold cryptography and secret sharing to ensure availability, confidentiality, integrity and authentication of routing information updates. However, their mechanism ultimately relies on a trusted certificate authority, whose public-key must be known by all nodes in the network. It is not clear that this is a realistic assumption for spontaneous ad-hoc networks that may span organisational boundaries. Another PKI mechanism is developed by Capkun et al. [42], who propose a mechanism, where every user holds a public-key certificate, which is certified by other users in the system. This is very similar to the mechanism implemented in PGP [43], but it doesn't rely on central key repositories. Instead, users certify each other's keys and a valid chain of certificates is needed when a user u wishes to verify the public-key of another user v. A certificate chain is valid if:

1. The first certificate in the chain can be verified directly by u using a public-key that u knows and trust (e.g., her own public-key).
2. Each remaining certificate can be verified using the public-key contained in the previous certificate of the chain.
3. The last certificate contains the public-key of the target user v.

This mechanism eliminates the need for a central trusted authority, but it still suffers from a bootstrap problem, i.e., newly arrived nodes in an area will be unknown to all nodes which means that their public-keys cannot be verified using the proposed mechanism. PGP solves the bootstrap problem by having key signing parties where users meet face to face, which allows them to physically verify the identity of other users and sign their keys. An online version of this mechanism is proposed by Stajano and Anderson [44], who have investigated secure collaboration among intermittently connected peers (they mainly focus on consumer electronic appliances). They identify the absence of a certificate authority (an online server) as a fundamental problem for secure communication in ad hoc networks. They propose a solution where two nodes come into physical contact in order to exchange cryptographic keys. While this may be appropriate for consumer appliances, e.g., a television and its remote control, it is unsatisfactory in general mobile ad-hoc networks. Moreover, it only addresses the problem of key exchange, which can be used to establish confidentiality and integrity of communications, but it provides little help to address the problem of authorisation.

The collaborative nature of ad-hoc routing protocols, where all nodes are part of the routing infrastructure, introduces the problem of routing security. Two solutions have been proposed to solve the problem of secure routing in mobile ad-hoc networks: detecting and avoiding misbehaving nodes and providing a fiscal incentive to behave correctly.

Marti et al. [45] investigate the ability to identify misbehaving nodes in mobile ad hoc networks. They focus on dynamic source routing (DSR) and propose a mechanism based on the ability of most network interfaces to enter "promiscuous mode" where all received packets are forwarded to the network layer. This enables each node to monitor whether the next node in the source route relays the packet as intended and to report misbehaving nodes back to the sender. This assumes that radio coverage is symmetric, which limits the stations' ability to manage their transmission power independently. Moreover, the authors themselves identify the inability of their mechanism to deal with Byzantine behaviour such as collusion and framing. The CONFIDANT protocol [46] extends the simple mechanism defined by Marti et al. The protocol relies on feedback (ALARMS) from trusted nodes (friends) in the network. Whenever a node observes that a router does not forward a packet, it sends an ALARM to all its friends and the sender of the packet, warning them about the misbehaving node. Relying on feedback from trusted entities reduces the problem of one node framing another node, but selection of these trusted nodes remain an unsolved problem. In fact, "the reputation system is based on negative experience", so there is no obvious way to bootstrap the system.

Buttyan and Hubaux [47] propose a virtual currency, called Nuglets, which is used to pay other nodes for forwarding packets. A sufficient amount of Nuglets should be included in each packet to pay all nodes on the route to the destination. In order to bootstrap the system, all nodes start with a predefined, but not necessarily equal, amount of Nuglets. Unless a node earns as many Nuglets by forwarding packets for other nodes as it spends sending its own packets, it will eventually run out of Nuglets and thereby be unable to send any packets. Another problem is that the Nuglet economy is a closed system, which requires that there is an equilibrium between the number of packets that a node needs to send and the number of packets it is able to forward for other nodes. This means that centrally placed nodes may eventually end up holding all the Nuglets, especially if they do not send many packets themselves, which may prevent other nodes from communicating with each other. This problem is addressed by Tewari and O'Mahony [48] who propose to use real micro-payments in order to create an open economy and provide a stronger incentive to forward packets, i.e., the reward for forwarding packets is paid in the same currency as the cost of forwarding the packets, namely the monetary cost of recharging the battery.

5. New Technologies needed

From all of the above discussion it should be clear that there is a need for some new, or at least, modified security services and mechanisms and that work on defining those is at an early stage. In this section we explore how two such technologies – so-called entity recognition and privacy enhancing technologies – may be useful in exotic networks.

5.1 Entity Recognition

It has been observed that authentication in pervasive computing systems is not necessarily enough to ensure security, because identity conveys no *a priori* information about the likely behaviour of the other entity [49, 50]. Entity recognition (ER) [50] has been proposed as a more general replacement for authentication that does not necessarily bind an externally visible identity to the recognised entity (i.e. authentication is a special case of recognition that binds an externally visible identity to the recognised entity). We conjecture that the ability to more-or-less reliably recognize the re-appearance of another entity is a useful security service more suited for exotic networks, and in particular that ER can provide a sound mechanism upon which higher level security decisions can be based. To allow for dynamic enrolment of strangers and unknown entities, we have proposed an entity recognition process, which consists of four steps:

1. *triggering* of the recognition mechanism
2. *detective work* to recognize the entity using the available recognition scheme(s)
3. *discriminative retention* of information relevant for possible recall or recognition
4. *action* based on the *outcome of recognition*

As an example of what is possible with this approach, we have developed an entity recognition component based on Pluggable Recognition Modules, which allows the integration of more or less secure recognition schemes (such as traditional authentication modules developed for PAM (Unified Login with Pluggable Authentication Modules) or "pure" recognition based schemes such as "A Peer Entity Recognition" (APER) [50] which uses signed claims broadcast periodically on a network to recognize entities. APER provides three levels of confidence in the recognised entity, depending on how much verification effort is applied to the claims – in increasing order of confidence APER allows for simple signature validation to be used, or additional checks on claim freshness, and finally defines a challenge response protocol to prove the current presence of the entity.

5.2 Privacy Enhancing Technologies

In order to address the serious security and privacy issues raised by mobile users in a ubiquitous computing infrastructure, a privacy driven security model is needed, which makes privacy the default. This implies the definition of a privacy model, which describes how to protect the privacy of the user, e.g., the user's identity and her preferences/profile, and the definition of a privacy driven security model, which extends the privacy model to describe how to protect personal information stored in the system. One way to develop such a privacy model is to rely on virtual identities and zero-knowledge authentication, which severs the link between the identity of the principal and the requested action. Virtual identities provides anonymity for the requesting principal, which makes it difficult to impose sanctions against principals who abuse the system, so the privacy model has to be extended with a security model that accommodates virtual identities. One solution would be to apply a trust-based security architecture [29], where autonomous entities establish trust in other entities based on collected evidence, such as reputation, recommendation and records of past experience. The level of trust in another entity is then used to decide whether to either request service from that entity or reply to a request from that entity.

5.2.1 Privacy model

Anonymity is not a goal in itself, but an important means to achieve privacy, but it is much more difficult to support anonymity or pseudonymity on an identified communications infrastructure than to support identification and authentication on an anonymous communications infrastructure [51]. However, anonymous identities are not sufficient to protect the privacy of users, because persistent use of the same virtual identity may eventually be linked to the real identity, e.g., prepaid phone cards allow traceability of a principal's actions but these actions cannot be linked to a particular identity. This illustrates the existence of different degrees of anonymity from fully anonymous and non-traceable to fully identified and traceable. It is therefore important to develop a privacy model based on virtual identities, which allows linkability between actions but makes it difficult to link actions to a particular identity. However, in order to reduce the risk of abuse, some identity escrow mechanism could be included into the system, which, under special circumstances, e.g., as the result of a court order, can be invoked to establish the link between the virtual identity and the principal's real identity. The requirements outlined above are quite similar to those of anonymous digital cash with detection of double spending and we conjecture that many of the same cryptographic techniques can be used to develop our privacy model. However, there are some important differences that require further investigation if these techniques are to be used as the basis of virtual identity scheme, e.g., double spending is normally detected at a single entity (the bank) that acts as a trusted party while we wish to divide the escrow mechanism between multiple (possibly less) trusted parties to avoid the accumulation of control by a single entity.

5.2.2 Privacy driven security model

Persistent use of pseudonymous virtual identities enables traceability, i.e., linkability between actions, which allows an entity to establish trust in other entities based on collected evidence, such as reputation, recommendation and records of past experience. Past experience is particularly important because it is the only objective element in the trust evaluation; all other elements originate with other entities that may themselves be trusted to varying degrees, i.e., recommendations are made by third parties, that may be themselves trusted to different degrees, and both personal observation and reputation is vulnerable to collusion among other entities in the system. The relative importance of these different forms of evidence will have to be assessed in order to establish and evolve trust in the other entity. Persistent use of the same virtual identity exposes an apparent conflict between security and privacy, because persistent use of the same virtual identity may eventually reveal the real identity, e.g., it may be possible to infer the address of a mobile entity through observing its movement patterns provided by a location service. It is therefore important to support multiple virtual identities and to allow the mobile entity to select a virtual identity according its current context [52]. We propose to design and implement a trust-based security architecture, which supports our privacy model and which integrates well with current security technologies proposed for distributed knowledge bases.

6. Conclusions

In this chapter we have described some of the types of exotic network which are being developed and we have considered how "standard" security requirements and services might be handled in those environments. This has shown that the "infrastructure" style security services and mechanisms to which we have become used, will likely not work in such networks, and that new security technologies are needed.

Finally, we also conclude that examining existing security requirements and technologies in the context of exotic networks is a useful way to highlight the limitations of these technologies, and seems to point at improvements (e.g. reducing infrastructure required at run-time) which can be made which could also be beneficial in standard networking environments.

References

[1]   GSM 03.20: "Digital cellular telecommunications system (Phase 2+); Security related network functions".
[2]   Howell, R. "WAP Security",
         http://www.vbxml.com/wap/articles/wap_security/default.asp

[3]   Cisco Systems, "A Comprehensive Review of 802.11 Wireless LAN Security and the Cisco Wireless
        Security Suite",
        http://www.cisco.com/warp/public/cc/pd/witc/ao1200ap/prodlit/wswpf_wp.pdf
[4]   Nihkil,   A,   "An   Overview   of   Bluetooth   Security",   February   2001,
        http://citeseer.nj.nec.com/nikhil01overview.html
[5]   Aime, M.D., Lioy, A., Mazzocchi, D. "On the Security of 802.11 Wireless Networks", in
        "Security and Privacy in Advanced Networking Technologies", B. Jerman-Blažič, W. Schneider, T.
        Klobučar (Eds.), IOS Press, 2004.
[6]   SeNDT project web site: http://down.dsg.cs.tcd.ie/sendt/
[7]   Z. J. Haas and M.R. Pearlman: "The Zone Routing Protocol (ZRP) for Ad Hoc Networks", IETF Internet
        Draft, draft-ietf-manet-zone-zrp-02.txt, June 1999.
[8]   D. B. Johnson and D.A. Maltz: "Dynamic Source Routing in Ad Hoc Wireless Networks", In Mobile
        Computing, T. Imielinski and H. Korth (Eds.), Kluwer Academic Publishers, 1996.
[9]   G. Pei, M. Gerla, and T.-W. Chen: "Fisheye State Routing: A Routing Scheme for Ad Hoc Wireless
        Networks", in Proceedings of the IEEE International Conference on Communications, pages 70--74, New
        Orleans, LA, June 2000.
[10]   C. E. Perkins and E. M. Royer: "Ad hoc On-Demand Distance Vector Routing", in Proceedings of the 2nd
        IEEE Workshop on Mobile Computing Systems and Applications, New Orleans, LA, February 1999, pp.
        90-100.
[11]   Akyildiz, I. F., Su, W., Sankarasubramaniam, Y., and Cayirci, E.,"A Survey on Sensor Networks," IEEE
        Communications Magazine, Vol. 40, No. 8, pp. 102-114, August 2002.
[12]   Chatterjea, S., Havinga, P. "A Dynamic Data Aggregation Scheme for Wireless Sensor Networks",
        ProRISC 2003, Veldhoven, The Netherlands, 26-27 November 2003.
[13]   Rahul C Shah, Sumit Roy, Sushant Jain, Waylon Brunette, "Data MULEs: Modeling a Three-tier
        Architecture for Sparse Sensor Networks" IEEE Workshop on Sensor Network Protocols and
        Applications (SNPA). May, 2003
[14]   http://www.intel.com/research/exploratory/motes.htm
[15]   Internet Research Task Force, Delay Tolerant Networking Research Group: http://www.dtnrg.org
[16]   Warthman,   F.   "Delay   Tolerant   Networks   (DTNs):   A   tutorial"   March   2003,
        http://www.dtnrg.org/tutorials/warthman-1.1.pdf
[17]   Cerf. et al. "Delay-Tolerant Network Architecture", Internet draft, March 2003, (work-in-progress)
[18]   Scott, K., Burleigh, S. "Bundle Protocol Specification", Internet draft. March 2003 (work-in-progress)
[19]   Durst. R., "Delay-Tolerant Networking: An Example Interplanetary Internet Bundle Transfer", Internet
        draft. March 2003 (work-in-progress)
[20]   CCSDS, "Advanced Orbiting Systems, Networks and Data Links: Architectural Specification". Blue
        Book. Issue 3. June 2001
[21]   http://www.dtnrg.org
[22]   Juang, P. et al, "Energy-Efficient Computing for Wildlife Tracking: Design Tradeoffs and Early
        Experiences with ZebraNet" appeared at ASPLOS-X conference. October, 2002. San Jose, CA.
[23]   Rice, J. "Telesonar Signalling and Seaweb Underwater Wireless Networks", Proc. NATO New
        Information Processing Techniques for Military Systems, October 2000.
[24]   Yang, X., et al. "Design of a Wireless Sensor Network for Long-term, In-Situ Monitoring of an Aqueous
        Environment", *Sensors* 2002, *2*, 455-472
[25]   Farrell, S. Jensen, C.D., "Scaling an Interplanetary Internet", in "Proceedings of the International
        Conference on Recent Advances in Space Technologies" (RAST2003), Istanbul, Turkey, November 2003,
        IEEE Catalog Number: 03EX743, ISBN 0-7803-8142-4.
[26]   Diffie, W., Landau, S. "The Export of Cryptography in the 20th Century and the 21st"
        ,http://research.sun.com/research/features/tenyears/volcd/papers/22Diffie.pdf
[27]   United States Department of Commerce, National Institute of Standards and Technology (1994),
        "Approval of Federal Information Processing Standards Publication 185, Escrowed Encryption
        Standard," Federal Register, Vol. 59, No. 27, February 9, 1994.
[28]   Raju Rajan, Dinesh Verma, Sanjay Kamat, Eyal Felstaine, and Shai Herzog. "A policy framework for
        integrated and differentiated services in the internet", IEEE Network, 13(5):36--41, September/October
        1999.
[29]   V. Cahill, E. Gray, J.-M. Seigneur, C. Jensen, Y. Chen, B. Shand, N. Dimmock, A. Twigg, J. Bacon, C.
        English, W. Wagealla, S. Terzis, P. Nixon, G. d. M. Serugendo, C. Bryce, M. Carbone, K. Krukow, and
        M. Nielsen, "Using Trust for Secure Collaboration in Uncertain Environments", in *Pervasive Computing
        July-September 2003*, vol. 2(3), IEEE, 2003, http://csdl.computer.org/comp/mags/pc/2003/03/b3toc.htm.
[30]   http://www.lanarchitect.net/Articles/Firewalls/Part1/default.htm

[31]   Farrell, S., Jensen, C.D., "Trajectory based addressing" 8th Cabernet radicals workshop October 2003
        http://www.newcastle.research.ec.org/cabernet/workshops/radicals/2003/papers/
[32]   Shirey, R., "Internet Security Glossary", Interent RFC 2828, May 2000.
[33]   Housley, R., Polk, T. "Planning for PKI: Best Practices Guide for Deploying Public Key Infrastructure",
        John Wiley & Sons; 1 edition (March 13, 2001) ISBN: 0471397024
[34]   WAP Forum, "WAP Public Key Infrastructure Specification" WAP-217-WPKI-20010424-a,
        http://www1.wapforum.org/tech/terms.asp?doc=WAP-217-WPKI-20010424-a.pdf
[35]   Housley, R. Et al "Internet X.509 Public Key Infrastructure - Certificate and Certificate Revocation List
        (CRL) Profile" Internet RFC 3280, April 2002.
[36]   Kohl, J., Neuman, C., "The Kerberos Network Authentication Service (V5)" Internet RFC 1510,
        September 1993.
[37]   Kent, S., Atkinson, R. "Security Architecture for the Internet Protocol" Internet RFC 2401, November
        1998.
[38]   Harkin, D. Carrel, D., "The Internet Key Exchange (IKE)" Internet RFC 2409, November 1998.
[39]   Kaufman, C. (ed), "Internet Key Exchange (IKEv2) Protocol" Internet-Draft, draft-ietf-ipsec-ikev2-12.txt,
        January 2004, work-in-progress
[40]   Dierks, T., "The TLS Protocol Version 1.0" Internet RFC 2246, January, 1999.
[41]   L. Zhou and Z. J. Haas: "Securing Ad Hoc Networks", IEEE Network Magazine, vol. 13, no.6,
        November/December 1999
[42]   S. Capkun, L. Butty an, and J.-P. Hubaux: "Self-organized public-key management for mobile ad hoc
        networks", in IEEE Transactions on Mobile Computing, 2(1), January-March 2003.
[43]   S. Garfinkel: "PGP: Pretty Good Privacy", O'Reilly & Associates, 1994.
[44]   F. Stajano and R. Anderson, "The Resurrecting Duckling: Security Issues for Ad-hoc Wireless Networks",
        in *Proceedings of the 7th International Security Protocols Workshop*, pp. 172-194, 1999,
        http://citeseer.nj.nec.com/stajano99resurrecting.html
[45]   S. Marti, T. Giuli, K. Lai, and M. Baker: "Mitigating routing misbehavior in mobile ad hoc networks", in
        Proceedings of the Sixth annual ACM/IEEE International Conference on Mobile Computing and
        Networking, pages 255--265, 2000.
[46]   S. Buchegger and J.-Y. Le Boudec: "Performance Analysis of the CONFIDANT Protocol", in
        Proceedings of MobiHoc 2002.
[47]   L. Buttyan and J. P. Hubaux: "Nuglets: a Virtual Currency to Stimulate Cooperation in Self-Organized
        Mobile Ad Hoc Networks", Technical Report No. DSC/2001/001, EPFL, January 2001.
[48]   H. Tewari & D. O'Mahony: "Real-Time Payments for Mobile IP", in IEEE Communications, Vol. 41, No.
        2, February 2003, pp 126-136.
[49]   S. Creese, M. Goldsmith, B. Roscoe, and I. Zakiuddin, "Authentication for Pervasive Computing", in
        Proceedings of the First International Conference on Security in Pervasive Computing, 2003.
[50]   J.-M. Seigneur, S. Farrell, C. D. Jensen, E. Gray, and Y. Chen, "End-to-end Trust Starts with
        Recognition", in *Proceedings of the First International Conference on Security in Pervasive Computing*,
        2003, http://www.cs.tcd.ie/publications/tech-reports/reports.03/TCD-CS-2003-05.pdf
[51]   Ian Goldberg: "A Pseudonymous Communications Infrastructure for the Internet", Ph.D. Thesis,
        University of California at Berkeley, Fall 2000
[52]   J.-M. Seigneur and C. D. Jensen, "Trading Privacy for Trust", in Proceedings of iTrust'04 the Second
        International Conference on Trust Management, LNCS, Springer-Verlag, 2004.

Security and Privacy in Advanced Networking Technologies
B. Jerman-Blažič et al. (Eds.)
IOS Press, 2004

Design, Implementation and Evaluation of Security Facilities for a Next Generation Network Element

Dušan GABRIJELČIČ, Arso SAVANOVIĆ[1], Borka JERMAN-BLAŽIČ
Jozef Stefan Institute, Laboratory for Open Systems and Networks, Jamova 39, Slovenia.
E-mail: dusan,arso,borka@e5.ijs.si

Abstract. Introducing new services in a network always represents a challenge from many aspects. Without a doubt, security is among the most important ones. In the following paper we will present a case study of needed security facilities of a heterogeneous, extensible and flexible network element. Security facilities of such system have to be again flexible and extensible, besides being general and complete, to cope with security issues raised. We will discuss their design and implementation, report on performance measurements and experimental results. The evaluation of the facilities shows, that strong security in such system is possible and that facilities developed can support the system features.

Introduction

In the era of new generation networks there is a strong tendency to introduce more functionality in the network and on the network elements (NE). New services on these elements can provide either a general functionality or a specific one tailored to the needs of a specific user. Services can operate in management, control and transport plane and therefore it is realistic that they can be implemented in heterogeneous environments. These services have to be deployed, instantiated and managed on NEs. All these issues raise security concerns that have to be addressed in a general, flexible and scalable way. For this purpose, we will present in this paper a study of a security architecture of a flexible, heterogeneous and scalable NE.

The study covers the development, implementation and experiments with the NE based on principles of active and programmable networks[1,2]. These principles are a powerful, flexible and scalable networking paradigm, which offer opportunities for innovative networking services but pose many security challenges. The NE or a node, in short, has been developed in the context of the FAIN project [3]. Its architecture advocates heterogeneity and support for multiple and different Execution Environments (EE). As such, it is a perfect example for the study purposes and we will urge here a need for a strong security and a baseline in a system design with a basic but complete, flexible and scalable communication security facilities, and a need for transparent authorization and policy enforcement framework on the node.

In the paper we present in Section 1 a brief introduction to the node and the system as a whole and in Section 2 threats, security requirements and architecture goals. Security issues related to needed security services are discussed in Section 3. In Section 4 we propose a high level security architecture and point out its relations to other node subsystems. Possible node implementations are presented in Section 5 and the security architecture design and implementation in Section 6. Performance measurements are reported in Section 7 and an

---

[1] Currently employed with Konel, Mlakarjeva 87, Šenčur, Slovenia, e-mail: arso.savanovic@konel.si

experiment with integrated existing active networking approach is presented in Section 8. An evaluation of the architecture and achieved results are presented in Section 9. Our conclusions and future work are stated in Section 10.

1. The system description

The FAIN active node is defined by a reference model [4], decomposing the node into four layers: router or hardware, node operating system (NodeOS), Virtual Environments (VE), and services. The NodeOS is a collection of basic node services, which perform tasks of demultiplexing, resource control, active service provisioning, security and management. The NodeOS functionality is exported through NodeOS API to Execution Environments (EE), which reside in VEs. A VE is a resource and user related abstraction on the node; one or more EEs and services reside in the VE. Services are a collection of components carrying out an application for its users. Service and service components as such are defined by a service descriptor [5] which is resolved in the network and on the node in one or more code modules, which can be instantiated into certain EE(s) where the component(s) becomes a runtime instance(s).

In the described network element, packets are interpreted as requests and evaluated on the node, within one or more service components, and can result in zero, one or more packets on the output of the node. Requests or the result of an evaluation can be either active or passive packets. We consider as active packets those packets that contain ANEP an header as defined in the ANEP draft standard [6]. Packet content or the service state on the node can be changed during evaluation. The code or data in the packet can result in action(s) regarding the API defined by dedicated component EE or NodeOS API.

A service can exist in a single node or can span over multiple nodes in the network. Packets exchanged between communicating entities can be processed only at the sender and receiver, or, depending on the nature of the service, on any suitable node in between. In the sense of the network structure, this structure is virtual. There can be also "passive" nodes in the network as well.

Code modules extending the programming environment of the node are a result of service deployment in the network and service resolution on the node. This approach is called out-of-band because the code is not transferred together with the data; to gain additional flexibility we also use an in-band approach in the SNAP Activator system [7]. But in the majority of cases in our approach the code can be considered as transferred out-of-band.

We can deduce the following set of entities in the system from the system description: network users, network nodes and services. An execution environment in the processing model is a technical term defining the required system elements for a successful evaluation, and it is not a real system entity. To be able to abstract the resources that the active network user has available on the node, and that its services are using, The Virtual Environment abstraction is used. VE represents the resources on the node and the environment needed for the service operation. The VE is a flexible abstraction; it can overlap tightly with a service, a specific user, or it can be used in the context of multiple services and users. In this sense the node represents the priviledged Virtual Environment (pVE). There can be a number of "external" entities that support the system operation, for example code producers, certification and attribute authorities etc.

2. Threats, security requirements and architecture goals

In the described system threats are considerably extended in comparison to traditional 'passive' systems where evaluation is more or less related to forwarding a packet through the network element. But threat consequences are not different from those in traditional systems. They are, as categorized in [8]: disclosure, deception, disruption and usurpation. A reasonable selection of threat actions that can cause a threat consequence applicable to a described system is presented in [9].

Entities in the system that can be a source of the threat action causing threat consequences are all entities presented in Section 1. The pVE represents a threat to all other entities in the system. While basic pVE services (security, resource control) can prevent threat actions between other entities, the threat represented by pVE can be prevented by strict control, which nodes can process, and evaluate packets.

Basic security related problems can be seen in the following areas: (a) startup of the node and its connection to the network, (b) partitioning of the node and the network resources, (c) deployment of new services, related code, configuration and policies in the network and on the node, (d) accessing, managing, control and observing services and related data, (e) control which data (packets) a service can access, (f) naming of the resources in the network and (g)providing traceability of the node state.

We have set the following general goals and requirements, for the security architecture, which addresses security problems and threats::

- *authorized use*, protect network element and user resources in the network. Network element resources can be functional, computational or communicational. User resources are the packet content and possible states on the network nodes. Only authorized users should be able to access these resources, and only authorized nodes can process the packets,
- *separation* between different VEs and their related services regarding access and resource usage should be enforced in the network and on the network elements,
- *communication security*, security architecture perimeter is a network element; communication between network elements should be protected and sufficient information about communicating entities in the system for security architecture operation should be provided in a secure manner,
- *verification*, code brought to the node must be verified either statically or dynamically, and must be protected on the node together with code related configuration and data against intentional or unintentional changes,
- *accountability* of security related events, audit service should be provided on the nodes and in the network,
- *common treatment* regarding security of: (a) network elements, like end, intermediate, management nodes, (b) VEs, services, components, (c) EEs and code modules, (d) and communication in between and across multiple network elements, (e) the same security mechanisms should be used in the management, control and transport planes,
- *transparency*, operation of security architecture should be transparent to its users and developers, either through well defined interfaces, protocol headers or architecture implicit operation, and should require minimal user intervention,
- *flexibility*, (a) multiple trust management approaches should be supported between entities in the system, (b) multiple types of security policies should be supported, (c) security architecture proposed should be general enough that it can be used for all developed technologies in FAIN, as well as existing established technologies,
- *sufficient and extensible*, basic security services should be sufficient for safe network element operation; but it should be possible to extend the security architecture by certain VEs or services to fulfil their specific needs.

Security architecture goals can be achieved mainly with authentication, authorization and policy enforcement, system/code/packet integrity service, code verification, controlling users' resource usage on the node and in the network, audit service, the right choice of selected security mechanisms, and system design. These issues are discussed in the next Section.

3.   Security issues

3.1   Authorization and policy enforcement

Access to the node and user resources should be subject to authorization. Node and user resources can be hardware, e.g. CPU, memory, storage and link bandwidth, or functional, like special purpose files, routing tables, policy and credentials entries and databases, VEs and service related data, etc. Important resources are possible service states on the nodes, which can be shared among multiple users, and user packet content.

Authorization is a process that provides an authorization decision about access of the subject to the object. A decision is provided to an enforcement engine. In general we assume that, when the subject accesses the object, the enforcement engine suspends the request and asks the authorization engine for an authorization decision. The information passed to the authorization decision is security context of the subject and object, action and possible environment of the access. Based on the information passed the authorization engine returns an authorization decision that is then enforced by the enforcement engine. Security context is all security relevant data available on the system regarding the subject and object. Of course, proper authentication is required to provide authorization.

Policies control which users can have access to a certain resource, and in what manner. Policies should be detached from the system and should not be hardwired in the application. Because the policies used in general can vary, the system should be flexible enough to support multiple kinds of policies.

In the context of policies users can be defined either by their identities or attributes like roles or groups. We will name both user attributes; users in the system should posses certain credentials which express these attributes. Multiple type of credentials should be possible to enable various ways of trust management between users. A scalable approach should be provided in the system to enable nodes to access user credentials. When transferring credentials through the network integrity must be provided. If credentials are referenced or included in the packet such information must be bound to the packet content. Replay protection for such packets should be provided.

It should be possible to generate and enforce certain policies by the system itself, independently of the user policies. Such policies can be understood as mandatory access policies that enable separation between system entities like VEs and services, and prevent their undefined and unneeded interaction.

Certain kinds of policies can require that the state of previous authorization decisions is known. The system should be able to define such state and keep it available for later authorization decision provisioning.

It is hard to believe that all policies and all users can be globally understandable. But we can assume that the users and the policy can be known in a single administrative domain or in the context of a certain service. The system should be able to provide functionality that can enable replacing, adding or removing of credentials at the administrative domain borders.

The enforcement process must have classic attributes of a reference monitor: it must be non-bypassable, tamperproof and analysable [10]. In addition, as correctly noted in [9], it has to be non-spoofable. Security context of the above-mentioned subject and object has to be bound to these in such way that it cannot be forged in the system. We can add to this that authorization decisions made, based on the security context, are only valid as far as the data in the context is valid. So the process of building a security context has to be carefully examined to be able to provide authorization decisions based only on the data we can trust.

3.2   Authentication

Authentication is a required service for authorization and also for other security services in the system. Authentication has to be provided per packet, connectionless, because of the assumed model of communication.

A major problem of authentication service in active networking approaches is how to authenticate an active packet on every node that it passes. Symmetric or asymmetric cryptography based solutions can be used for authentication. The use of symmetric cryptography solutions requires that a session key is negotiated or provided to two or more parties in communication. Asymmetric based approaches do not require such step, but trust must be managed between the active packet sender and the nodes that the packet traverses. Symmetric approaches do not provide non-repudiation; this fact is important if two or more nodes use the same session key, and any of them can become a source of the authenticated packet. In such setup, if one node is compromised, this can be a serious security problem. Also, the session key can be seen as a hard state on the node; if it is not available, the communication will fail. Symmetric techniques that negotiate separate session keys with each node in their path and provide authentication data for every node in the packet are too costly in terms of bandwidth and negotiation time. Both asymmetric and symmetric based approaches must tackle the issue of packet integrity as described in section 3.3.

Symmetric cryptography approaches are still very useful when used properly; neighbour nodes can identify each other in this way after they have established a trust relationship and negotiated a security association (SA). In addition to authentication of a peer they can provide integrity and confidentiality for the packets exchanged, dependent on protection mechanisms used in a SA,. Such type of communication is called a session; two entities in communication exchange data over a negotiated and set up secure connection for a limited period of time. The concept of sessions can be supported in various ways, it can be based for example on IPSec [11] or SSL [12].

Data origin authentication is related to the data integrity; there can be no data origin authentication if data integrity is not provided as well.

3.3   Packet integrity

Packet content can be changed in the network and this change raises the question of data origin. If the packet originates on one node but the content is added to the packet (for example, data is collected on nodes), or something is removed (for example some part of the code or data), this data as a whole cannot be authenticated any more for its data origin on the rest of the nodes that the packet can pass. The logical consequence is to split the packet in the part that can change, e.g. the part that is variable, and in the part that is static during the packet lifetime in the network.

The variable part of the packet can be used by the service to store or modify the packet content. But we still want to protect somehow this variable part from the unauthorized or malicious modifications. The first countermeasure is to control which nodes can process and evaluate such packet. With this approach we can avoid unauthorized modification between two authorized nodes. We will call such protection per hop protection in contrast to the protection that can be applied end-to-end for static parts of the packet. Per hop protection is similar to sessions, introduced in section 3.2 and can be understood as system level protection of active packets exchanged between two nodes. Under the term system level we understand protection on the level of nodes, e.g. NodeOS or pVEs. Another question is how to control additions or modifications. Because of the diversity of approaches and internal service knowledge of the data structure this responsibility must probably be shifted from the system layer to the service layer.

If the active packet contains a code and data intermixed the integrity of such packets is difficult to provide, and it is difficult to decide which part of the packet data is static and which is variable. Protecting such packets in between hops is helpful, but not enough. We will propose later in Section 8 a solution for a SNAP Activator system.

3.4   System integrity

The system integrity service is one of the core services that must be provided on a network element. It must be provided from the ground up, from the first piece of code run on the node. System integrity guarantees, together with other security services, notably authorization, policy enforcement and code and service verification, that the node will perform its intended function in an unimpaired manner.

The task of system integrity is threefold: firstly, when the node programming environment is extended the state of the code after authorization and possible results of verification are stored safely, secondly, during the node operation it enables mechanisms that enable preventing malicious, unintentional and unauthorized system changes, and thirdly, it must keep previous states of the code and related data, so that the extensions and modifications of the node environment can be traced or rolled back if required.

3.5   Code and service verification

Code and service verification is a security service, which verifies the correctness of a service and code modules operation. We can divide the verification into two broad groups: dynamic and static. Static verification is done prior to the injection of the service into the network. Dynamic verification happens prior to or during the evaluation; it must be extremely fast in contrast to the static verification.

As stated in Section 1, the majority of the code comes into a node out-of- band. For out-of-band approaches it is possible to verify the code in the static way. Many kinds of verification are possible, like source code inspection, code testing, generating proofs [13], which can be verified on the node prior to code installation and use, etc. For static verification it is important that trust between the verifier and the code user (node or VE) is established.

Dynamic verification is usually performed by interpreters, like in the case of Java bytecode verification. When the interpreter model is extended the verification must be extended, too. Dynamic verification is important in the case of in-band deployment of the code.

Specific to our approach to service verification is how services are composed; many code modules can be composed into a single service when the service descriptor is resolved on the particular active network node. While a service can be verified for the desired properties at the network level, final verification of the service must be carried out at the node level. For every piece of code a verification is needed; a common approach should be chosen because of the various active networking technologies we use.

3.6   Accountability

Accountability is an important property of the system; it enables us to track and analyze possible security breaches through an audit service. Accountability should not be provided only on the node; active services span over many nodes and can be influenced by many external subsystems, and audit traces should be collected in a single administrative domain in such a way that analyzing can be possible from a central point.

4. FAIN architectural model and high level security architecture

A high level security architecture is presented in Figure 1 Basic security services are positioned in the privileged VE because of the following reasons: we want to treat all possible technologies and their implementation, implementing VE and services, in one and only one manner, reducing the risk of multiple implementation. The services offered in the pVE are protected again by the same services and mechanisms. This does not preclude VEs or services from implementing their own security services or mechanisms when it is reasonable to do so.

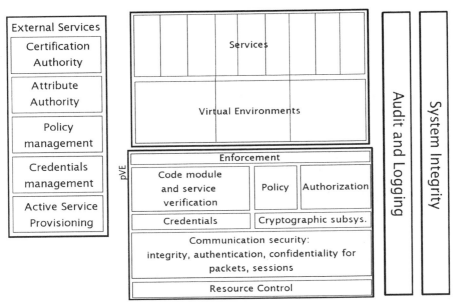

Figure 1. High level security architecture

Resource control is not really part of the security architecture. It is a required element of any reasonable network node. Using such element, security architecture can efficiently enforce separation between VEs and services regarding the resource usage.

The core of the architecture is the active network node. Basic functions of the NodeOS were decomposed into the following subsystems: demultiplexing (DEMUX), resource control framework (RCF), active service provisioning (ASP), management and security. Each subsystem is also related to security

- The DEMUX subsystem is responsible for the management of input and output channels to VEs and services. At this point the security perimeter of the architecture starts and the security context of the incoming packets is built. At the output channels the packets leave the perimeter, and here is the point where external security representation can be added to the packet. On the other hand DEMUX exports interfaces to set up or tear down the channels; these interfaces are part of NodeOS API,

- The RCF subsystem is responsible for resource allocation and enforcement of the resource usage. It enables separation of system entities regarding the communicational and computational resources. A guaranteed share of the resources has to be provided to pVE, so the basic services can operate without interruption. RCF exported interfaces enable resource reservation and report resource usage,

- The ASP subsystem is responsible for deploying the code for the service operation to the node; it must cooperate with the security subsystem to ensure system integrity and static service code modules verification,
- The management subsystem is responsible for the management of the basic node services, VEs, its services and service components. It exports interfaces for their initialization, setup, control, suspension, observation and termination in a common manner irrespective of their implementation. These interfaces become a part of NodeOS API.

High-level security architecture was decomposed into system elements performing the required architecture tasks and mechanisms:

- *principal manager*, which is responsible for principal related operations: adding to, removing from and searching for a principal in principal database. Principal entries are a collection of principal related data: principal attributes, list of his/her credentials, and a pointer to principal secure store,
- *credential manger* that manages principal related credentials in a uniform way irrespective of the credential type. It is responsible for parsing and validating credentials and extracting principal related credential information: user attributes, credential time validity or possible policies embodied in the credential. The credential manager also provides utilities for principal credentials and keystores generation,
- *policy manager* that manages in a uniform way various policies on the node. The policy manager provides also policy engine(s) that can provide an authorization decision related to the particular policy,
- *security manager,* which is a central point of the subsystem. It is responsible for building of the security context of the subjects and objects on the node; security contexts are kept in the security subsystem and never leave the subsystem,
- *authorization engine* that provides authorization decision to node enforcement engines. An authorization decision is based on one or more policy engine decisions. The authorization engine also keeps the state of the authorization which can be exported to the audit subsystem or stored if certain policies require such state,
- *enforcement layer*, which enforces the authorization engine decision. The enforcement layer is separated into enforcement engines, where the authorization decision is enforced, and the mechanism, which enables secure gathering of the subject and object information on the node,
- *audit subsystem*, which provides an audit service on the node through audit channels to audit the database,
- *system integrity subsystem* that collects all code modules, service, EEs and VEs related data, and reacts to code or service changes, code time validity or code related policy changes,
- *verification manager*, which enables dynamic or static verification of the code or services,
- *cryptographic subsystem*, which offers required mechanisms for all cryptographic operations,
- *secure store,* which holds principal related cryptographic information, and provides asymmetric cryptography mechanisms together with a cryptographic subsystem in a manner that the principal related private keys never leave the store,
- *communication security facilities*, with *external security representation subsystem* that can build and extract principal (packet) security context related information in a uniform manner, mechanisms to fetch the principal related credentials on the node, *neighbour discovery protocol* to enable *connection manager* to build in a secure,

trusted and dynamic way the security associations with its neighbour nodes, used by *integrity subsytem* to provide hop protection between nodes.

5.   FAIN node implementation

The FAIN node, as described in Sections 1 and 4, can have varied implementation. Indeed, three types of nodes have been developed that conform to the same architectural principles. All nodes have a common base NodeOS layer with management software that wraps a specific functionality of the particular node, and is able to access, control and manage these systems and their resources. NodeOS is based on Linux and its subsystems like Netfilter[2] and OS resource control features, Java[3] EE and CORBA.[4] CORBA and Java were used to enable communication between node subcomponents through a set of well-defined interfaces in IDL. Node implementations are: a Software router extended with Active SNMP system; High performance active node with extensible and dynamic in kernel router based on PromethOS [14]; and Hybrid node, Hitachi based GR2000 router[5] extended with active node, and Active SNMP.

Tied together with the common NodeOS layer, systems like SNAP, Active SNMP, PromethOS, Java based EE, commercial and software routers can be used in a synergistic way to support or complement each other with the aim to provide new services in the network in a flexible and extensible way.

6.   Security architecture design and implementation

Security architecture requirements and goals as described in Section 2 come in full light when security architecture is to be applied to a heterogeneous and extensible network element as presented in the previous Section. Common treatment, transparency and flexibility are clearly strong requirements in such case. From the security perspective it is most important that an abstraction component oriented model was used for the main system [15]. Everything on the node, including base pVE services, VEs, EEs, services and their components, and active packets are treated equally through this model. Modularity, the same treatment of all system components, object oriented implementation and fine granularity of the approach are beneficial to the security.

6.1   Security context, enforcement layer, authorization and policy enforcement

During component initialisation and startup, security context is assigned to each component in the system. In the cases when a new VE is created a component is transitioned to a new entity and components belonging to a VE are then labeled accordingly with a VE identifier and with a corresponding service identifier. The service identifier is based on a service descriptor that defines a service. If a security policy is specified for a component, this policy is set. Components, or subjects treated like components, for example active packets, ports initiated trough SSL session and sessions between nodes, are handled in a similar way as VEs and are assigned contexts based on their external representation. When assigning a security context each component gets a unique opaque security identifier (SID), which relates it to the security context stored in the database. Java language object oriented features are used, so that only

---

[2]   See http://www.netfilter.org.
[3]   See http://java.sun.com.
[4]   See http://www.omg.org.
[5]   See http://www.hitachi.co.jp/Prod/comp/network/gr2000_eng/index.html.

trusted code can get access to this database and that the component SID cannot be modified. The security context links through its data structures the component with its parent, VE and service data, data about components implementing the service, user data like credential(s) information and the audit vector. In this way we have in one place security related data, which can be used to provide a security related decision like an authorization decision.

Communication between or access to the components is controlled with the help of CORBA interceptors. A transparent enforcement layer has been implemented that extracts the subject SID, the called interface (action) and the possible environment of the call, and pass it together with the object SID to the security manager authorize interface.

The authorization engine first compares components VE identifiers and then service identifiers. If both values match, the action and possible environment of the call is evaluated in the policy engine, specified by policy type. The authorization decision is returned to the enforcement layer where the decision is enforced.

Security again benefits from the component-oriented model, object oriented environment and transparent enforcement layer. All components are treated in one and the same manner regarding security. The component developer has no security related work, and security issues are transparent to him/her in this sense. The management environment must prepare the desired security policies which are later enforced on the nodes. To ease security policy development we have followed the object oriented nature of the components. When the security policies are defined for the basic set of components, inherited components can reuse the basic policies. In this way the policy has to be specified only for the extensions that the inherited component provides. For our simple security model, which was based on principal roles (e.g. user, manager, vemanager and observer), we have provided a simple set of utilities that use annotated IDL specification to be able to provide policies in an automated way.

Additionally, in the enforcement layer, we collect the stack of SIDs if the request of the subject passes more than one component or an interface. Although we use at the moment only a flat model, e.g. only the first SID in the stack is used to provide an authorization decision, the feature could be used to reason also about the compound principal and combination of different principals' privileges.

6.2   Communication security facilities

As the basis for *external security representation* we use the ANEP [6]. The solution is applicable to any active networking approach that can be encapsulated with the ANEP protocol. Regarding the discussion in section 3 we have defined six new options to carry security related information over untrusted connections. These options carry the VE and service identifier, hop protection and credentials option related information, service variable data and resource usage information. From the original ANEP options only the source and destination addresses are used.

The hop protection is defined by the Security Association (SA) identifier, sequence replay protection field, and keyed hash. The keyed hash covers the entire ANEP packet except the keyed hash itself. The hop protection protects all active packets exchanged between two neighbour active nodes. As system layer protection, these fields are removed from the packet after a successful check; only information about the previous hop node is kept for the packet. If the packet leaves the node a new hop option is built regarding the next hop SA.

The credential option is defined by: the credential identifier and type; credential location field, specifying where it can be fetched; the target field where the user can specify specific targets as nodes, the system layer or a packet itself; optional time stamp, which protects from replays; and the digital signature. The digital signature is applied to static data of an active packet: the first 32 bits of ANEP header, source address, VE and service ID, ANEP payload and credential option itself, except digital signature data. The digital signature mechanism enables authentication of data origin, provides a data integrity service for the covered data end-to-end and enables non-repudiation. The time stamp in the credential option is an additional measure of protection against misbehaved or subverted node or service. Per hop replay protection in this case is not sufficient. For such a service it is easy to store and replay the packet later. This measure requires roughly synchronized node clocks. There can be zero, one or more credential options in a single active packet. Credential types can vary, from X.509 certificates or attribute certificates, SPKI [16] certificates to Keynote credentials [17].

Credentials can be fetched in multiple ways, if not included directly in the packet: either from a DNS, LDAP or any other suitable store. In our case we have designed and implemented a simple *protocol for fetching credentials* from the previous hop node. In this way, it is the responsibility of the packet originator entity to supply all credentials required that can be validated later on the nodes that packet traverses. To be able to supply credentials on the intermediate nodes we have designed and implemented node *credentials cache*. After successful validation, the credentials are cached on the node for the time of their validity or regarding the cache policy about cache size and maximum time period of the cache entry. Caching a credential has other benefits. If the cache entry is valid, there is no need to validate the credentials. In this way we can reduce the required digital signature validation to only one per credential option in the packet, which results in a significant speed improvement after the first principal packet has passed the node. Additionally, we also cache bad credentials in a separate cache in the cases where the credentials cannot be verified. Packets with such credentials are discarded immediately.

VE and service identifiers are used by the demultiplexer to divert the packets to the specified service. A variable option is used by the service to store data that can change in the network, which can be a service state, collected data, etc. At the moment the resource related option is only a simple counter of the passed nodes.

For the *cryptographic subsystem* we used a Java based and Sun JCE compliant cryptographic library.[6] The part of cryptographic operations is performed inside a *secure store* that wraps digital signature related operations and Java keystore functionality in such a way that users' private keys never leave the store. Only pVE security subsystem components have access to the stores; user stores can be managed directly by the users and are password protected.

The *connection manager* is responsible for setting up Secure Associations between neighbour nodes. It exports interfaces so that the SAs can be managed either manually or by triggering key exchange by the Network Management System. Additionally, a protocol was designed to exchange the keys automatically. The protocol reuses the same mechanisms and possible credentials as discussed at the beginning of this Section, and Station to Station protocol as described in [18]. The protocol is modified to the extent that entire protocol messages are covered by the digital signature in the credential option. Messages are addressed to a channel that does not provide hop protection but access to it is authorized. Two nodes, as protocol entities establishing a SA, must supply their credentials, that contain suitable authorization information regarding the channel policy, for the SA establishment to succeed. To be able to support the per hop protection and connection manager operations dynamically, the neighbour discovery protocol was designed and developed.

6.2.1   Neighbour discovery

The per hop integrity protection requires each active node to keep an up-to-date list of all neighbour active nodes. Manual configuration of active node neighbour lists is not acceptable due to scalability issues and dynamic nature of active networks. We have

---

[6] Bouncycastle Java Crypto library, http://www.bouncycastle.org.

therefore developed a protocol, which enables active nodes to automatically create a list of neighbour active nodes and to update it whenever necessary due to changes in the network infrastructure [19].

The protocol has three operation modes, as depicted in Figure 2: node advertisements, discovery handshake, and heartbeat exchange. Active nodes advertise themselves by periodically transmitting the advertisement message to an emulated communications bus, which distributes the advertisement to all active nodes. The implementation of an emulated communications bus can be multicast-based, with one dedicated multicast group per overlay, server-based, or a combination of both. Upon reception of an advertisement an active node starts a discovery handshake with the sender with probability p only in order to limit the load on the sender of the advertisement. The discovery handshake is the main protocol mechanism for neighbour discovery and detection of network changes. It involves an exchange of two messages between the node, which initiates the handshake (poller), and the node, which responds (responder). Both messages carry the address of the previous hop active node, which is used by the active nodes en route for updating their neighbour tables when necessary. A node periodically sends the heartbeat message to each of its known neighbours to indicate that it is still alive. Neighbour active nodes use this message to refresh the soft state in their neighbour tables.

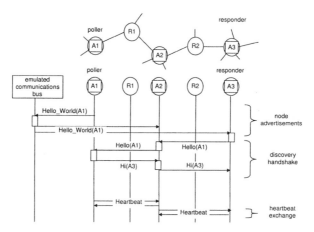

Figure 2. Neighbour discovery protocol

We note that neighbour discovery protocol employs packet interception, where an intermediate active node intercepts and processes the protocol message, even though the message is addressed to some other node. Packet interception is inherently supported by active network nodes, contrary to traditional routers.

6.3   Verification manager

For static verification a digital signature mechanism was chosen as the most common one. Static verification is used in the process of out-of-band code deployment to the node in conjunction with the Node level ASP manager. The cryptographic hash of the code is digitally signed and code digital certificate issued by either code producer, verifier, or trusted archive. The verification manager verifies the certification path and the signature; the authorization decision about possible code deployment is made with a common developed authorization mechanism regarding the local node code repository policy. Dynamic verification can be added as part of the Verification manager functionality as described in Section 8 for Active SNMP system.

6.4   Security manager and security area interfaces

The Security Manager is the central point of the security architecture that exports minimal set of interfaces. Internal interfaces are receive and send check with demultiplexing system, interfaces for assigning and releasing security context, authorize interface with enforcement layer and interface for static code modules verification. External interfaces, available also to non pVE entities, are interfaces for managing a component policy and audit vector and interfaces for managing trusted anchors and manual configuration of SAs. The internal interfaces are accessible only to certain subsystem components and the external have defined a policy and requests to them are strictly authorized.

6.5   General active packet security events

In general, we can divide active packet security events into three parts: entry-level checks, evaluation level checks and exit level checks.

Entry level check steps are, as follows: After an active packet is diverted by the demultiplexing subsystem, if recognized as an active packet, the packet is passed to the security subsystem. Based on the SA identifier in the hop protection option, the right SA is selected and sequence replay protection is checked. The option keyed hash is verified and, if the verification is successful, the resource option is checked for the maximum number of hops. Then the credential option is parsed, credentials are fetched from the previous node if they are not in the credentials cache already. If credentials are successfully validated they are stored in the cache and the digital signature in the option is verified. If present, the credential timestamp is compared to the local clock. The security context is built from this credential option. The procedure is repeated for every credential option in the packet. VE and service identifiers in the packet are compared to those stated in the credentials. If they match, the packet as a request is authorized against the security context of the input channel. At least one security context must be authorized positively for the packet, otherwise the packet is dropped. If the incoming channel requires code verification the code is verified. If the packet passes all checks it is returned to the demultiplexer, which sends it to the service.

Evaluation level checks are performed if the packet evaluation results in access to NodeOS interfaces, service state or packet itself. In these cases actions are authorized and the service or the node policy enforced as described in the Section 6.1.

Exit level checks. Basically, when the packet is sent by the service to the exit channel the demultiplexing subsystem invokes the security send check interface, and the packet resource counter is increased, the right SA is selected based on the packet's next hop destination, and the hop option is built and inserted in the packet. If the packet has a credential option initialized, but not yet built, the option is built and the digital signature computed for the packet. The sending entity must own the secure store pointed to in the initialized option. The packet is returned to demultiplexing and sent to the wire. Also other checks are possible. The exit channel can have a policy set that can be evaluated regarding the packet security context(s). The resource counter is divided among outgoing packets when the evaluation on the node results in multiple packets.

7.   Security architecture performance

We were primarily interested in the security architecture performance in the case where an active packet passes the node. For this purpose we assume that the suitable VEs and services are already set up on the node and that the user can access secure store and his/her credentials, and the related key pair to be able to create ANEP packets and corresponding credential options in the packet. The originating node should have already established SA with its neighbour node. On the nodes that the packet passes security costs are related to the general scenario as described in section 6.5.

The testing environment was a commodity PC, with Intel P4 2.2 Ghz processor with 512 MBit RAM, Red Hat Linux 8.0, kernel 2.4.18-14, Java SDK 1.3.1_3, Bouncy Castle crypto-library version 1.17 and FAIN network node code. The active packet in the test case hadq a basic ANEP header, hop option, option for VE and service identifier, one full credential option, resource option and zero length variable option and payload. The hop option keyed hash was HMAC-SHA-1 [20] on the receiving and sending sides. The credential used in this case was a X.509 based certificate with RSA encryption with MD5 hash signature. The issuer key length was 1024 bits. X.509 V3 extensions were used to encode user attributes and VE and service identifiers. The signature in the credential option, computed on originating node, was RSA encryption with SHA-1 hash. The RSA key length was 768 bits. The certification path length was one.

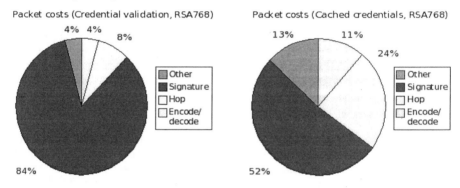

Figure 3. Breakdown of the packet costs

Figure 3 represents a breakdown of the measured security costs related to the ANEP packet passing the node. The *hop* part represents costs of validating the hop option on the receiving side and building a new hop option on the sending side. The *encoding/decoding* part represents costs of decoding a packet at receiving side and encoding it together with a new hop option on the sending side. The *other* costs are related to the process of building a security context on the node, verifying user statements about VE and service IDs regarding those in the credential and access control decision regarding the security context of the input channel. The *signature* costs are costs of validating a credential and verifying the digital signature in the packet.

On the left hand side of the Figure 3 is a case where the user credential is contained in the packet and is validated on the node. On the right hand side are the security costs of the case when the user credential is already cached in the cache. As expected, the largest overhead is due to validation of the credential option. It involves costly asymmetric cryptography, the RSA signatures verification. With no caching, the cost of validating the credential option is large, and represents over 84% of all security costs. Validating the hop option represents only 8%. With cached credentials these costs can be decreased to 52%, because of reducing the credential option validation to only one packet digital signature verification and the timestamp validation. All the other costs remain the same but their percentage raises because of the reduced overall costs.

In the absolute numbers, the node can handle 396 packets per second with the credential validation. When the credential is already cached, the security costs are reduced by a factor of three and 1190 packets per second can be processed. Our measurements show that per packet related costs are not drastically related to the RSA key size in the current setup; in the case of RSA512 the node can handle 1340 and in the case of RSA1024 1003 packets per second. With only per hop protection, like in case of inter-node communication, the node can handle over 11000 packets. The size of the variable option has an impact on the decoding/encoding costs and per hop protection costs, which are proportional to the time needed to compute hash of the packet data. The payload size additionally increases costs to calculate the hash used to verify the digital signature in the credential option.

We have also looked into the ways of improving the Communication facilities performance. A comparison of the results with the OpenSSL[7] library shows that the OpenSSL library is twice as fast as the Bouncy castle library for digital signature verification (1770/3550 per sec). The use of cryptographic accelerators like Broadcom based BCM5821[8] shows additional speed improvements with very light utilization of the main CPU (8142 signatures verification per sec, less than 1% CPU). Using native libraries or accelerators should improve the performance of the communication facilities to a few thousands active packets per second, even with costly checking of digital signatures.

With regards to the neighbour discovery, we were mostly interested in the speed of neighbour discovery, i.e. the delay between the network change and the corresponding updates of active node neighbour tables. By varying different protocol parameters in our tests we were able to achieve convergence delay in the range of 30--40 seconds, i.e. our target range. We chose this target value because the convergence delay of current routing protocol implementations ranges from around 30s for OSPF [21] to several minutes for BGP [22]. We find the comparison with the routing protocols interesting due to the following. As far as the authors are aware, no results on convergence delay are currently available for related efforts in the area of automatic discovery of neighbour active nodes [23]. On the other hand, routing protocols provide analogous functionality to neighbour discovery protocol: after a perturbation occurs in the network, the routing protocol has to accordingly reconfigure the physical network (i.e. routes in the network) as soon as possible in order to minimise the disruption in communication caused by the perturbation.

8. Architecture applicability

The security architecture as designed and implemented should be applicable to any active networking approach. To evaluate this assumption we have applied the security architecture to the case of SNAP Activator [7],also developed in FAIN. We call the adaptation of the SNAP activator to the FAIN architecture Active SNMP.

Snap Activator is a SNAP based solution for controlling and managing active node resources. SNAP is used in this solution as a carrier and a finite state machine to program a series of active network nodes through SNMP enabled network devices.

SNAP itself provides a high level of safety and it even provides resource usage guarantees per packet. In our case the evaluation of a SNAP packet can result in composition with a system that is known to have security problems [21] and the actions requested can be

---

[7] See http://www.openssl.org.
[8] See http://www.broadcom.com/products/5821.html.

security critical. Every action should be authorized and the policy for the action enforced on the nodes that the packet traverses.

There are two distinct problems in integrating the SNAP activator in the common framework. The first is how to provide protection for the SNAP packets while they are in transit over the network. SNAP is a pure active networking approach and contains intermixed code and data in the same packet. SNAP packets can legally change in the network during the evaluation on the node. Therefore, for the packet as a whole, its data origin cannot be cryptographically verified on the nodes that the packet passes. The second issue is how to integrate SNAP daemon into the node environment and how to use the designed and implemented mechanisms for the authorization and policy enforcement.

SNAP packet integrity issues were tackled in the following way: after compiling a SNAP program the originating node produces a fingerprint of the program, extracting from the program the static part of SNAP packet data. Static parts are SNMP commands and related data, which will be invoked on the node during the packet evaluation. The fingerprint is stored in the ANEP packet payload while the entire SNAP packet is put into a variable option. The originating node builds a credential option and digitally signs the static parts of the packet, including the fingerprint in the packet payload.

At the intermediate nodes the general scenario of the packet passing the node is exactly the same as described in the Section 6.5. The packet fingerprint with a known data origin is submitted to the verification subsystem together with the SNAP program itself, the fingerprint of the program is produced again and compared to the one that was verified. If they match, the packet will be injected into the system, otherwise it is dropped. Verification in this way ensures that the security critical parts of the SNAP code have not changed in the network; the commands and the data, their position and occurrence is protected against unauthorized modifications.

The integration with the node services is in part covered by the integration of the SNAP daemon with the management framework. In this way it is treated as any other node component, security issues, its installation, initialisation and management included. SNAP daemon environment was extended on the node with a trap system that intercepts SNAP packet requests and invokes actions on the node corresponding to these requests. Additionally a helper component was designed and implemented that takes care of resubmitting and intercepting the packets going in and coming from SNAP daemon. The component also takes care of synchronizing the SNAP packet evaluation with its security context, built from the active packet external representation. In this way, SNAP packet actions can be authorized in the general way, as described in section 6.1. SNAP packet security context is compared with a security context of the trap system and an authorization decision is enforced.

9.   Evaluation of the security architecture

Security architecture was evaluated through comparisons with related work, experiments, performance measurements, and number of properties, namely flexibility, reliability, scalability and security.

In the context of *related work* our architecture can be compared to the U. Penn SANE [25],[26],[27], the SANTS [9][28][29] and the Bees [30]. The SANE is one of the first quite complete active networks security architectures. They have proposed a two level model with a "safe" language for active code, called PLAN [31] and more heavy-weight active extensions, which can be invoked by authenticated and authorized packets. Their authorization and policy enforcement framework is based on namespace thinning. For communication security they have used only symmetric cryptography in the packet context, with little discussion about how to negotiate shared secrets for the packet that traverse many nodes. They did not specify how they handle possible changes in the packet content and their hop protection is more unstructured, on the level of a service.

The SANTS is a reference implementation of the DARPA Active Networks Security working group security architecture [9]. Their prototype is based on ANTS [32] and provides an authorization and policy enforcement framework and partial communication security facilities for its support. Their work does not cover other security related tasks. For active packets they provide both the hop protection and the protection regarding the originator. The supporting ANEP options are similar to ours, but they do not provide replay protection in credential option. We have explicitly labelled the service and VEs in the packet and in the credentials. There is little discussion about the hop protection and no examples of how the both types of the protection are used. We have set the hop protection on the system level, to support control, which nodes can process active packets, and we support it with additional neighbour discovery. Their authorization and policy enforcement is achieved through namespace thinning and invoking of a policy engine to gain additional flexibility. The example policy engine used was the Keynote [17], which has been additionally wrapped to support policy dynamics [29]. Our example policy and policy engine is much simpler, but because of the component model, clear interfaces in IDL and inter-communication system used, we were able to better detach the security architecture from the rest of the system and make it more transparent. For example, our authorize interface is available only to the enforcement layer while their checkPermission interface [29] has to be available to anybody. In our approach, the system can be only policy driven.

The Bees is one of the most recently developed active networking approaches. It is a rework of the ANTS system with new security architecture and strong resource control support in their own Java implementation. Interestingly, they have minimized their reliance on cryptographic mechanisms on the system level, but they are available on service level, like the hop protection or sealing of data. Authorization mechanism is based on capabilities, which raises the issue of their revocation. Besides ours, their system is the only one that has addressed the need to protect entities' cryptographic data on the nodes.

In general, our solution is the only one that can support multiple Execution Environments simultaneously running on a node and protecting it with a common set of security services and mechanisms. On the other hand our system is also the only one that can support multiple implementations of the same architecture, as presented in Section 5, without any changes in the security architecture itself.

The *evaluation through experiments* has shown, as in the case of SNAP explained in the Section 8, that the security architecture design allows reuse of a existing active networking approach without its modification. Even more importantly in the same sense is that the architecture itself has not been modified, there was only a small, controlled addition of the dynamic verification. On the other hand, the architecture was successfully evaluated in network experiments with all types of the nodes in a FAIN setup pan-European testbed.

The *performance measurements* show, as presented in Section 7, that the security architecture performance is adequate for the management and control plane, even with the use of costly asymmetric cryptography. It is hard to compare the results of performance evaluation with the other approaches. The only measurements on active networking security costs that the authors are aware of are reported in [27]. Though the report is extensive, packet security cost are reported only for authentication based on symmetric cryptography and in relative values only. The authors are not aware of any measurement reports on the costs of authentication based on asymmetric cryptography.

The *flexibility* of the approach is shown in (a) an ability to support simultaneously multiple EEs, existing active networking approaches and multiple implementations of the architecture, (b) possibility to add a new functionality to the system in the sense of a new component functionality or interfaces without any changes to the architecture because of the transparent authorization framework implementation, (c) possibility to extend the policy framework with new policy engines, (d) support for multiple credential options in the packet and possibility to link multiple entities with single request and (e) same mechanisms are used on the node for management and control plane.

The *reliability* was addressed in many points of security architecture design: (a) the positioning of basic security services at system layer, protecting all services with the same mechanisms, (b) the minimal interweaving with the rest of the system keeping the trusted computing base small, (c) the separation with labeling in between VES/services so misbehaviour of one of them cannot influence the others, (d) the control of joining the nodes to the network, so only trusted nodes can process active packets and (e) the RCF can guarantee the reserved share of the computational and communicational resources which enables the system to operate even when the resources are scarce.

The *scalability* was addressed with selection of mechanisms and design: (a) the per originator protection is unidirectional and scales to large number of nodes, (b) the per hop protection performance is adequate and should scale to large number of neighbour nodes, (c) the neighbour discovery protocol enables automatic and dynamic adaptation of neighbour lists, which facilitates scalability, and (d) the management plane is supported either through sessions or active packets and it can provide either centralized management or scalable and distributed management because of the distributed nature of active technology used.

From the *security* point of view the architecture can be evaluated through high level goals. Authorized use can be enforced for important system and user resources, a separation between VEs and services is enforced by the system itself. The required communication security facilities are in place and complete to support data origin authentication and integrity services for the exchanged packets. Additionally, sessions to node are treated in the same manner with similar security mechanisms. Considering this and the fact that the security architecture is positioned on the system layer, we believe that storm security has been achieved.. Common treatment and transparency are achieved with the unified component model, inter-communication mechanism, clear definition of interfaces and security architecture design. These features have enabled us to support heterogeneous node environment and system extensibility without any changes to the security architecture itself. Verification of the code deployed to the node is done in the static case by inter-working with node level ASP. Dynamic verification cases can be supported as shown in the case of Active SNMP system. With the example of Active SNMP we have shown that the base security services should be sufficient and that the system can be extended with additional security mechanisms as SNAP Activator program fingerprinting and verification.

10. Conclusions and future work

The presented security architecture was designed as a general and flexible system. Strong security on a flexible and heterogeneous network node is possible and we have achieved most of our basic goals. Through experiments we have shown that security architecture, as designed and implemented, can be applied to three types of nodes at least in the management plane, and security architecture performance should be sufficient for operations in the management and control planes. But there is still a lot of research, implementation work and experiments that need to be done. The node component model should be formalized together with the security architecture operations. The flat security model assumed regarding system entities in interaction should be extended to multiple entities and a proper model proposed to treat them as compound principals. The security state of the node that can be exported through the authorization engine should be kept on the node and continuously analysed; the same mechanism should be used for security related protocols and operation of security subsystems as the verification manager, system integrity subsystem, connection manager etc. Authentication in the case of active packets has performance problems and more solutions, preserving existing flexibility, should be proposed, designed and evaluated. Although tightly integrated with the FAIN node architecture, the security architecture was designed and implemented in such a way that it should be possible to apply it to other active networking implementations. Only parts of it should be reimplemented in a different environment, like the enforcement layer.

References

[1]   A.T. Campbell, H.G.D. Meer, M.E. Kounavis, K. Miki, J.B. Vicente, and D. Villela. A Survey of Programmable Networks. ACM SIGCOMM Computer Communication Review, 29(2):7--23, April 1999.
[2]   J.M Smith and S.M Nettles. Active Networking: One view of the Past, Present and Future. IEEE - Transactions on Systems, Man and Cybernetics, Special Issue on Technologies that promote computational intelligence, openness and programmability in networks and Internet services, 2003. In print.
[3]   FAIN project home page. http://www.ist-fain.org.
[4]   S. Denazis, S. Karnouskos, T. Suzuki, and S. Yoshizawa. Component-based Execution Environments of Network Elements and a Protocol for their Configuration. IEEE - Transactions on Systems, Man and Cybernetics, Special Issue on Technologies that promote computational intelligence, openness and programmability in networks and Internet services, 2003. In print
[5]   M. Bossardt, L. Ruf, B. Plattner, and R. Stadler. A Service Deployment Architecture for Heterogeneous Active Network Nodes, In proceedings of 7th Conference on Intelligence in Networks (IFIP SmartNet 2002), Saariselkä, Finland. page~, Kluwer Academic Publishers, April 2002.
[6]   D.S. Alexander, B. Braden, C.A. Gunter, A.W. Jackson, A.D. Keromytis, G.J. Minden, and D. Wetherall. Active Network Encapsulation Protocol (ANEP). July 1997.
[7]   W. Eaves, L. Cheng, A. Galis, T. Becker, T. Suzuki, S. Denazis, and C. Kitahara. SNAP Based Resource Control for Active Networks, IEEE GLOBECOM 2002 Proceedings. November 2002.
[8]   R Shirey. RFC 2828: Internet Security Glossary. May 2000.
[9]   Active Networks Security Working Group. Security Architecture for Active Nets. November 2001.
[10] DoD. Trusted Computer System Evaluation Criteria. December 1985.
[11] S. Kent and R. Atkinson. RFC 2401: Security Architecture for the Internet Protocol. November 1998.
[12] T. Dierks and C. Allen. RFC 2246: The TLS Protocol Version 1. January 1999.
[13] G. Necula. Compiling with proofs. School of computer science, Carnegie Mellon University, September 1998.
[14] R. Keller, L. Ruf, A. Guindehi, and B. Plattner. PromethOS: A Dynamically Extensible Router Architecture Supporting Explicit Routing, Proceedings of the Fourth Annual International Working Conference on Active Networks (IWAN 2002). page~, Springer Verlag, Lecture Notes in Computer Science, December 2002.
[15] M. Solarski, M. Bossardt, and T. Becker. Component-based Deployment and Management of Services in Active Networks, Proceedings of Fourth Annual International Working Conference on Active Networks (IWAN2002). page~, December 2002.
[16] C. Ellison, B. Frantz, B. Lampson, R. Rivest, B. Thomas, and T. Ylonen. RFC 2693: SPKI Certificate Theory. September 1999. Network Working Group.
[17] M. Blaze, J. Feigenbaum, J. Ioannidis, and A.D. Keromytis. RFC 2704: The KeyNote Trust-Management System, Version 2. September 1999.
[18] B. Schneier. Applied Cryptography: Protocols, Algorithms, and Source Code in C. John Wiley and Sons, Inc., Second edition, 1996.
[19] A. Savanovič and B.J. Blažič. A Protocol for Adaptive Autoconfiguration of Active Networks. WSEAS Transactions on Communications, 2:78--83, 2003.
[20] H. Krawczyk, M. Bellare, and R. Canetti. HMAC: Keyed-Hashing for Message Authentication. February 1997.
[21] A. Basu and J. G. Riecke. Stability Issues in OSPF Routing. Proceedings of SIGCOMM 2001, pages 225--236, August 2001.
[22] C. Labovitz, A. Ahuja, A. Bose, and F. Jahanian. Delayed Internet Routing Convergence. Proceedings of SIGCOMM 2000, pages 175--187, 2000.
[23] S. Martin and G. Leduc. RADAR: Ring-based Adaptive Discovery of Active neighbour Routers. Proceedings of IWAN 2002, pages 62--73, December 2002.
[24] CERT. Multiple Vulnerabilities in Many Implementations of the Simple Network Management Protocol. February 2002,.

[25] D.S. Alexander, W.A. Arbough, A.D. Keromytis, and J.M. Smith. A Secure Active Network Environment Architecture: Realisation in SwitchWare. IEEE Network, Special Issue: Active and Programmable Networks:37-45, May/Jun 1998.

[26] D.S. Alexander, W.A. Arbaugh, A.D. Keromytis, and J.M. Smith. Security in Active Networks. Lecture Notes in Computer Science State-of-the-Art. Springer-Verlag, 2000.

[27] D.S. Alexander, P.B. Menage, A.D. Keromytis, W.A. Arbaugh, K.G. Anagnostakis, and J.M. Smith. The Price of Safety in an Active Network. Journal of Computers and Networks, 3(1), March 2001.

[28] S.Murphy, E.Lewis, R.Puga, R.Watson, and R.Yee. Strong Security for Active Networks, IEEE OPENARCH 2001 Proceedings. April 2001.

[29] S.L. Murphy, E.T. Lewis, and R.N.M. Watson. Secure Active Network Prototypes, DARPA Active Networks Conference and Exposition Proceedings, DANCE 02. May 2002.

[30] T. Stack, E. Eide, and J. Lepreau. Bees: A Secure, Resource-Controlled, Java-Based Execution Environment. December 2002.

[31] M. Hicks and A.D. Keromytis. A Secure PLAN, Proceedings of International Workshop for Active Networks (IWAN) 1999. Pages 307-314, June/July 1999.

[32] D. Wetherall, J. Guttag, and D. Tennenhouse. ANTS: Network Services Without Red Tape. IEEE Computer, pages 42-48, Apr 1999.

Security and Privacy in Advanced Networking Technologies
B. Jerman-Blažič et al. (Eds.)
IOS Press, 2004

Critical Infrastructure Protection
– Some Telecom Operators' Point of View –

Paul FRIEßEM

Fraunhofer Institut für Sichere Telekooperation SIT
Rheinstr. 75, D-64295 Darmstadt, Germany
paul.friessem@sit.fraunhofer.de

Heinz SARBINOWSKI

Fraunhofer Institut für Sichere Telekooperation SIT
Rheinstr. 75, D-64295 Darmstadt, Germany
heinz.sarbinowski@sit.fraunhofer.de

Reinhard SCHWARZ

Fraunhofer Institut für Experimentelles Software-Engineering IESE,
Sauerwiesen 6, D-67661 Kaiserslautern, Germany
reinhard.schwarz@iese.fraunhofer.de

Abstract. CIP considerations and publications tend to focus on the government's or society's perspective: the "service continuity" of a CI. In a study carried out in 2002–2003 we talked to telecom operators in order to better understand their point of view. The study revealed that an operator's view focuses on the "business continuity" of a CI. The relevant CIP issues such as critical dependences, threats, vulnerabilities, and risks were dealt with having this focus in mind. Not surprisingly, many of the traditional "service continuity" CIP issues are judged in a different way when emphasising the "business continuity" paradigm. In addition, the "business continuity" orientation causes some CIP issues to be strongly re-emphasised, like for example outsourcing or external supply chains.

1. Introduction

As part of the ACIP [1] project (Analysis & Assessment for Critical Infrastructure Protection), funded by the European Commission under the "Information Society Technology" programme (project IST-2001-37257) a case study was carried out in 2002–2003 with five telecom operators (fixed and mobile networks). The aim of the study was to identify the operators' position concerning the "criticality" of their business, the processes they consider most critical, the threats and risks they see for their operations, the protection methods and measures they use, and their requirements and expectations for new protection and recovery methods and tools. During the study individual interviews and a joint workshop with the telecom operators were carried out.

The case study was based on the assumption that the operators use the following widely accepted procedural model for their security processes:

- In a first step a CI operator will analyse which processes and procedures are critical for providing its services.

- In a second step the operator has to find out whether there are critical dependences, for example on ICT components or ICT services, within the critical processes.
- For these critical dependences the relevant threats and risks have to be determined.
- For risks that cannot be accepted suitable countermeasures have to be determined and implemented, and their adequacy continuously monitored.

This paper gives an overview of the (concurring) results of the case study. In addition some conclusions for a general approach to develop new methods and tools for ICT-oriented critical infrastructure protection are suggested.[1]

2. Threats and risks for critical processes

In analysing critical processes one can at first differentiate between the perspective of a CI operator and the perspective of a governmental/regulatory institution. While an operator takes all measures to ensure the "business continuity", government or society are more interested in "service continuity". That means that from a society's point of view it does not matter if one CI operator goes out of business, as long as other CI operators provide sufficient service. During the interviews, of course, the „business continuity" point of view turned out to dominate.

2.1 Critical processes

The main critical processes were identified as:
- The operational network including the network management components.
  This is the "cash cow" which must be kept running to produce the revenue. Running the operational network is certainly a highly complex task with a lot of local sources for errors or disruptions. But considerable technical and organisational effort is dedicated to continuous operation. In addition (at least in Germany) there exists an exhaustive redundant service coverage by independent operators. Astonishingly, operators judge the availability of the operational network – seen from a global perspective – as rather uncritical: merely regionally limited crises or a crisis of a single operator is to be expected. A national or European crisis scenario seems to be unrealistic.
  Nevertheless there exist critical components in the telecom networks that can be identified and localized with moderate effort. A physical attack on these key components could cause trouble in a limited region for several days.
- The production network with components like IT support, supply chain, billing, customer relationship management.
  This network and its components are more susceptible to disruption than the operational network. A breakdown of one of these components represents a considerable economic problem to the operator. But due to redundant service provision from competing operators this would not harm society in a major dimension.

---

[1] A more general discussion on the perspectives of the different stakeholders and different responsibilities for communications security is included in the ETP report „Security Issues for European Communications Providers" [2]

2.2 Critical dependences

The critical dependences that we identified can be grouped into the following categories:
- Dependences internal to the enterprise
  - Critical dependences are handled as much as possible under the control of the CI-operator itself (i.e., outsourcing is avoided for critical process elements).
- Dependences under external control
  - Energy supply

    This is the biggest single dependence. Short-term outages will be compensated by battery and emergency power supply devices. But wide-area or long lasting energy shortage cannot be compensated for. However, the European energy supply network is very robust and difficult to injure in large-scale areas. Experience also shows that often the end users are faced with energy shortage long before the telecom networks run out of energy. A large-scale energy shortage would assume a catastrophic damage scenario in which a telecom shortage is only a minor evil.
  - Spare Parts

    Spare part supply is a potential bottleneck. But a large crisis relevant for society assumes a huge damage, such as an EMP. The consequences would be equally huge for all other critical infrastructures, so that an effective protection seems not possible.
  - Third party software

    The far most feared and seen most realistic threat is due to software dependence in both the operational and the production network. So far there is no viable approach to judge the quality or even integrity of complex software in an adequate way. Operators restrict themselves to probe-oriented black box testing. There remains a strong discomfortable feeling with blackbox software components. In practice parts of the software functionality become operational untested. This causes severe concerns to the operators. Because all operators receive important key components from only a few vendors, a malfunction of a judiciously chosen, widely used software component may cause large-scale, simultaneous outages for many operators. An accidental breakdown of this kind seems unrealistic due to the complexity and diversity of the systems. But a well-prepared strategic software attack seems not unrealistic, although difficult to carry out.

Human resources create both internal and external dependences. The employees of the CI-operators and their vendors represent critical resources to the successful operation of telecommunication services.

2.3 Threats, vulnerabilities and risks

Threats and vulnerabilities are distinguished according to business-oriented and service-oriented scenarios. The telecom services are offered in a highly distributed, highly redundant/robust and competitive way. This means that until now natural disaster or other events could not harm the general service provisioning. At most a local or regional breakdown of services happened so far. Even the so-called „Elbe Flood" (Germany 2002) was not considered a telecom crisis: telecom service essentially remained intact. Telecom service providers are used to handle such incidents in their daily operation, for example, that cable trunks are cut during road repair, or that a switching centre breaks down due to fire or energy loss. From a service point of view, crises so far were limited to regional effects only.

Operators do not really fear a "real crisis" – defined as a threat to survivability, that means a threat to the core functionality of the operational network – because of their past experiences. This was common understanding in the interviews and the workshop.

From a CIP point of view, the dependence on vendor software (possibly infiltrated with malfunctions) constitutes a much higher potential risk than fire or even bombing attacks by terrorists. This is because with clever and long-term software "preparation" you may produce damage not only on a regional but also on national/transnational level.

3. CIP methods and measures currently in use

There exists a so-called industry standard of "best practices" on how to operate a robust and failure-resistant telecommunication network (key concepts are, e.g., emergency power supply, redundancy, fault limitations, decentralization, backups). All operators comply with these standard measures. In addition there exist a body of legal and regulatory rules that have to be obeyed. Current practices do not require special crisis management exercises. But when an accident happens, it also serves as an opportunity to re-examine and train the procedures. According to telecom operators, even the tools for running the operational network are considered as sufficient and need no major further research. The cooperation between the operators is so well-established that inter-carrier-exercises are considered unnecessary for "normal" emergency situations. This might change when dramatic crises should ever emerge, in which several networks are affected.

The measures can broadly be divided into technical and procedural measures, and into organizational infrastructure measures such as a "certified security culture" – e.g., according to ISO 19977. There were no systematic or even tool-based procedures identifiable for the conception or for the assessment of protection measures.

The main method in use to identify and take measures against threats is to use the human expertise. Tools are only used for small functional scopes and on a rather low technical level (e.g. intrusion detection, port scanning, log file analyses). Decision support tools to provide assistance during a crisis, or to prevent a crisis, seem to be not required – or impossible to build. Decision support tools make only sense if decision takers are used to these tools, and if the tools provide a feedback loop. That means the tool use has to be continuously exercised. This can be accomplished in crisis simulation training. On the other hand, any crisis may be different, and the tool value correspondingly vague. A better approach may be the integration of security tools into the day-to-day use of network operation tools, to ensure that users are prepared for proper tool application when a crisis arrives.

It seems as if the telecom community had not to face a real crisis so far. It might even be that managing the smaller crises with only limited, regional effects has trained the organizations in preventing real disaster under all realistic circumstances.

3.1 Methods for risk assessment and risk management

Risk assessment for physical risks is very well understood (e.g., protecting buildings against water, fire, unauthorised access). In addition, these risks are typically limited to local or regional impact.

Such risks are typically considered under commercial, business-oriented aspects. Commercial risks may hit one operator, but typically they do not impact society. ICT-induced risks are much more difficult to assess. According to the telecom operators, current tools turned out to be not very useful. Rather, simple checklists are used. Methods that encompass the internal process structure of an operator are difficult to transfer, because the process structure that differs significantly between operators.

4. CIP method/tool requirements and expectations

The interview partners do not build but operate their equipment. Therefore, our study did not expect to elicit requirements for constructive measures, but rather for operational and analysis measures. On a fundamental level the expertise of human experts cannot be substituted. It has to form the basis for all methods and tools. Tools may provide various levels of expertise aggregation. Among the operators that we interviewed, there was a general agreement that quantitative methods are not very promising. Tools that "know to much" are even considered potentially harmful. They provide a huge potential for misuse. Practitioner's expectations encompass concrete and generic functions:

- Requirements for the operational and strategic level include
    - Budget optimisation for security measures (how to get for a given budget the maximum of security?) and cost-benefit analyses of security measures (ROSI: Return of security investment).
    - "Crisis simulation tool" to train the employees.
    - Improved scoring rates for logging, monitoring and intrusion detection tools (e.g. less false positives / negatives).
    - Improvements in assessing software quality and integrity.
    - Three-dimensional model with dimensions for functionality, economy of operation and risk. (Each dimension should use no more than 15 parameters.)
    - An approach to make risks more transparent, and to better include them into economic business models.
    - Integration of existing monitoring tools (e.g., network management, intrusion detection) with a unified data exchange format and corresponding import/export interfaces, so that different vendors can provide different computations / interpretations on the different sets of basic data.
- Generic tool and method requirements include
    - Short set-up time
    - Low data intensity (for input and output)
    - Independence of organizational structure
    - Predictable quality and completeness of results
    - Comprehensiveness and maintainability
- Rather sceptical judgements are concerned with:
    - Security benchmark figures
      They are easily misinterpreted and lead security management into unbalanced considerations. They may be misused to damage the reputation of a company.
    - Decision support
      The trust in knowledge management and decision support tools is rather low. The effort for providing the input data, for information maintenance, and the necessary training of users is considered too high.
    - Modelling and simulation tools
      The effort of model preparation to make them comply with reality is considered too high.

5. Conclusions

- Operators address critical infrastructure protection from a business-oriented position, which may differ significantly from the viewpoint of the government or the society. This general tendency can be attributed to the ongoing privatisation in the CI sectors.
- Society accepts the unavailability of critical infrastructures as long as the problems are restricted in space and time (energy blackouts, traffic jams, mobile phone dead zones etc.). Thus, availability under all (even the most unrealistic) circumstances is not necessary.
- Driven by business-orientation there is a tendency to outsource non-core business parts (and also backup provisions). That is, physical/technical safeguards are increasingly replaced by service-level agreements with third parties; this seems to aggravate critical dependences, often beyond the control of the operators.
- Concerning threats and risks, operators know how to deal with local day-to-day incidents. Real disaster is beyond imagination, as for such a situation there is no (financially realistic) way to protect against, so why think about it?
- Telecom operators are more or less satisfied with state-of-the-art or standard CIP procedures. Consequently, all competitors follow about the same procedures, which means about the same investment in protection. To the mutual advantage of all operators, strong competition for higher investments in infrastructure protection is avoided, as there is no business disadvantage in case of emergency: All competitors will be affected by a crisis to roughly the same degree!
- There is a strong demand for methods and tools for security budget optimisation Operators need quantitative data on ROSI (return of security investment).
- Modelling and simulation tools are received rather sceptically: the effort for model preparation and updates is considered (too) high.

Final remark

Research in the area of CIP must take the operators' viewpoint into account – not as the only one, but as a major one. Otherwise the results will not be accepted by practitioners.

References

[1] Analysis & Assessment for Critical Infrastructure Protection. Project number IST-2001-37257 by the IST research programme of the European Community, managed by the European Commission DG Information Society: www.eu-acip.de
[2] European Telecommunications Platform: Security Issues for European Communications Providers (Final Draft)

Firewalls, Intrusion Detection and Biometrics

Security and Privacy in Advanced Networking Technologies
B. Jerman-Blažič et al. (Eds.)
IOS Press, 2004

Network Firewall Technologies

David W. CHADWICK

IS Institute, University of Salford, Salford, M5 4WT, England

Abstract. This paper provides an overview of the topic of network firewalls and the authentication methods that they support. The reasons why a firewall is needed are given, plus the advantages and disadvantages of using a firewall. The components that comprise a firewall are introduced, along with the authentication methods that can be used by firewalls. Finally, typical firewall configurations are described, along with the advantages and disadvantages of each configuration.

1. Security Threats from connecting to the Internet

Most organisations today have an internal network that interconnects their computer systems. There is usually a high degree of trust between the computer systems in the network, particularly if the network is private. However, many organizations now see the benefits of connecting to the Internet. But, the Internet is inherently an insecure network. Some of the threats inherent in the Internet include:

- **Weak or No Authentication required**. Several services e.g. rlogin, require no password to be given when a user logs in. Other services provide information with no or little authentication e.g. anonymous FTP, and WWW. Other services trust the caller at the other end to provide correct identification information e.g. TCP and UDP trust the IP address of the remote station; whilst other services grant access at too large a granularity e.g. NFS grants access to anyone from a particular remote host. Finally many services require passwords to be transmitted in the clear across the network, which make them vulnerable to capture and replay.
- **Insecure software**. Internet software, particularly shareware, free or low cost packages, often have bugs or design flaws in them usually as a result of poor design or insufficient testing of the software. But due to their ready availability and low cost, many people still take the packages. Examples include: the UNIX sendmail program which has had numerous vulnerabilities reported in it, and a freeware FTP product which contained a Trojan Horse that allowed privilege access to the server. Unscrupulous people are always ready to exploit these weaknesses.
- **Sniffer programs**. In 1994 the CERT reported that thousands of systems on the Internet had been compromised by hackers, and sniffer programs installed on them. Sniffer programs monitor network traffic for usernames and passwords, subsequently making these available to the hacker.
- **Cracker programs**. These programs, widely available on the Internet, run in background mode on a machine, encrypting thousands of different words and comparing these to the encrypted passwords stored on the machine. These so called dictionary attacks (because the words are held in a dictionary) are often very successful, providing the hacker with up to a third of the passwords on a machine.
- **Port Scanners**. These programs, again available freely from the Internet, will send messages to all the TCP and UDP ports on a remote computer to see if any of them are

open and waiting to receive a call. Once an open port has been located, the hacker will then try to get in to the computer through it.

- **Ease of Masquerade (Spoofing)**. The above make it relatively easy for the hacker to exploit the trust inherent in the Internet, or to capture passwords and replay them. Other security weaknesses include: the SMTP protocol uses ASCII messages to transfer messages, so a hacker can TELNET into an SMTP port and simply type in a bogus Email message; a feature called IP source routing allows a caller to falsify its IP address, and to provide the recipient with a return path directly back to itself.

So how can an organization securely connect to the Internet? One solution is to use one or more network firewalls.

2. What is a Firewall ?

A firewall is a secure Internet gateway that is used to interconnect a private network to the Internet (see Figure 1).

The Firewall

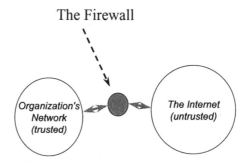

Figure 1

There are a number of components that make up a firewall:

i) the Internet access security policy of the organisation. This states, at a high level, what degree of security the organisation expects when connecting to the Internet. The security policy is independent of technology and techniques, and should have a lifetime independent of the equipment used. An example of statements from such a security policy might be: external users will not be allowed to access the corporate network without a strong level of authentication; any corporate information not in the public domain must be transferred across the Internet in a confidential manner, and corporate users will only be allowed to send electronic mail to the Internet - all other services will be banned.

ii) the mapping of the security policy onto technical designs and procedures that are to be followed when connecting to the Internet. This information will be updated as new technology is announced, and as system configurations change etc. For example, regarding authentication, the technical design might specify the use of one-time passwords. Technical designs are usually based on one of two security policies, either:

- permit any service unless it is expressly denied, or
- deny any service unless it is expressly permitted.

The latter is clearly the more secure of the two.

iii) the firewall system, which is the hardware and software which implements the firewall. Typical firewall systems comprise a IP packet filtering router, and a host computer (sometimes called a bastion host or application gateway) running application filtering and authentication software.

Each of these firewall components are essential. A firewall system without an Internet access security policy cannot be correctly configured. A policy without enforced procedures is worthless as it is ignored.

3. Advantages of Firewalls

Firewalls have a number of advantages.

- They can stop incoming requests to inherently insecure services, e.g. you can disallow rlogin, or RPC services such as NFS.
- They can control access to other services e.g.
  - bar callers from certain IP addresses,
  - filter the service operations (both incoming and outgoing), e.g. stop FTP writes
  - hide information e.g. by only allowing access to certain directories or systems
- They are more cost effective than securing each host on the corporate network since there is often only one or a few firewall systems to concentrate on.
- They can control the spread of viruses by filtering messages as they pass through the firewall
- They are more secure than securing each host due to:
  - the complexity of the software on the host - this makes it easier for security loopholes to appear. In contrast, firewalls usually have simplified operating systems and don't run complex application software,
  - the number of hosts that need to be secured (the security of the whole is only as strong as the weakest link).

4. Disadvantages of Firewalls

Firewalls are not. the be all and end all of network security. They do have some disadvantages, such as:

- They are a central point for attack, and if an intruder breaks through the firewall they may have unlimited access to the corporate network.
- They may restrict legitimate users from accessing valuable services, for example, corporate users may not be let out onto the Web, or when working away from home a corporate user may not have full access to the organization's network.
- They do not protect against back door attacks, and may encourage users to enter and leave via the backdoor, particularly if the service restrictions are severe enough. Examples of backdoor entrance points to the corporate network are: modems, and importing/exporting floppy discs. The security policy needs to cover these aspects as well.
- They can be a bottleneck to throughput, since all connections must go via the firewall system.
- Firewall systems on their own cannot protect the network against smuggling i.e. the importation or exportation of banned material through the firewall e.g. games programs as attachments to Email messages. Smuggling could still be a significant

source of virus infection if users download software from external bulletin boards etc. The recent Melissa and Love Bug viruses were smuggled inside Email messages unbeknown to the recipients. This is an area that the security policy needs to address. There are software packages that can help in this e.g. Mimesweeper runs in the firewall and will check Email attachments before letting them pass. It will remove potentially dangerous attachments or stop the Email altogether.

−   The biggest disadvantage of a firewall is that it gives no protection against the inside attacker. Since most corporate computer crime is perpetrated by internal users, a firewall offers little protection against this threat. E.g. an employee may not be able to Email sensitive data from the site, but they may be able to copy it onto a floppy disc and post it.

Consequently organizations need to balance the amount of time and money they spend on firewalls with that spent on other aspects of information security.

4.1 Firewalls have weaknesses too

A vulnerability in Checkpoint's Firewall was reported in July 11, 2001 as follows: A VULNERABILITY IN Check Point Software's Firewall-1 and VPN-1 firewalls may allow intruders to tunnel illegitimate traffic into or out of corporate networks.

The hole was discovered in June 2001 by Inside Security, a spin-off of the University of Stuttgart's security team in Germany. The hole could be exploited to passively snoop inside corporate networks or to launch certain types of denial-of-service attacks, according to the CERT Coordination Center security response team at Carnegie Mellon University, which issued a bulletin on the vulnerability.

"This is a pretty serious vulnerability [because] Check Point is one of the most widely deployed firewalls on the Internet," said Ian Finlay, a member of the CERT team.

The vulnerability involves a proprietary protocol called RDP that is used in Check Point's firewalls for internally communicating between software components. By default, VPN-1/ FireWall-1 allows RDP packets to traverse firewall gateways to simplify encryption setup, according to Check Point's advisory on the topic. Under some conditions, malicious packets with RDP headers could be constructed that would be allowed across the firewall, according to the Check Point bulletin.

Users can get around the problem by installing a patch from Check Point. Until the patch can be applied, users can reduce their risks by configuring their routers to block access to the port that is exploited by the vulnerability, CERT said in its advisory.

Although there have been no reported security incidents related to this vulnerability, CERT is recommending that all affected sites upgrade their software as soon as possible. "The thing to keep in mind is that the very nature of a firewall is to block traffic from reaching your internal network. This is a situation where that assumed fundamental protection [is breached]" said Shawn Hernan, a CERT member.

5. Models, Layers and Firewalls

ISO uses a 7 layer model for Open Systems Interconnection, whereas the Internet can be regarded as having a 5 layer model. Whereabouts in these models are firewall systems placed?

Firewalls, Layers and Models

ISO 7 Layer Model	Internet 5 Layer Model	Firewalls
Application (7)	Application (5)	Proxy Service
Transport (4)	TCP/UDP (4)	Packet Filtering Router/Packet
Network (3)	IP/ICMP (3)	Screening Router
		Stateful Inspection
Link (2)	Link (2)	
Physical (1)	System Interface (1)	none

Figure 2

Firewall systems are usually placed at layers 3, 4 and 5 of the Internet model, (3, 4 and 7 of the ISO model), see Figure 2. Their purpose is to control access to and from a protected network. Note that a firewall can be placed between any two networks, for example between a corporate business network and its R&D network. In general, a firewall is placed between a high security domain and a lower security domain.

A firewall system operating at layers 3 and 4 is sometimes called a packet filtering router or a screening router. Its purpose is to filter IP and ICMP packets and TCP/UDP ports. The router will have several ports and be able to route and filter the packets according to the filtering rules. Packet filters can also be built in software and run on dual homed PCs, but whilst these can filter packets they are not able to route them to different networks.

A firewall at layer 5 Internet (7 ISO) is sometimes called a bastion host, application gateway, proxy server or guardian system. Its purpose is to filter the service provided by the application.

It is also possible to operate a firewall system at Layer 2 (the link level) e.g. by configuring an Ethernet bridge to only forward certain packets, but this is not very common. The Inspection Module from Checkpoint's Firewall 1 product operates between the link and network layers and inspects packets before letting them pass through the firewall.

Packet Filtering Firewall

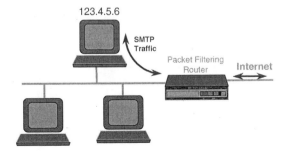

Figure 3

6. Packet Filtering Router

Packet filtering routers were the first type of firewall to be invented. A packet filtering router should be able to filter IP packets based on the following four fields:

- source IP address
- destination IP address
- TCP/UDP source port
- TCP/UDP destination port

Filtering is used to:

- block connections from specific hosts or networks
- block connections to specific hosts or networks
- block connections to specific ports
- block connections from specific ports

When configuring a router, it is usually possible to specify all ports or hosts, as well as specific ones. Packet filtering routers have fast performance, since the IP packets are either forwarded or dropped without inspecting their contents (other than the address and port fields). Packet filtering routers are equivalent to guards who ask someone "where are you from and where are you going to" and if the answer is OK, the person is let into the building.

For example, suppose an Internet access security policy stated that the only Internet access allowed was incoming and outgoing Email. Assuming that the organisation's Email server was located on host 123.4.5.6, then the router would be configured in the following way:

Type	SourceAddr	DestAddr	SourcePort	DestPort	Action
tcp	*	123.4.5.6	>1023	25	permit
tcp	123.4.5.6	*	>1023	25	permit
*	*	*	*	*	deny.

Note. * means any address.

Note. It is conventional for SMTP mail switches to always listen for incoming messages on port 25 (the well known port number), and to send messages on port numbers 1024 upwards.

The first rule allows incoming Email from any address to be sent to the Email server, the second rule allows outgoing Email to be sent from the Email server to any address, whereas the last rule forbids any other traffic from passing through the router.

7. Problems with Packet Filtering Routers

Packet filtering routers are a vital component of a firewall system, but they should only be considered as a first line of defence, since they do have a number of deficiencies.

1. They can be complex to configure (the rule set can be large, particularly when many services are supported), and there is no automatic way of checking the correctness of the rules i.e. that the rules correctly implement the security policy. Furthermore, if the router does not support logging of calls, there is no way of knowing if supposedly disallowed packets are actually getting through via a hole in the rules.

2. If some members of staff have special requirements for Internet access, then new rules may have to be added for their machines. This further complicates the rule set, maybe making it too complex to manage. Furthermore this access is at the wrong level of granularity, since the machine rather than the user is being given permission. Users are not authenticated, only the packets are checked.

3. Some basic routers do not allow TCP/UDP filtering, and this makes it impossible to implement certain security policies e.g. the one given in the example above.
4. You cannot filter between different ISO protocols running over TCP/IP. RFC 1006 specifies how ISO applications such as X.500 and X.400 may run over TCP/IP. However, all of the ISO applications must connect to port 102, on which the RFC 1006 service sits.
5. Finally, packet filtering routers are not very secure, since the contents of the packets are not inspected (only their headers) so anything can be being passed through e.g. viruses, unauthorised delete commands etc. Finally, the senders of the packets are not authenticated.

In order to overcome some of these deficiencies, more of the contents of the packets need to be inspected. This led to application level firewalls and more recently to the stateful packet inspection module from Checkpoint.

8. Stateful Packet Inspections

This is a software module that runs in the operating system of a Windows or Unix PC firewall, and inspects the packets that are arriving. The inspection is driven by security rules configured into the machine by the security officer. Headers from all seven layers of the ISO model are inspected, and information about the packets is fed into dynamic state tables that store information about the connection. The cumulative data in the tables is then used in evaluating subsequent packets to make sure they are on an existing connection or are new allowed connection attempts.

Whilst this technology is more secure than simple packet filtering routers, it is not as secure as application gateways, as the full application layer data is not inspected. However, it does perform faster than application proxies. Stateful inspection is similar to a security guard that asks who are you, where are you going, and what are you carrying, before he lets you into the building.

Note that this technology is patented by Checkpoint, the manufacturers of FireWall-1.

9. Application Level Firewalls

An application level firewall is created by installing a (bastion) host computer running the appropriate application(s), between the packet filtering router and the intranet. The packet filtering router directs all calls from the Internet to the application level firewall.

The application(s) running on the host are not usually full blown versions of the application(s), but rather are slimmed down proxy services that simply filter the messages at the application level, letting some messages through, rejecting other messages, and modifying others before accepting them.

If the host does not run a particular application proxy service, then calls to this application will not usually pass through the firewall to/from the Internet. In other words, all services not running on the firewall are blocked. Common application proxies, supported by most application firewalls suppliers are FTP, SMTP, HTTP and Telnet.

Application proxies are similar to a security guard who asks you why you want to enter the building and what are you carrying, and if he does not like your answer he will refuse you entry, or he may direct you to another person, or even remove some of your items or substitute them before letting you pass through. He may even take things off you before you can leave the building.

FTP poses a security threat because confidential information may be exported from the organisation, or bogus information may be deposited in the organisation's file store. The FTP proxy allows FTP commands to be selectively blocked according to source and destination addresses. For example, if the organisation has information that it wishes to publish on the Internet, the proxy would forbid sending *put* commands (i.e. writing) to the relevant FTP server and directory. If the organisation wishes customers to send files to it, then the FTP proxy can ensure that *dir* and *get* commands are blocked, and that the FTP connection is sent to the correct system and directory.

SMTP poses a security threat because mail servers (often the buggy *sendmail* program on UNIX systems) run with system level permissions in order to deliver incoming mail to users' mailboxes. Hackers can initiate an interactive session with a mail server (by hand typing in commands or writing their own programs) and exploit its system level privileges. The SMTP proxy which runs on the firewall isolates the internal Email system from incoming Internet mail, thereby preventing Internet users from directly interfering with a mail server. Incoming mail is spooled in a reserved directory on the firewall host, by the proxy SMTP mail program that runs without system privileges. The remote Email sender is then disconnected before any harm can be done. Another process picks up the mail from the reserved directory and forwards it to the internal Email system.

TELNET allows users to login to remote machines. This can be a security risk if remote users are allowed to login to the organisation's computers with standard username/password pairs, given the inherent weaknesses with password based systems. The Telnet proxy can be configured to state which systems can make calls to it, and which systems it will permit to be called. A typical configuration will be to allow internal users to call the Internet, but not vice versa.

HTTP accesses remote web pages. HTTP proxies can filter the various HTTP commands (methods) such as POST, PUT and DELETE as well as filter the URLs (e.g. forbid connections to .com sites)

In addition, all of the application proxies will provide logging of the incoming and outgoing sessions, and will authenticate the users. However, rather than each proxy having its own authentication service, it is beneficial if all proxies can make use of a common authentication module that runs on the firewall.

We also want to make sure that the data being transferred is virus free, therefore we need Content Filtering as well.

10. Content Filtering

With content filtering, the application data is handed over to a content filtering server that unpacks the data to see what is inside, and harmful content is then disposed of. For example, zipped files are unzipped first to see what is inside them. If the content contains a virus it will be discarded or disinfected. (Note, this requires that organisations regularly update their virus checking software, as new viruses are found daily.) File types are identified (not from the filename extension but from their content) and undesirable types e.g. executables can be removed, according to the security policy. Alternatively, if imported code is digitally signed, the author/signer can be checked to see if he is on a trusted list of signers and then the file can be accepted. Text files can be scanned for a list of undesirable key words (e.g. swear words or explicit sexual language). Finally, incoming http Java or ActiveX applets can be removed if this is company policy. Content filtering is like the security guard that empties your pockets, and gives you a full body check both on entering and leaving a building.

The biggest vendor of content checking software is Checkpoint with its MIMEsweeper family of products (that include MAILsweeper and WEBsweeper).

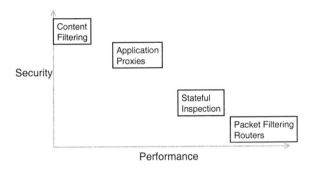

Performance vs. Security

Figure 4

The biggest problem with scanning and filtering all the packet contents as they pass through the firewall, is the amount of processing time this takes, see Figure 4. Consequently, large servers are needed if all incoming data is to be screened.

11. Inspecting Logs is Important

Logging of all calls that pass through the firewall is important, both incoming and outgoing, but just as important is inspecting the logs on a daily basis. Automated tools will be helpful for this, dependent upon the volume of traffic passing through the firewall. Administrators should look out for the following:

- probes to ports that have no applications running on them (this could be a sign of hackers looking to install Trojan horses on these ports)
- IP addresses that are always rejected (this could be a sign that hackers are trying to find a way in)
- unsuccessful logins (this could be a hacker running a password cracker)
- unusual outgoing calls (this could mean you have already been hacked as a DDOS zombie site)

12. Authentication

It has already been noted that simple passwords can not be relied upon to provide authentication information over the Internet. Something stronger is needed. The logical place to site the strong authentication functionality is in the firewall. An increasingly common authentication method is the use of one-time passwords or hashed passwords. But digital signatures are also becoming more popular as PKIs get implemented. Digital signatures rely on asymmetric encryption. The sender digitally signs a message, by appending to it a digital summary of the message (called a message digest), encrypted with his private key. The firewall can decipher the digital signature using the sender's public key. The firewall can also compute the message digest and compare this to the deciphered one. If both digests are the same, the message is authentic (it must have come from the owner of the private key and it has not been tampered with during transfer).

SOCKS authentication was one of the first general authentication mechanisms to be placed in a firewall, that allows remote applications to authenticate to the firewall. RADIUS is the Internet draft standard for dial in user authentication to a firewall.

12.1 SOCKS Authentication

SOCKS provides an authentication layer for the firewall that can be used by all application proxies. Calls come into the SOCKS service, are authenticated by it, then a call is opened up to the application proxy which does further application level filtering before making a call to the application on the intranet, see Figure 5.

SOCKSv5 operates as follows. A TCP client opens up a connection to a SOCKS server at port 1080 in the firewall. The client negotiates an authentication method, then authenticates to the SOCKS server. If successful, the client sends a Relay Request to the SOCKS server. The SOCKS server then either relays the request to the requested server or rejects the request. If accepted, thereafter messages between the application server and the client are relayed via the SOCKS server. A full description of SOCKSv5 can be found in [1].

SOCKS Authentication Service

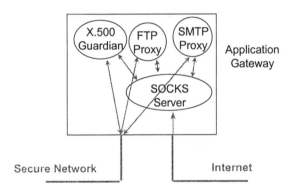

Figure 5

A disadvantage of SOCKSv5 is that it requires modified TCP software in the client system. Fortunately this is now widely implemented, and is supported for example in Netscape and Internet Explorer, plus freely available implementations of the SOCKS library and server are available for download from the Internet.

Authentication methods primarily supported by SOCKS are username password and GSS-API. But this is not such a wide range, and the password is sent in the clear so it is open to sniffing attacks.

12.2 RADIUS

The Remote Authentication Dial In User Service (RADIUS) is specified in RFC 2865 [2]. The mode of operation is as follows:

1. The user dials into the network via a modem. The network can be the corporate network running its own modems, or it could be an Internet Service Provider.
2. The receiving computer acts as a RADIUS client, and will usually ask the user for his username and password.
3. The RADIUS client sends an Access Request message to the RADIUS server including the username and password (which is encoded using MD5 to stop sniffing - see later).
4. The RADIUS server authenticates the user using its local database and sends back an Access Accept or Access Reject message to the RADIUS client. If the message is an accept, it can include other information such as servers and ports the user is allowed to access.

Where Challenge/Response authentication is supported, the Access Request message will contain the user's name, and the RADIUS server will return an Access Challenge message containing a random number/string. This is sent to the user by the RADIUS client and the user must type in the correct reply. This is typically calculated using a one time password device (card or software). The RADIUS client then sends a second Access Request message containing the user's reply as the password. The server can determine if this is the correct reply and if so send an Access Accept message.

Remote Authentication Dial In User Service (RADIUS)

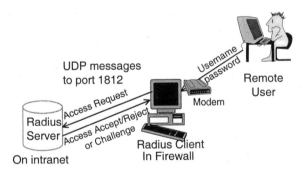

Figure 6

The RADIUS client and server share a secret (such as a long password) so that they can authenticate each other. When password based user authentication is being used, the Access Request message sent by the RADIUS client contains a 16 octet random number (called the authenticator), generated by the client. Then, in order to authenticate itself and the user to the server, it takes the authenticator and the shared secret, and hashes them using the MD5 algorithm. This produces a 16 octet (128 bit) number which is then XOR'ed with the user's password to produce another 16 octet number. This is carried in the Access Request message as the value of the password attribute (see Figure 7).

The authenticator is used in the Access Accept/Reject message so that the RADIUS client can authenticate the reply from the RADIUS server. Only this time the whole response message, the request authenticator and the shared secret are concatenated and hashed to form a 128 bit number which is sent as the response authenticator.

If the authentication method is challenge-response, then the first Access Accept message will not have a valid user's password (as it has not been computed yet). Therefore the password attribute can be blank or set to a fixed string such as "challenge required".

All messages are sent using UDP, and the RADIUS well known port number is 1812.

The advantages of RADIUS are that it is an open protocol, an Internet Draft Standard, supports a wide range of authentication mechanisms, is widely supported by vendors, and is extensible. RADIUS protocol messages contain a series of attributes (type, length, value tuples). These are standardised and registered with the ICANN (formerly IANA), and new attributes can be added as the Internet community agree on a need for them. Already defined attributes include: user's name, user's password, RADIUS client's IP address, call-back number (for modem's which call the user back at home) etc.

RADIUS Password
Based Authentication

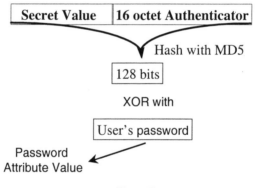

Figure 7

12.3 Hardware Based One Time Passwords

An increasingly common authentication method is the use of one-time passwords. There are two popular variants of one-time passwords, one is based on a challenge response mechanism, the other on synchronised clocks.

With the challenge response mechanism, the user logs into the firewall, and the firewall passes the user a challenge, usually in the form of a numeric string. The user responds to the challenge with a one-time password that is computed from the string by his hardware/software according to a pre-defined encryption algorithm that is also known to the firewall (see Figure 8). One such system (SecureNet from Digital Pathways) relies on the user having a one-time password card the size of a credit card that is capable of computing the passwords. The card has a digital display, and requires a PIN number to be entered before it can be used. Another system (S/key from Bellcore) relies on software in the remote user's PC to compute the password (see next section).

With the clock synchronised mechanism (e.g. SecureID from RSA Security), both the card and the firewall authentication system compute a new password every 60 seconds, according to a pre-defined encryption algorithm which uses the date and time, and a shared secret. This eliminates the need for a challenge string (see Figure 8). With the SecureID system, the user must transfer a PIN number plus the computed password, so that if the card is stolen it cannot be used by anyone else. This mechanism is sometimes referred to as Two Factor Authentication, as it is based on something I possess (the card) and something I know (the PIN).

12.4 Software Based One Time Passwords - S/Key

S/Key is a challenge-response one time password mechanism, and is widely supported by firewall vendors. Free S/Key implementations are available from the Internet. S/Key works as follows.

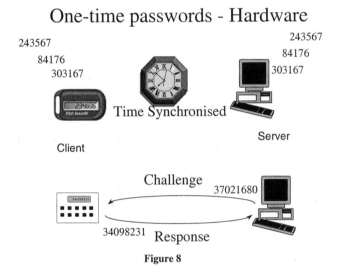

Figure 8

The server hashes up the user's password plus a random seed word a large number of times (say a thousand times) and stores the resulting 128 bit number. When the user asks to log in, the server returns a challenge comprising the seed word and the number 999 (one less than the nth hash stored). The user is asked for his password, then his PC computes a hash of the password and seed word, then repeats this another 998 times and sends the resulting 128 bit hash to the server. This number is usually sent as ASCII words rather than binary, to stop the eight bit of each byte possibly being corrupted during transfer. The server takes the incoming number, hashes it once and compares it with its stored value. If they are the same it knows the user is authentic and allows the login. It then stores the hash it has been given. The next time the user wants to login, the server returns the seed word and the number 998, and the whole process is repeated. The user can login another 997 times until number 1 is reached. The server then has to invent a new random seed word and hash this with the password a thousand times and store it. The whole process then starts again.

One-time passwords - Software

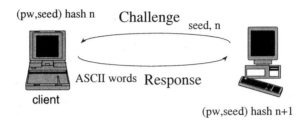

Figure 9

The system works against sniffers, since it is not possible to compute the (n-1)th hash (you can never work out what the input to a hashing algorithm is). Therefore if an attacker captures the one time password this will not help him, as he cannot work out what the next one will be (he can only determine what the previous one was).

12.5 Virtual Private Networks

Virtual private networks connect two intranets, or an intranet and a remote user, together via an authenticated and encrypted link (see Figure 10). This secure tunnel makes the traffic confidential, authentic and un-replayable as it traverses the Internet. Most firewall vendors now provide VPN software as part of their firewall offerings.

      The security is provided at the IP layer, by encapsulating each IP packet within an outer IP packet. The outer IP header directs the packet through the Internet to the remote firewall. Immediately after the outer IP header is an IPsec header that describes the security that has been applied to the encapsulated IP packet. (This is either an Authentication Header for packet authentication, anti-replay and integrity, or an Encapsulated Security Payload header for authentication, confidentiality, anti-replay and integrity.) The encapsulated packet contains the IP header for the final destination, followed by the payload (usually higher layer headers and higher layer data).

      If the encapsulated data has been encrypted using symmetric encryption and a shared secret key, then this key has to be made available to both ends of the VPN. This can either be manually configured into both firewalls or it may be automatically generated by using the Internet Key Exchange protocol, which uses public key cryptography to distribute the key to the two firewalls.

      Whilst IP Security (IPsec) [3] is optional in IPv4, it is mandatory in IPv6.

Virtual Private Networks (VPNs)

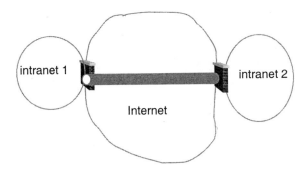

Figure 10

13. Firewall Configurations

13.1 The Dual Homed Gateway

This is a secure firewall design comprising an application gateway and a packet filtering router. It is called "dual homed" because the gateway has two network interfaces, one attached to the Internet, the other to the organisation's network. Only applications with proxy services on the application gateway are able to operate through the firewall. Since IP forwarding is disabled in the host, IP packets must be directed to one of the proxy servers on the host, or be rejected. Some manufacturers build the packet filtering capability and the application proxies into one box, thereby simplifying the design (but removing the possibility of having an optional info server and modems attached to the screened subnet, see Figure 11). The disadvantages of the dual homed gateway are that it may be a bottleneck to performance, and it may be too secure for some sites (!) since it is not possible to let trusted applications bypass the firewall and communicate directly with peers on the Internet. They must have a proxy service in the firewall.

13.2 The Screened Host Gateway

The screened host gateway is similar to the above, but more flexible and less secure, since trusted traffic may pass directly from the Internet into the private network, thereby bypassing the application gateway. In this design the application gateway only needs a single network connection (see Figure 12).

The IP router will normally be configured to pass Internet traffic to the application gateway or to reject it. Traffic from the corporate network to the Internet will also be rejected, unless it originates from the application gateway. The only exception to these rules will be for trusted traffic that will be allowed straight through.

Dual Homed Gateway Firewall

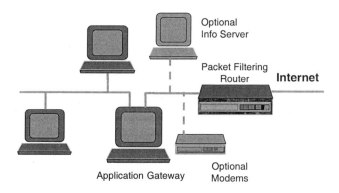

Figure 11

Screened Host Gateway

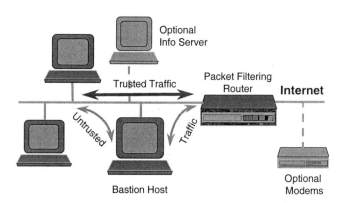

Figure 12

13.3 The Screened Subnet Gateway

This configuration creates a small isolated network between the Internet and the corporate network, which is sometimes referred to as the demilitarised zone (DMZ), see Figure 13. The advantages of this configuration is that multiple hosts and gateways can be stationed in the DMZ, thereby achieving a much greater throughput to the Internet than the other configurations; plus the configuration is very secure as two packet filtering routers are there to protect the corporate network.

Screened Subnet Gateway

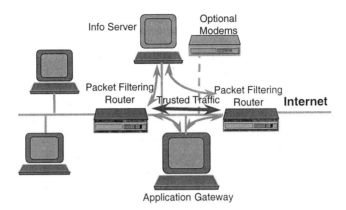

Figure 13

The IP router on the Internet side will only let through Internet traffic that is destined for a host in the DMZ (and vice versa). The IP router on the corporate network side will only let site traffic pass to a host in the DMZ (and vice versa).

This system is as secure as the dual homed gateway, but it is also possible to allow trusted traffic to pass straight through the DMZ if required. This configuration is of course more expensive to implement!

13.4 Double Proxying and a DMZ

Double Proxying and a DMZ

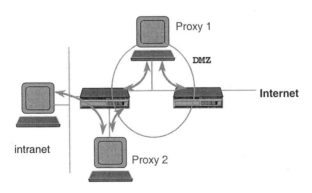

Figure 14

The configuration shown in Figure 14 is even more secure that the screened subnet seen in the previous section. It is used by a bank to protect its internal network from direct access from the Internet. Users from the Internet have to pass through two application proxies before they can access the bank's intranet.

This shows that there really is no limit to how complex a firewall configuration can be. The only limitations are the cost and performance implications of building ulta-secure firewall configurations.

References

[1] SOCKS Protocol Version 5. M. Leech, M. Ganis, Y. Lee, R. Kuris, D. Koblas & L. Jones. RFC 1928, April 1996. (Status: PROPOSED STANDARD).
[2] Remote Authentication Dial In User Service (RADIUS). C. Rigney, S. Willens, A. Rubens, W. Simpson. RFC 2865, June 2000. (Obsoletes RFC2138) (Status: DRAFT STANDARD).
[3] Security Architecture for the Internet Protocol. S. Kent, R. Atkinson. RFC 2401, November 1998.(Status: PROPOSED STANDARD).

Security and Privacy in Advanced Networking Technologies
B. Jerman-Blažič et al. (Eds.)
IOS Press, 2004

161

Intrusion Detection Systems –
Introduction to Intrusion Detection and
Analysis

Hervé DEBAR

herve.debar@francetelecom.com

France Télécom R&D, 42 rue des Coutures, F-14000 Caen

Abstract. Information systems security has been a research area for a long time. Initial viruses and worms propagated slowly through the exchange of magnetic containers. With the development of TCP/IP, security problems have become more frequent and taken very different forms, and have lead to the development of new security techniques.

Very early in the development of the Internet, vulnerabilities affecting operating systems have allowed attackers to move from system to system. Detecting attackers has been a necessity for military environments. Insufficient access control measures have led to the development of intrusion-detection systems (IDS).

These IDS have been developed to detect abnormal behaviour of information systems and networks, indicating a breach of the security policy. Two families of techniques have been developed, *misuse-detection* and *anomaly-detection*, to analyze a *data stream* representing the activity of the monitored information system. Misuse-based analysis detects known violations of the security policy, explicitly specified by the security officer. Anomaly-based analysis detects deviations from the normal behaviour of the monitored information system.

The objective of intrusion-detection systems today is to inform operators on the security health of information system. This mostly improves accountability but does not protect the information system from attacks. The development of dependable analysis techniques, particularly reduction of false alarms and identification of attack context, should in the future enable the migration to efficient intrusion protection systems, merging access control at the network layer with access control at the application layer. Distributing IDS components onto single workstations should create an efficient multi-layered approach to information security in the near future.

1. Introduction

1.1 Problem statement

Attacks against information systems have been occuring in increasing numbers for years, according to an increase in the number of published vulnerabilities. Publication in semi-official forums is often accompanied by sample exploit code, allowing would-be attackers with limited capabilities quick access to attack tools.

1.1.1   Difficulty in implementing protective measures

Preventive measures such as access control conflict with operational necessities in real environments. Firewalls protect the majority of internal networks, but they leave open a number of communication protocols, such as DNS or HTTP, which are infection vectors for worms and attack opportunities when vulnerabilities targetting them are published. Reactive security actions such as patching remain largely ineffective today, due to the cost of rolling out patches in large environments and the low quality of these very patches.

In addition, it is extremely difficult today to assess the efficiency of firewalls. The audit trails generated by the filtering engine are obscure and unrelated to the high-level security policy. IDS qualify the filtered trafic and provide a more explicit vision of the trafic to the operator.

1.1.2   Complexity of filtering technologies

The development of complex IP-based protocols for telephony and video-conferencing leads to difficulties in configuring firewalls, because open ports are not known in advance. As a result, open configurations are required for these services to function properly, or the firewall must be application-aware, resulting in the same false alert problem that has plagued IDS until today.

1.1.3   Objectives of intrusion-detection systems

The objective of intrusion-detection systems is to monitor an information system and analyze its behaviour to detect attacks. It retrieves information about the activity of the information system through one or several data sources, analyzes the resulting events for conformance with a given security policy, and provides alerts to a management console in the case of breaches. Data stream and analysis method are the two prime characteristics of an intrusion-detection system today, and should be carefully weighted in a purchase decision.

1.2   Description of an intrusion-detection system

1.2.1   Standards

The Intrusion Detection exchange format Working Group1 (IDWG) of the Internet Engineering Task Force (IETF) develops a standard alert message format. The first document [16] provides a definition of terms used in the intrusion-detection area. The main concepts are described in 1.2.2.

An IDS in the IDWG sense is build by a set of blocs with a precise function, linked to each other by information flows. Two humans are included in the operation, the administrator and the operator. An intrusion-detection *probe* retrieves information (*activity*) from a *data source* using a *sensor*. The *activity* is a sequence of bytes, later segmented into network packets, log lines or records, to create *events* that are checked by the *analyzer*.

---

[1]http: //www.ietf.org/html.charters/idwg-charter.html

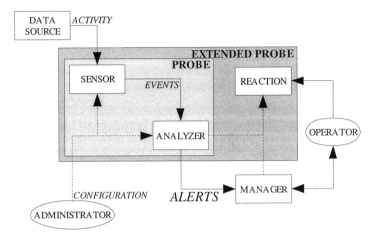

Figure 1 : Components of an intrusion-detection system

The *administrator* is in charge of the security policy, particularly to define what event constitutes an alert. As such, he is responsible for choosing the location of the probe, configuring the sensor and the analyzer, and maintainig this configuration when updates become available. The *operator* is in charge of the monitoring, receiving alerts and applying the proper counter-measure (*reaction*). Note that the appropriate reaction may have to be specified by the administrator. For efficiency reasons, some counter-measures have to be automated and handled by the probe. The best example is the injection of additional network trafic to reset a communication stream; the probe is better located than the manager to do this, and the insertion has to take place immediately, for the reaction to be efficient. This leads to the concept of *extended probe*, not standardized by the IDWG, but frequently encountered in the litterature about intrusion *prevention* systems.

The IDWG description is limited to the detection environment. The objective of the standard is even more restricted, since its goal is only to standardize the format and protocol of the *alert* information stream. Control architecture is clearly excluded from the standard. As such, this does not constitute a complete intrusion-detection system.

1.2.2 Components

An intrusion-detection *system* has the following components:

- **Probes** are the active components of the IDS. They collect and analyze information to provide alerts.
- **Management consoles** configure and update the probes. In particular, the analysis software and knowledge bases need to be frequently updated by the administrator. Management consoles are pentium-class machines. They must have an Internet connection for frequent updates from the vendors websites.
- **Alert concentrators** gather and correlate alerts, generally from a relational database. They can also include presentation software such as a web server.
- **Analysis consoles** allow the operator to process the alerts, generate periodic reports, and follow incidents. They also include mining tools for forensics analysis of the alert database.

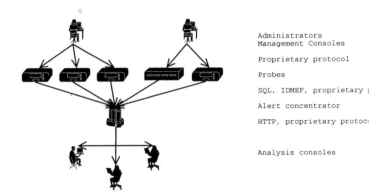

Administrators
Management Consoles

Proprietary protocol

Probes

SQL, IDMEF, proprietary]

Alert concentrator

HTTP, proprietary protoc·

Analysis consoles

Figure 2: Typical configuration of an intrusion-detection system

Figure 2 displays a possible arrangement of these components. Two management consoles handle five probes, that are all sending their alerts to a single concentrator. This concentrator offer services to three analysis consoles. Separation in probe management is likely to follow organisation-related separation of duties. However, there is in many cases only one concentrator, because this component is expensive to monitor and maintain.

Probes are either software components or hardware appliances, sized according to the bandwidth of the data stream. They dialog with management console mostly though proprietary protocols. Probes and concentrators dialog today using private protocols on network management protocols, but this dialog should migrate to IDMEF [3] over IDXP [7] as soon as the standard is officially published. Finally, analysis consoles access information on the concentrator mostly though HTTPS-enabled web servers or java environments.

1.2.3   History

Intrusion detection systems have initially been designed as passive listening devices, due to the initial complexity of understanding the behaviour on information systems. As such, they required human intervention to validate the analysis and react to the threat. Since time to react effectively is limited, and the number of alerts large, automated countermeasures can be configured in most IDS. Of course, this requires trust in the result of the analysis process.

The founding principle for data analysis in intrusin detection comes from the IDES project [4,5,6], led in the early eighties by Dorothy Denning at SRI. This project has defined two families of analysis techniques:

- **Misuse-detection** explicitly describes the undesirable behaviour of the monitored system, and provides an alert when this undesirable behaviour occurs. The objective of this technique is to use the body of knowledge about computer break-ins, and ensure that known attack patterns are properly identified, since attackers are extremely likely to reuse known, existing flaws. Recent studies on incident origins [2] show that many system compromises occur through known, established and corrected vulnerabilities.

- **Anomaly-detection** explicitly describes the appropriate behaviour of the monitored system, and provides an alert when events not compatible with this appropriate behaviour are encountered.

This classification is used both by commercial products and research prototypes. Although not ideal, it does provide a baseline for understanding the alerts that you will have to deal with. The analysis technique is a strong differentiator between IDS. The following section will explore in more details these two families, including advantages and drawbacks.

2.　　Analysis technologies

2.1　　Misuse detection

Misuse detection takes advantage of the body of knowledge related to security vulnerabilities and penetration of information systems and networks. The IDS contains information about these vulnerabilities and looks for attempts to take advantage of them. When such an attempt is detected, an alert is sent to the management console. In other words, any action that is not explicitly identified as an innapropriate usage of the information system is considered acceptable.

Note that misuse detection does cover more than known attacks and vulnerabilities. If a security policy explicitly bans certain activities, these activities can be linked to alerts in an IDS. The best example would be banning IRC activity from a network. Any connection using the IRC port would trigger an alert. SNMP is also banned from certain environments and its innapropriate usage by network management tools can easily be detected. Also, recurrent attack mechanisms have been analyzed to abstract generic attack methods, covering not a single vulnerability but a class of them. These abstract models allow detection of broad attack patterns covering even some unknown vulnerabilities, or at least ensure that the detection mechanism does not rely on specificities of some attack tools.

2.1.1　　Signature description

In a misuse-based approach, one needs to define the trigger that, when found in the event stream, will generate an alert. This trigger is usually refered to as an attack *signature*, although the terms *scenario* and *rule* have been used to describe these triggers as well. The term *signature* will be used throughout this paper.

Initially, trigger description in IDES [5] took the form of facts entered into an expert system. User actions abstracted from the event stream wera also represented as facts, while the detection process was described as production rules. This procedure was extremely costly, because of the processing needed to abstract several low level audit events into a single user action. Snapp and Smaha found that instead of abstracting system or network events to the expert system, it was easier to express vulnerabilities as sequences of events found in the event stream, named signatures [14].

A signature is the expression of some sequence of events characterizing the exploitation of a vulnerability. The detection process is thus simplified, and the cost is transferred to the definition and test of the signature for all the possible event stream formats that the IDS intends to support. This is sometimes a costly trade-off, if the event stream does not contain all the data that is being looked for, or if multiple encodings have to be taken into account.

In practice, a signature is expressed by a sequence of bytes being matched in the event stream [1], or in more complex cases by regular expressions [15]. These expressions are easier to write than the initial sequences of bytes proposed by [14], but it is still somewhat difficult to implement. Difficult because even for the same event stream format and the same exploited vulnerability, attacks can show under very different forms: attackers can mask their attempt under specific encodings or variate sequencing by introducing irrelevant events in the data stream. Applying signatures to the data stream requires the sensor to remove protocol-specific encodings or operating-system related dependancies. This phase can be complex and costly performance-wise.

2.1.2 Misuse detection and false positives

The misuse detection approach should be able to generate very few false positives, if any. This however postulates that the attack is effectively detectable from the data stream, and that at least one signature properly characterizes the exploit.

False positives in misuse detection mainly come from an erronous characterization of the vulnerability. This erronous characterization often occurs when the IDS attempts to detect the execution of an application without differentiating between normal usage and the actual malicious attempt. For example, detection of CGI attacks is often based on the detection of the script name in the HTTP request, and identically-named scripts induce false positives.

Moreover, it is ofter difficult to differentiate the interactions between an attacker and a vulnerable information system from the interactions between normal users and the same information system. It is thus important to analyze alerts with the knowledge of the configuration of the monitored system, to ensure proper evaluation of the severity of these alerts.

2.1.3 Misuse detection and false negatives

Clearly, false negatives in misuse detection occur on new attacks, when there is no signature associated to the vulnerability. Collecting vulnerability information of sufficient quality to write adequate signatures is a time-consuming task, and validation of this information is often limited, due to the sheer number of attack combinations possible. Most often than not, IDS vendors obtain sample event stream information containing the attack and ensure that their tools can detect the occurence of the sample data in the event stream. This is a long and tedious task.

Let's take a few numbers to illustrate this fact. An IDS today contains between 500 and 2000 signatures. Public vulnerability databases contain anywhere between 6000 and 20000 different vulnerability reports. Hence, there is roughly a one to 10 factor between what an intrusion-detection system knows about vulnerabilities, and what is publicly available. This ratio seems to be fairly stable; one counts between 100 and 150 new vulnerability announcements per month, associated with 10 to 20 new signatures announced by IDS vendors over the same period. This difference is the product of two factors:

- Not all vulnerabilities are of interest to IDS users, because they affect only rare, specific environments or tools, or they do not provide the attacker with access to the vulnerable system, only limited denial of service. In addition, some of these vulnerabilities are old and affect very old software revisions that are not available anymore.

- A vulnerability may only leave some tracks in specific event streams. If the IDS does not recover this particular event stream, the vulnerability exploit cannot be detected.

Finally, there is the possibility of generic signatures, that trigger on multiple vulnerabilities. This happens because attack code is reused from exploit script to exploit script, or because variations resulting in multiple vulnerabilities affect the same operating system or application and result in a single signature. Vendors are focusing on these generic signatures, hoping to cover not only vulnerabilities but also attack principles. Many products include generic buffer overflow detection, hoping to catch new exploits if they fit the attack technique.

Note that misuse-detection techniques are usually less-well suited for the detection of internal malicious activity. Registered users have access to the information system, and are likely to possess enough privileges on this information system to carry out most malicious activities without resorting to the exploitation of known vulnerabilities.

2.1.4 Misuse detection and counter-measures

Misuse detection allows a contextual analysis of the attack and its effects on the monitored information system. This facilitates the understanding of the problem and the decision-making process for corrective or preventive action. Current research in alert correlation includes correlation between vulnerability assessment tools and intrusion-detection tools. Automated lookup of alert references in vulnerability reports will provide the operator with a mean to rank alert severity not only with respect to the attacker's potential gain, but also with the target's potential risk.

When target machine and target service are identified, it is reasonably easy to detect if the attack has some probability of succeeding, and if its effects are incompatible with the site security policy. The operator is able to evaluate the trade-off between the reliability and business objectives of the service, and the security policy objectives. *This is fundamental in counter-measures*: it could be legitimate to let the information system provide services even if compromised.

2.1.5 Evolution of misuse detection

Misuse detection prototypes have been initially implemented using first-order logic and expert systems. Current commercial products follow the so-called "signature-based" approach. There are also petri-nets-related implementations and state transition analysis implementations.

Signature-based intrusion-detection systems usually rely on string or regular expression matching to detect specific pieces of information occuring in the data source. The matching mechanism is constrained further by specifying additional characteristics of the event stream, such as specific communication ports or protocol states. Each of these characteristics describes a particular facet of the vulnerability.

The expression of the signature depends of the level of detail available in the data source during exploitation of the vulnerability. For example, if a web server stops functioning during an attack before log entries can be written to disk, an intrusion-detection system based on log file analysis will not be able to detect the attack. Product vendors today tend to provide extremely wide signatures that will trigger on anything from normal usage to simple scanning, encouraging the notion that intrusion-detection systems cry wolf without cause.

2.2   Anomaly detection

The general objective of anomaly detection is to define the correct behaviour of the monitored information system. An alert is generated when an event cannot be explained by the model of correct behavior. This method assumes that an intrusion will induce a deviation from the normal usage of the information system.

2.2.1   Description of the correct behaviour model

The model of correct behaviour can be constructed either from past samples of observed behaviour, of from explicit policy declarations. When an event occurs, the intrusion detection system compares the current activity with the model. An alert corresponds to the deviation of one or several measures between the current activity and the model.

As such, *anything that does not correspond to an explicitely-defined acceptable activity is considered anomalous*. Of course, the efficiency of such a system strongly depends on the capability of the model to represent the activity of the information system. For example, only using measures of CPU activity to model the normal behaviour of an information system would not allow straightforward detection of denial-of-service attacks filling disks or memory. It also assumes that the measures discriminate normal activity and malicious activity, as postulated by Denning [4,6]. Unfortunately, this postulate has not been validated theoretically. Experimental systems show that it is possible to detect some malicious activity by anomaly-based techniques, but do not qualify the coverage of this detection process.

The first models were based on learning techniques. A set of variables is defined that represents the interesting factors of the information system. Acceptable ranges for these variables is defined through observation of past data. A range here can be an association of average and standard deviation, or more complex statistical measures [10]. The model is trained during an observation period, and should converge towards stable values at the end of the observation period.

This area is still a research subject. New models and detection methods are regularly proposed, that improve constantly on existing technologies.

2.2.2   Advantages of anomaly detection

Anomaly detection has, at least in principle, several advantages over misuse detection. First of all, it should be able to detect usage of unknown vulnerabilities. This is particularly important, as it does not rely on explicit security knowledge.

It also does not rely (or only in a limited way) on operating system specific knowledge, or application-specific knowledge. This is a great advantage when monitoring heterogenous systems. After measures have been collected for the model, the intrusion detection system performs the modeling and detection process autonomously.

Finally, it can also detect abuse of privileges and insider attacks. Insiders usually have access to the monitored information system and do not need to use well known vulnerabilities to compromise the system and get access to the information they need. Misuse detection seldom detects insider attacks, whereas anomaly detection could show deviations from normal usage patterns.

2.2.3   Anomaly detection and false positives

Anomaly detection techniques often have a high false positive rate. This phenomenom arises from the fact that deviations from the model are often observed for any incident occuring on the monitored information system. Deviations also occur with configuration changes. Hence, the workload for processing alerts is large, and the operators have a frequent feeling that alerts are irrelevant to security.

   This feeling is aggravated by the lack of explanation coming with the alerts. The root cause of the phenomenom is unknown, and the information provided seldom helps in resolving the issue.

2.2.4   Anomaly detection and false negatives

False negatives in anomaly detection have two main causes, corruption of the behaviour model and absence of measurement.

   Corruption of the behaviour model occurs when the model learns an intrusive behaviour and incorporates it in its coverage. The intrusion detection system becomes incapable of detecting occurences of the attack that has been accepted as part of the normal behaviour of the information system. Learning intrusive behaviour as normal occurs in particular in intrusion-detection systems where the model is constructed using past samples. Such systems need to be retrained periodically, and unfiltered training data could include malicious behaviour. Current research is therefore going away from learning technologies, and developing specification-based techniques to construct the model of normal behaviour.

   Also, attacks sometimes do not impact the measures used by the model of normal behaviour. Let's take the very simple example of an intrusion-detection system that would monitor CPU usage and not disk usage. An attack that would fill the disk would not be detected by such a system. Of course, intrusion-detection systems make use of much more complex measures, including dynamic ones. As such, the exact coverage of the monitoring is difficult to establish.

2.2.5   Anomaly detection and counter-measures

Alerts coming from an anomaly-based intrusion-detection system are often difficult to analyze. Counter-measures are difficult to deploy because neither target nor attack source are clearly identified, as well as the attack principle. Without an explicitely identified attack principle, counter-measures become extremely hazardous.

   A new approach based on honeypot-like technology has recently been developped to improve identification of attack sources. When suspicious requests are identified, the response provided by the intrusion-detection system contains uniquely-identifiable information. When these specific tags come back, the intrusion-detection system can clearly identify the anomaly and its source.

3.   Data sources

The detection techniques are applied to a data source (or several, although this cannot be considered the general case). However, the intrusion-detection system rarely uses the raw information coming from the data source. It generally applies the detection algorithm to a normalized and pre-filtered version of the information. This section not only describes the capture process, but also this pre-processing stage which is extremely important for the proper performance of the detection algorithm.

3.1   Network traffic observation

Network traffic is the most used data source in intrusion-detection. Such systems are known as Network Intrusion Detection Systems (NIDS) [11].

3.1.1   Retrieval of network packets

The sensor collects information by listening to the network and analyzing headers and payload of network packets. The Ethernet card is usually placed in *promiscuous* mode, and collects not only the packets that should arrive to the machine on which the NIDS runs, but any packet passing on the physical medium. This data source was extremely popular with coaxial Ethernet networks, because it was then extremely easy to observe a whole subnet from a single workstation.

Recently, a new kind of NIDS has appeared, that does not use the promiscuous facility. They only analyze packets that should arrive on the machine, and are called Network Node Intrusion Detection Systems (NNIDS). This technology is interesting because it naturally distributes the monitoring application rather than letting a single point cope with all the traffic. It also reuses the operating system IP stack for packet interpretation, which naturally removes operating system particularities.

Physically, dedicated sensors mostly take the form of hardware appliances with two network interfaces, one for capture and the other for management. The capture interface is not bound to an IP address and cannot be addressed by attackers, limiting the risk of sensor compromise. It is expected that the management interface is connected to a separate link than the capture interface, at least logically if not physically.

3.1.2   Advantages of network traffic as data source

The use of network packets allows the detection of network-specific attacks. Several attacks, particularly denial-of-service attacks, are based on the manipulation of network headers to introduce conflicting flags in the network packet. Only a network listening device can pick up such packets.

This data source minimizes (in most cases) the impact and deployment cost on the monitored information system. Application servers need not be modified, and network overload is controled. The intrusion-detection system can therefore be installed with minimal changes to the information system. This is less true in high speed networks, where traffic duplication can impact switch and router performance, and capture requires additional hardware such as derivation taps.

This data source provides a homogenous format for the information. It is (at least on surface) independant of the monitored operating systems. The TCP/IP standard allows easy acquisition, formatting and analysis of the data, even in an heterogenous environment. Unfortunately, this must be tempered by the fact that TCP/IP is loosely standardized, and that the implementors have interpreted the standard in different ways. The NIDS needs to have knowledge of these divergences to properly pre-process the retrieved network packets.

3.1.3   Drawbacks of network traffic as a data source

Several network-specific issues occur in NIDS:

- **Address masking**. Network Address Translation (NAT) does not provide the IP address of the endpoint to the NIDS.
- **Encryption**. Encrypted protocols defeat NIDS because most of their detection process requires access to headers (sometimes encrypted) and to payload (always encrypted). Popular protocols such as SSL and SSH render NIDS unusable.
- **Fragmentation**. IP fragmentation is a rare phenomenom normally. It can be used to fragment the payload in such a way that the NIDS will not see the attack in one piece.
- **Reliability of the source address**. Many attacks can be realized while using fictitious IP addresses (IP *spoofing* [13]) when no answer from the target is necessary. An attacker can also use *stepping stones* [17] to mask the origin of the attack. Finally, it can also use *reflectors* [12] to trick unwilling agents into carrying out the attack on its behalf.
- **Transience of address information**. In many organizations, and ISPs in particular, IP addresses are handed out dynamically via DHCP. Identification of a particular customer through the IP address requires log analysis and can therefore be costly, or even impossible if logs have been rolled over.

The interested reader will find more detailed information in [9, 13].

3.1.4   Preparation of network data

Application protocols encode the information in the packet payload. Hence, exploitation of the payload requires that the IDS recognizes the possible encodings. The attacker can hide its actions through the use of specific encodings that are not understood by the NIDS.

For example, the http protocol allows the replacement of any character by its ascii hexadecimal code, prefixed with the % character [8]. This replacement is mandatory for special characters, obliously % but also space, and others. Ptacek and Newsham have shown that NIDS in 1998 did not understand this encoding and could not detect encoded attacks [13]. This particular problem has been solved for a long time, but others regularly appear.

Also, NIDS can include more intelligence than simple decoding, and incorporate a recognition of protocol states, refered to as *protocol awareness*. A protocol aware NIDS recomposes the target protocol finite state machine and applies the detection algorithm to only the appropriate state. A NIDS that does not understand protocol states (often refered to as *network grep*) applies its detection algorithm to the payload of the packet regardless of the protocol state or history, and is much more likely to create false positives. Of course, keeping protocol states is costly, and these NIDS include safeguard mechanisms to avoid memory saturation, falling back to stateless detection if needed.

3.2   System audit trail analysis

The system audit trails cover all the data sources that are made available by the operating system. The intrusion detection systems using host data sources are named Host Intrusion Detection Systems (HIDS).

3.2.1   Acquisition of system audit data

Syslog on UNIX systems and the NT event log under microsoft windows operating systems provide to applications a service for identifying, timestaming and storing information. Using this kind of facility is very easy for application developpers, and they are used by several HIDS as a tool to collect, correlate and present system-related information.

Several operating systems also offer a so-called "C2 audit", to conform to the US government requirement for computer purchases. Such an audit aims at providing a trace of all privileged operations realized on a given computer, usually through the recording of system calls. It offers a strong user identification capability and an extremely fine-grained action description. Unfortunately, this C2 audit system is rarely properly documented and has a strong performance impact, so it has been abandonned by most HIDS.

Recent HIDS have developed specific interception software, similar to anti-virus technology. This interception software allows the HIDS to recover only the information that can be analyzed, at lesser cost. Of course, these interception mechanisms are operating-system dependant, which results in a smaller number of offerings in the product space.

3.2.2   Advantages of system audit data

The main advantage of host audit data is the precision of the information. On this basis, an HIDS is able to reduce the number of false positives, while providing detailed information about the circumstances of the attack.

In particular, actors (both target and perpetrator) are correctly and precisely identified. As such, the counter-measures can be appropriately tailored to the situation. Contextual information, related to the success of the attacker's activity, allows the operator to evaluate the risk and determine the appropriate level of counter-measures.

3.2.3   Drawbacks of system audit data

The main drawback of system audit data is that the HIDS has to reside on the same host, or a large volume of data has to be transported for remote analysis. Performance is such degraded through consumption of either bandwidth or processing power for security. Moreover, The behaviour of HIDS under stress heavily relies on the capabilities of the underlying operating system, and there is a real risk that denial-of-service attacks will either incapacitate the HIDS (if the original application has priority) or be facilitated (if the HIDS has priority).

Moreover, an application needs to be installed on the host. This has a strong impact on server deployment when servers have to be qualified before being placed in a production environment. Also, the signature updates may be problematic if software updates are also included in the signature updates.

3.3 Application logs

Application logs cover all the traces maintained by the applications. The intrusion detection systems using application logs are considered as HIDS, even though an application log could provide information about a distributed environment, spanning multiple machines.

3.3.1 Retrieval of application logs

A typical example of application logs is the HTTP server log files storing requests presented to the server (usually in the *access.log* file) and error messages (usually stored in the *error.log* file. Each line stores the request presented to the server, and statistics about the response. The format of these log lines is reasonably easy to parse, making the data source an attractive proposition for developpers.

Retrieval of the information generally consists of watching the file and parsing additional information into the data structures of the HIDS. Since these logs may ignore local information, constant information such as host names may be added on the fly to obtain an autonomous message.

3.3.2 Advantages of application logs

Application logs are often more precise and dense than both system audits and network traffic, because they contain information that is atomic from the point of view of the application, while multiple packets or several thousand system calls may be necessary to realize the function.

Also, they provide more accurate information with the inclusion of return codes and error messages. These return and error messages are extremely important for the intrusion detection system, because they provide effective diagnostic of the issue and its impact on the monitored information system.

3.3.3 Issues with application logs

As already mentionned with network traffic, applications may use specific encodings. Depending on the log, decoding may also be required to normalize the information.

The biggest issue with application logs is that they are often targetting debugging and abnormal termination cases. As such, these files may not contain enough data for the HIDS. In certain cases, it is necessary to collect the entire transaction log, because even error-free transactions may contain attack-related activity that needs to be analyzed.

4.   Deployment and operation

Multiple parameters need to be taken into account when deploying an intrusion-detection system. In this section, we will first review the main orientation choices that need to be tackled early in deployment. We will then dig into alert management, which forms the core of an intrusion-detection system efficiency.

4.1   Orientation choices

The following choices determine the orientation that an organisation will take when deploying an intrusion detection system.

- **Managed service or self-handled deployment**. Intrusion-detection is an extremely technical area, requiring in-depth knowledge of IP networking, operating systems and security vulnerabilities. For smaller organization not able to devote specific and trained personnel, outsourcing the monitoring of their network (particularly internet access) may be a wise choice. Bigger organizations with 24x7 system and network management may prefer internal IDS management to avoid leaking sensitive information in alerts.
- **HIDS vs NIDS**. The second choice to make is to choose what kind of data source will be used for deployment. There is no answer valid for every situation. In fact, there are numerous practical factors that constraint the choice of technology. In some cases, network monitoring may not be possible on the switching or routing equipment used. In particular, spanning may reduce switching performance or may already used for other non-security monitoring functions such as debugging or performance measurement. In others, servers may need to be qualified in such a way that deployment and management of additional software is considered incompatible with the objectives of performance or down-time.
- **Localization**. Placing the sensors properly has an extreme impact on signatures and on the number of alerts generated. A sensor located close to Internet access points is likely to generate 10 or 100 times the volume of alerts of one located internally. This is due to two factors, the number of random security attempts on the Internet and the number of random system failures inducing IDS alert noise.
- **IDS Evaluation**. Several publications are available that evaluate intrusion detection systems. The publications from the NSS Group, available for a fee, do provide a reasonableindependant insight on the capabilities and drawbacks of IDS products. On the other hand, testing with a vulnerability assessment product is of little value, as vendors verify their products with these tools.
- **System maintenance**. An intrusion-detection system needs frequent maintenance operations to maintain operational efficiency. In addition to signature updates, the configuration of the intrusion-detection system needs to take into account the evolution of the information system configuration (new systems, new services, service upgrade, ...).

The IDS deployment team need to define who will be responsible for the different aspects of IDS localization and maintenance.

4.2   Alert management

Alert management is a crucial issue in the deployment and operation of intrusion detection systems. Multiple parameters need to be taken into account when receiving and processing an alert:

Event significance. Intrusion detection alerts often have limited significance for security. For example, the Simple Network Management Protocol is in itself an insecure protocol, and implementation of SNMP services also suffer from implementation vulnerabilities. Thereofore, intrusion-detection systems watch for SNMP traffic. Yet, SNMP is a widely used tool for network and system management and its occurence on a network is not rare. The same stands true for ICMP, which is used for denial of service attacks, but also for many network control functions. The *significance* issue arises from the fact that attack traffic is indistinguishable from normal traffic. In both cases, an attack can be perpetrated simply using the fact that the traffic can traverse the firewall or the service is enabled on the system.

In such cases, the preferred response by IDS practitionners is to disable the signature. A better response would be the provision of a statistical measure of the alert flow, enabling the separation of background noise from significant deviations in traffic pattern indicating potential security issues.

Event relevance. Intrusion detection systems generally have little knowledge of the environment in which they are inserted. As such, a pure windows shop could completely ignore linux vulnerabilities (or vice versa). The *relevance* of the intrusion-detection system relates to the knowledge it has about its surroundings. This implies that accounting properly defines the role and configuration of monitored systems, so that transient servers or services are not inadvertently inserted for testing purposes and then left there providing potential unknown backdoors or attack paths for determined attackers. Again, instead of removing irrelevant alerts, one should requalify them to ensure that they do not bother the operators, but also provide some statistical qualification of this background noise to ensure that persistent attackers are not perturbing the information system.

Event severity. Intrusion-detection systems provide an evaluation of the *severity* of every alert. This severity is, in general, a function of the privileges gained by the attacker if he succeeds. Vulnerabilities resulting in administrative access are rated high, while denial-of-service attacks are rated at lower levels. This rating does not take into account the actual form of the attempt by the attacker. The attempt may take three forms, normal usage, scan and actual compromise attempt. In the first two forms, compromise of the information system is impossible, so a high rating should not be associated with the alert.

The only true solution for this issue is a fix from intrusion detection system vendors. A temporary solution is to re-evaluate the ratings of the alerts in the light of the signature data, when accessible.

Event pertinence. The *pertinence* of the alert measures the exposure of the information system. The objective here is to indicate whether the monitored system was actually vulnerable to the attack. This is often realized by correlating the alert information with the result of a vulnerability audit (or even by realizing an audit on the spot for the specific attack). Note that even though this capability is very much hyped by intrusion-detection vendors, it does not provide a solution for the severity issue described above. Effectively, if an attacker scans a vulnerable system, there will be knowledge gained by the attacker, but no system compromise. Therefore, the actual action of the attacker needs to be evaluated to understand whether a compromise was attempted.

Event return code. The *return* code of an event characterizes the answer that the information system returned to the attacker. Even if the attacker attempted to compromise a vulnerable system, he could fail to do so, for many reasons. Unfortunately, this information is also not provided by intrusion-detection systems, and is a critical data point in assessing the actual risk and gain of the attacker.

Alert management should also include response management. In most modern intrusion detection systems, alert response is a fire-and-forget technology, which does not verify the effectiveness of the response. Measuring response effectiveness includes both verifying that the attack has effectively ceased or did not have the response expected by the attacker, and verifying that the information system still performs properly.

4.3   Intrusion Prevention systems

The current trend of security products is incorporating intrusion-detection technologies in so-called *Intrusion Prevention Systems* (IPS). Intrusion Prevention Systems are also sometimes called inline IDS, and do not represent a radically new technology. They allow current protection tools such as firewalls to include application-level protection, and improve the reporting capability of these protection tools. With increases in IDS reliability, IPS are able to detect attacks and block them, instead of simply reporting alerts. There are two side effects of this trend. First, the independence between enforcement and detection may be lost, if organizations replace their firewalls and intrusion-detection systems with an IPS. Second, these IPS also become single points of failure. They are clearly a marketing evolution of the intrusion-detection area rather than a technical evolution, and they also bear witness of the importance of informing operators about the security state of their information systems.

5.   Conclusion

Intrusion-detection technology provides an important function, monitoring the enforcement and efficiency of an information system security policy. These systems have matured to a point that makes them manageable by security-aware personnel, although they are still requiring a pretty strong technical knowledge. Alert flooding remains an issue today, although a lot of research activities are going on related to alert vizualization and correlation.

The most important advantage of intrusion-detection systems from a security standpoint is that they provide a separation of enforcement and monitoring duties. Monitoring of the security policy must be separate from the enforcement point as much as possible, so that failure of the enforcement can be detected by an independant technology. In this light, the NIDS is almost the perfect tool, invisible to the attacker and completely distinct from firewalls and authentication servers. Using HIDS technology often provides a more precise diagnostic, but could be defeated by a compromise of the server on which the HIDS resides.

One of the current challenges of intrusion-detection technology is performance, both in terms of capacity and in terms of quality of diagnostic. With faster servers and networks, the amount of information to analyze becomes huge. The coming intrusion-detection systems must accomodate gigabit networks, and they are starting to do so through the availability of dedicated hardware appliances.

IDS/IPS products are being deployed in operational environments today, and are begining to shed light on security issues facing information systems today. They use advanced techniques that once mature are incorporated in protection products. As such, security officers are likely to face such technologies, and use them to better understand risks and solve security incidents.

References

[1] Boyer, R. S. and J. S. Moore: 1977, 'A fast string searching algorithm'. *Communications of the ACM* 20(10), 762–772.

[2] Browne, H., W. A. Arbaugh, J. McHugh, and W. L. Fithen: 2001, 'A Trend Analysis of Exploitations'. In: *Proceedings of the 2001 IEEE Symposium on Security and Privacy*. Oakland, CA, pp. 214 – 229.

[3] Curry, D. and H. Debar: 2003, 'Intrusion Detection Message Exchange Format Data Model and Extensible Markup Language (XML) Document Type Definition'. Internet Draft (work in progress). http: //search.ietf.org/internet-drafts/draft-ietf-idwg-idmef-xml-10.txt.

[4] Denning, D.: 1987, 'An intrusion-detection model'. *IEEE Transactions on Software Engineering* 13(2), 222–232.

[5] Denning, D. E., D. L. Edwards, R. Jagannathan, T. F. Lunt, and P. G. Neumann: 1987, 'A Prototype IDES — A Real-Time Intrusion Detection Expert System'. Technical report, Computer Science Laboratory, SRI International.

[6] Denning, D. E. and P. G. Neumann: 1985, 'Requirements and Model for IDES - A Real-TIme Intrusion Detection Expert System'. Technical report, Computer Science Laboratory, SRI International, Menlo Park, CA.

[7] Feinstein, B., G. Matthews, and J. White: 2002, 'The Intrusion Detection Exchange Protocol (IDXP)'. Internet Draft (work in progress), expires April 22nd, 2003.

[8] Fieldings, R., J. Gettys, J. Mogul, H. Frystyk, L. Masinter, P. Leach, and T. Berners-Lee: 1999, 'Hypertext Transfer Protocol – HTTP/1.1, rfc 2616'. Technical report, IETF.

[9] Handley, M., C. Kreibich, and V. Paxson: 2001, 'Network Intrusion Detection: Evasion, Traffic Normalization, and End-to-End Protocol Semantics'. In: *Proceedings of the 10th USENIX Security Symposium*. Washington, DC.

[10] Javitz, H. S., A. Valdez, T. F. Lunt, A. Tamaru, M. Tyson, and J. Lowrance: 1993, 'Next Generation Intrusion Detection Expert System (NIDES) - 1. Statistical Algorithms Rationale - 2. Rationale for Proposed Resolver'. Technical Report A016–Rationales, SRI International, 333 Ravenswood Avenue, Menlo Park, CA.

[11] Northcutt, S. and J. Novak: 2003, *Network Intrusion Detection*. QUE, 3 edition. ISBN 0735712654.

[12] Paxson, V.: 2001, 'An Analysis of Using Reflectors for Distributed Denial-of-Service Attacks'. *Computer Communication Review* 31(3).

[13] Ptacek, T. H. and T. N. Newsham: 1998, 'Insertion, Evasion, and Denial of Service : Eluding Network Intrusion Detection'. Secure Networks, Inc.

[14] Snapp, S. R. and S. E. Smaha: 1992, 'Signature Analysis Model Definition and Formalism'. In: *Proc. Fourth Workshop on Computer Security Incident Handling*. Denver, CO.

[15] Thomson, K.: 1968, 'Regular Expression Search Algorithm'. *Communications of the ACM* 11(6), 419 – 422.

[16] Wood, M. and M. Erlinger: 2003, 'Intrusion Detection Message Exchange (IDMEF) Requirements'. Internet Engineering Task Force - IDWG. Work in progress, expires April 22nd, 2003.

[17] Zhang, Y. and V. Paxson: 2000, 'Detecting Stepping Stones'. In: *Proceedings of the 9th USENIX Security Symposium*. Denver, CO.

Security and Privacy in Advanced Networking Technologies
B. Jerman-Blažič et al. (Eds.)
IOS Press, 2004

On Usability (and Security) of Biometric Authentication Systems

Václav MATYÁŠ JR.
Department of Computer Science, University College Dublin, Ireland
&
Faculty of Informatics, Masaryk University Brno, Czech Republic
E-mail: matyas@fi.muni.cz

Zdeněk ŘÍHA
Faculty of Informatics, Masaryk University Brno, Czech Republic
E-mail: zriha@fi.muni.cz

Abstract. Biometric authentication systems identify users by their measurable human characteristics. This paper outlines our views on usability and security of biometric authentication systems, summarizing our findings after several years of studying biometric authentication systems and their security. Proper user identification/authentication is a major building block of any system's security. Our paper provides an insight into applicability of some biometric authentication methods, and discusses pros and cons of these methods with respect to their application environment.

Introduction

Biometrics are automated methods of identity verification or identification based on the principle of measurable physiological or behavioural characteristics such as a fingerprint, an iris pattern or a voice sample.
User identification/authentication has been traditionally based on:

- something that the user knows (typically a PIN, a password or a code) or
- something that the user has (e.g., a key, a token, a magnetic or smart card, a badge, a passport).

These traditional methods of the user authentication unfortunately do not authenticate the user as such. Traditional methods are based on properties that can be forgotten, disclosed, lost or stolen. Codes, PINs, and passwords often are easily accessible to colleagues and even occasional visitors and users tend to pass their tokens to or share their passwords with their colleagues to make their work easier. Biometrics, on the other hand, authenticate humans as such – in case the biometric system used is working properly and reliably, which is not so easy to achieve. Biometric characteristics are (or rather should be) unique and not duplicable or transferable. While the advantages of biometric authentication definitely look very attractive, there are also many problems with biometric authentication that one should be aware of.

Biometric characteristics are (or rather should be) unique and not duplicable or transferable. While the advantages of biometric authentication definitely look very attractive, there are also many problems with biometric authentication that one should be aware of.

1. What to measure?

Most significant difference between biometric and traditional technologies lies in the answer of the biometric system to an authentication/identification request. Biometric systems do not give simple yes/no answers. The person's signature never is absolutely identical and the position of the finger on the fingerprint reader will vary as well.

One could build a system that requires a 100% match each time. Yet such a system would be practically useless, as only very few users (if any) could use it. Most of the users would be rejected all the time, because the measurement results never are the same.

We have to allow for some variability of the biometric data in order not to reject too many authorized users. However, the greater variability we allow the greater is the probability that an impostor with a similar biometric data will be accepted as an authorized user. The variability is usually called a (security) threshold or a (security) level.

2. Error rates and their usage

There are two kinds of errors that biometric systems do:
- False rejection (Type 1 error) – a legitimate user is rejected (because the system does not find the user's current biometric data similar enough to the master template stored in the database).
- False acceptance (Type 2 error) – an impostor is accepted as a legitimate user (because the system finds the impostor's biometric data similar enough to the master template of a legitimate user).

In an ideal system, there are no false rejections and no false acceptances. The number of false rejections/false acceptances is usually expressed as a percentage from the total number of authorized/unauthorized access attempts. These rates are called the false rejection rate (FRR)/false acceptance rate (FAR). For the purpose of FAR computations the so-called zero-effort unauthorized authentication attempts are taken. In this case the unauthorized users are not actively changing their biometric characteristics (e.g., in the case of dynamic signature systems they sign as them-selves).

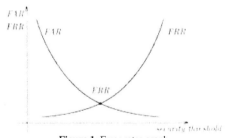

Figure 1: Error rates graph.

Although the error rates quoted by manufactures (typically ERR < 1%) might indicate that biometric systems are very accurate, the reality is rather different. Namely the false rejection rate is in reality very high (very often over 10%).

3. Biometric techniques

There are lots of biometric techniques available nowadays. A few of them are in the stage of the research only (e.g. the odour analysis), but a significant number of technologies is already mature and commercially available.

3.1 Fingerprint technologies

Fingerprint identification is perhaps the oldest of all the biometric techniques. Systems that can automatically check details of a person's fingerprint have been in use since the 1960s by law enforcement agencies.

3.1.1 Fingerprint readers

Before we can proceed any further we need to obtain the digitalized fingerprint. The traditional method uses the ink to get the fingerprint onto a piece of paper. This piece of paper is then scanned using a traditional scanner. This method is used only rarely today when an old paper-based database is being digitalized, a fingerprint found on a scene of a crime is being processed or in law enforcement AFIS systems. Otherwise modern live fingerprint readers are used. They do not require the ink anymore. These live fingerprint readers are most commonly based on optical, thermal, silicon or ultrasonic principles.

Optical fingerprint readers are the most common at present. They are based on reflection changes at the spots where the finger papillary lines touch the readers' surface. The size of the optical fingerprint readers typically is around 10 x 10 x 5 centimetres. It is difficult to minimize them much more as the reader has to comprise the source of light, reflection surface and the light sensor. Optical readers are relatively cheap and are manufactured by a great number of manufacturers. Optical fingerprint readers are also often embedded in keyboards, mice or monitors.

Silicon technologies are older than the optical technologies. They are based on the capacitance of the finger. The dc-capacitive fingerprint sensors consist of rectangular arrays of capacitors on a silicon chip. One plate of the capacitor is the finger; the other plate is a tiny area of metallization (a pixel) on the chip's surface. The ridges of the fingerprint are close to the nearby pixels and have high capacitance to them. The valleys are more distant from the pixels nearest them and therefore have lower capacitance. Such an array of capacitors can be placed onto a chip as small as 15 x 15 x 5 mm and thus is ideal for miniaturization. A PCMCIA card (the triple height of a credit card) with a silicon fingerprint reader is already available. Integration of a fingerprint reader on a credit card-sized smartcard was not achieved yet, but it is expected in the near future. Silicon fingerprint readers are popular also in mobile phones and laptop computers due to the small size.

The finger moisture affects the fingerprint bitmap obtained from the silicon reader as the moisture significantly influences the capacitance. This often means that too wet or dry fingers do not produce bitmaps with a sufficient quality and so people with unusually wet or dry fingers have problems with these silicon fingerprint readers.

Ultrasonic fingerprint readers are the newest and least common. They use ultrasound to monitor the finger surface. The user places the finger on a piece of glass and the ultrasonic sensor moves and reads whole the fingerprint. This process takes one or two seconds. The dirt on the fingers does not disturb ultrasound so the quality of the bitmap obtained is usually fair. The readers are relatively big (15 x 15 x 20 centimetres), heavy, noisy and expensive.

3.1.2 Fingerprint processing

Fingerprints are not compared and usually also not stored as bitmaps. Fingerprint matching techniques can be placed into two categories: minutiae-based and correlation based. Minutiae-based techniques find the minutiae points first and then map their relative placement on the finger. Minutiae are individual unique characteristics within the fingerprint pattern such as ridge endings, bifurcations, divergences, dots or islands. In the recent years automated fingerprint comparisons have been most often based on minutiae. The problem with minutiae is that it is difficult to extract the minutiae points accurately when the fingerprint is of low quality.

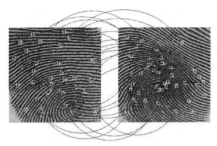

Figure 2: Minutiae matching.

3.2 Iris

The iris is the coloured ring of textured tissue that surrounds the pupil of the eye. Even twins have different iris patterns and everyone's left and right iris is different, too. Research shows that the matching accuracy of iris identification is greater than of the DNA testing. A near infrared grey-scale camera in the distance of 10 – 40 cm takes the iris pattern from the camera. The camera is hidden behind a mirror, the user looks into the mirror so that he/she can see his/her own eye, then also the camera can "see" the eye. Once the eye is stable (not moving too fast) and the camera is focused properly, the image of the eye is captured. The iris scanning technology is not intrusive and thus is deemed acceptable by most users. The iris pattern remains stable over a person's life, being only affected by several diseases.

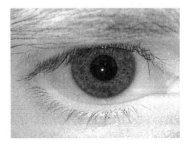

Figure 3: Iris is the coloured ring of textured tissue that surrounds the pupil of the eye.

Once the grey-scale image of the eye is obtained then the software tries to locate the iris within the image. If an iris is found then the software creates a net of curves covering the iris. The software then creates the iriscode, which characterizes the iris. When computing the iriscode two influences have to be taken into account. First, the overall darkness of the image is influenced by the lighting conditions so the darkness threshold used to decide whether a given point is dark or bright cannot be static, it must be dynamically computed according to the overall picture darkness. And second, the size of the iris dynamically changes as the size of the pupil changes. Before computing the iriscode, a proper transformation must be done.

3.3 Retina

Retina scan is based on the blood vessel pattern in the retina of the eye. Retina scan technology is older than the iris scan technology that also uses a part of the eye. EyeDentify launched the first retinal scanning systems in 1985.

The main drawback of the retina scan is its intrusiveness. The method of obtaining a retina scan is personally invasive. A direct source of light must be directed through the cornea of the eye. Also the operation of the retina scanner is not easy. A skilled operator is required and the person being scanned has to follow his/her directions.

A retina scan produces at least the same volume of data as a fingerprint image. Thus its discrimination rate is sufficient not only for verification, but also for identification. In the practice, however, the retina scanning is used mostly for verification. The size of the eye signature template is 96 bytes.

The retinal scanning systems are said to be very accurate. For example the EyeDentify retinal scanning system has reputedly never falsely verified an unauthorized user so far. The false rejection rate, on the other side, is relatively high as it is not always easy to capture a perfect image of the retina.

3.4 Hand geometry

Hand geometry is based on the fact that nearly every person's hand is shaped differently and that the shape of a person's hand does not change after certain age. Hand geometry systems produce estimates of certain measurements of the hand such as the length and the width of fingers. Various methods are used to measure the hand. These methods are most commonly based either on mechanical or optical principle. The latter ones are much more common today. Optical hand geometry scanners capture the image of the hand and using the image edge detection algorithm compute the hand's characteristics. There are basically 2 sub-categories of optical scanners. Devices from the first category create a black-and-white bitmap image of the hand's shape. This is easily done using a source of light and a black-and-white camera. The computer software then processes the bitmap image. Only 2D characteristics of the hand can be used in this case. Hand geometry systems from the other category are more sophisticated. They use special guide markings to position the hand better and have two (both vertical and horizontal) sensors for the hand shape measurements.

3.5 Signature dynamics

The signature dynamics recognition is based on the dynamics of making the signature, rather than a direct comparison of the signature itself. The dynamics is measured as a means of the pres-sure, direction, acceleration and the length of the strokes, number of strokes and their duration. The most obvious and important advantage of this is that a fraudster cannot glean any information on how to write the signature by simply looking at one that has been previously written.

Pioneers of the signature verification first developed a reliable statistical method in 1970s. This involved the extraction of ten or more writing characteristics such as the number of times the pen was lifted, the total writing time and the timing of turning points. The matching process was then performed using standard statistical correlation methods. Newer sequential techniques treat the signature as a number of separate events, with each event consisting of the period between the pen striking the writing surface and lifting off again. This approach is much more flexible. If the majority of the signature is accurate and only one event (e.g. the dot over it) is missing or added then this event can be easily ignored.

There are various kinds of devices used to capture the signature dynamics. These are either traditional tablets or special purpose devices. Tablets capture 2D coordinates and the pressure. Special pens are able to capture movements in all 3 dimensions. Tablets have two significant disadvantages. First, the resulting digitalized signature looks different from the usual user signature. And second, while signing the user does not see what he/she has written so far. He/she has to look at the computer monitor or another display and to see the signature. This is a considerable drawback for many (inexperienced) users. Some special pens work like normal pens, they have ink cartridge inside and can be used to write with them on paper.

A person does not make a signature consistently the same way, so the data obtained from a signature from a person has to allow for quite some variability. Most of the signature dynamics systems verify the dynamics only; they do not pay any attention to the resulting signature. A few systems claim to verify both (i.e. the signature dynamics as well as the resulting signature look itself). Our experience shows that if the system does not verify the resulting signature, then the signature that is accepted as a true match may look significantly different from the master template. The speed of writing is often the most important factor in the decision process, so it is possible to successfully forge a signature even if the resulting signature looks so different that any person would notice.

3.6 Facial recognition

Facial recognition is the most natural means of biometric identification. The method of distinguishing one individual from another is an ability of virtually every human.

Any camera (with a sufficient resolution) can be used to obtain the image of the face. Any scanned picture can be used as well. Generally speaking the better the image source (i.e. camera or scanner) the more accurate results we get. The facial recognition systems usually use only the grey-scale information. Colours (if available) are used as help in locating the face in the image only. The lighting conditions required are mainly dependent on the quality of the camera used. In poor light condition, individual features may not be easily discernible. There exist even infrared cam-eras that can be used with facial recognition systems.

The first task of the processing software is to locate the face (or faces) within the image. Then the facial characteristics are extracted. Facial recognition technology has recently developed into two areas: facial metrics and eigenfaces.

Facial metrics technology relies on the measurement of the specific facial features (the systems usually look for the positioning of the eyes, nose and mouth and the distances between these features).

Another method for facial recognition has been developed in the past three years. The method is based on categorizing faces according to the degree of fit with a fixed set of master eigenfaces. This technique is in fact similar to the police method of creating a portrait, but the image processing is automated and based on a real picture here.

The image processing and facial similarity decision process is done by the computer software at the moment, this processing requires quite a lot of computing power and so it is not easy to assemble a stand-alone device for face recognition. There are some efforts (by companies like Siemens) to create a special-purpose chip with embedded face recognition instruction set.

These systems have problems to distinguish very similar persons like twins and any significant change in hair or beard style requires re-enrolment. Glasses can also cause additional difficulties. The quoted accuracy of facial recognition systems varies significantly; many systems quote the crossover accuracy of less then one percent. The numbers from real systems are not so pleasant; the crossover accuracy is much higher and indicates that these systems are not suitable for identification.

3.7 Speaker verification

The principle of speaker verification is to analyse the voice of the user in order to store a voiceprint that is later used for identification/verification. Speaker verification and speech recognition are two different tasks. The aim of speech recognition is to find what has been told while the aim of the speaker verification is who told that.

The greatest advantage of speaker verification systems is that they do not require any special and expensive hardware. A microphone is a standard accessory of any multimedia computer; speaker verification can also be used remotely via phone line. A high sampling rate is not required, but the background (or network) noise causes a significant problem that decreases the accuracy. The speaker verification is not intrusive for users and is easy to use.

The system typically asks the user to pronounce a phrase during the enrolment; the voice is then processed and stored in a template (voiceprint). Later the system asks for the same phrase and compares the voiceprints. Such a system is vulnerable to replay attacks; if an attacker records the user's phrase and replays it later then he/she can easily gain the user's privilege. More sophisticated systems use a kind of challenge-response protocol. During the enrolment the system records the pronunciation of multiple phrases (e.g. numbers). In the authentication phase the system randomly chooses a challenge and asks the user to pronounce it. In this case the system not only compares the voiceprints, but also deploys the speech recognition algorithms and checks whether the proper challenge has really been said.

Speaker verification is a biometric technique based on behavioural characteristic and as such can be negatively affected by the current physical condition and the emotional state. The accuracy of the speaker verification can also be affected by the background and network noise in the input signal. This increases the false rejection rate. During the tests of a speaker verification system in the Sandia Labs the false acceptance rate after a single attempt was 0.9% and the false rejection rate after three attempts was 4.3%.

3.8 Other biometric techniques

Palm print: Palm print verification is a slightly different implementation of the fingerprint technology. Palm print scanning uses optical readers that are very similar to those used for finger-print scanning, their size is, however, much bigger and this is a limiting factor for the use in work-stations or mobile devices.

Hand vein: Hand vein geometry is based on the fact that the vein pattern is distinctive for various individuals. The veins under the skin absorb infrared light and thus have a darker pattern on the image of the hand taken by an infrared camera.

DNA: DNA sampling is rather intrusive at present and requires a form of tissue, blood or other bodily sample. This method of capture still has to be refined. So far the DNA analysis has not been sufficiently automatic to rank the DNA analysis as a biometric technology. The analysis of human DNA is now possible within 10 minutes. As soon as the technology advances so that DNA can be matched automatically in real time, it may become more significant. At present DNA is very en-trenched in crime detection and so will remain in the law enforcement area for the time being.

Thermal imaging: This technology is similar to the hand vein geometry. It also uses an infrared source of light and camera to produce an image of the vein pattern in the face or in the wrist.

Ear shape: Identification of individuals by the ear shape is used in law enforcement applications where ear markings are found at crime scenes. Whether this technology will progress to access control applications is yet to be seen. An ear shape verifier (Optophone) is produced by a French company ART Techniques. It is a telephone-type handset within which is a lighting unit and cam-eras that capture two images of the ear.

Body odour: The body odour biometrics is based on the fact that virtually each human smell is unique. The smell is captured by sensors that are capable to obtain the odour from non-intrusive parts of the body such as the back of the hand. Methods of capturing a person's smell are being explored by Mastiff Electronic Systems. Each human smell is made up of chemicals known as volatiles. They are extracted by the system and converted into a template. The use of body odour sensors brings up the privacy issue as the body odour carries a significant amount of sensitive personal information. It is possible to diagnose some diseases or activities in the last hours (like sex, for example) by analysing the body odour.

Keystroke dynamics: Keystroke dynamics is a method of verifying the identity of an individual by their typing rhythm that can cope with trained typists as well as the amateur two-finger typist. Systems can verify the user at the log-on stage or they can continually monitor the typist. These systems should be cheap to install, as all that is needed is a software package.

Fingernail bed: The US company AIMS is developing a system which scans the dermal structure under the fingernail. This tongue and groove structure is made up of nearly parallel rows of vascular rich skin. Between these parallel dermal structures are narrow channels, and it is the distance between these that is measured by the AIMS system.

4. Advantages of biometric authentication

The primary advantage of biometric authentication methods over other methods of user authentication is that they really do what they should, i.e., they *authenticate the user*. These methods use real human physiological or behavioural characteristics to authenticate users. These biometric characteristics are (more or less) permanent and not changeable. It is also not easy (although in some cases not principally impossible) to change one's fingerprint, iris or other biometric characteristics.

Users cannot pass their biometric characteristics to other users as easily as they do with their cards or passwords.

Biometric objects *cannot be stolen* as tokens, keys, cards or other objects used for the traditional user authentication, yet biometric characteristics can be stolen from computer systems and networks. Biometric characteristics are not secret and therefore the availability of a user's fingerprint or iris pattern does not break security the same way as availability of the user's password. Even the use of dead or artificial biometric characteristics should not let the attacker in.

Most biometric techniques are based on something that *cannot be lost or forgotten*. This is an advantage for users as well as for system administrators because the problems and costs associated with lost, reissued or temporarily issued tokens/cards/passwords can be avoided, thus saving some costs of the system management.

Another advantage of biometric authentication systems may be their *speed*. The authentication of a habituated user using an iris-based identification system may take 2 (or 3) seconds while finding your key ring, locating the right key and using it may take some 5 (or 10) seconds.

5. Disadvantages of biometric authentication

So why do not we use biometrics everywhere instead of passwords or tokens? Nothing is perfect, and biometric authentication methods also have their own shortcomings. First of all the performance of biometric systems is not ideal (yet?). Biometric systems still need to be improved in the terms of accuracy and speed. Biometric systems with the false rejection rate under 1% (together with a reasonably low false acceptance rate) are still rare today. Although few biometric systems are fast and accurate (in terms of low false acceptance rate) enough to allow identification (automatically recognising the user identity), most of current systems are suitable for the verification only, as the false acceptance rate is too high. Note that both the FAR and FRR are functions of the threshold value and can be traded off, but the set of usable threshold values is limited. For example a system with the ERR of 1% may be set to operate at the FAR of 0.01%, but this would imply the FRR to jump over 90 or 95%, which would make system unusable.

The fail to enrol rate brings up another important problem. Not all users can use any given biometric system. People without hands cannot use fingerprint or hand-based systems. (The FTE rate is estimated at 2% for fingerprint-based systems and 1% for iris-based systems. Real values of the FTE rate are dependent on the input device model, the enrolment policy and the user population.)

Visually impaired people have difficulties using iris or retina based techniques. As not all users are able to use a specific biometric system, the authentication system must be extended to handle users falling into the FTE category. This can make the resulting system more complicated, less secure or more expensive. Even enrolled users can have difficulties using a biometric system. The FTE rate says how many of the input samples are of insufficient quality. Data acquisition must be repeated if the quality of input sample is not sufficient for further processing and this would be annoying for users.

Biometric data are not considered to be secret and security of a biometric system cannot be based on the secrecy of user's biometric characteristics. The server cannot authenticate the user just after receiving her correct biometric characteristics. The user authentication can be successful only when user's characteristics are fresh and have been collected from the user being authenticated. This implies that the biometric input device must be trusted. Its authenticity should be verified (unless the device and the link are physically secure) and user's liveness would be checked. The input device also should be under human supervision or tamper-resistant. The fact that biometric characteristics are not secret brings some issues that traditional authentication systems need not deal with. Many of the current biometric systems are not aware of this fact and therefore the security level they offer is limited.

Some biometric sensors (particularly those having contact with users) also have a *limited lifetime*. While a magnetic card reader may be used for years (or even decades), the optical fingerprint reader (if heavily used) must be regularly cleaned and even then the lifetime need not exceed one year.

Biometric systems may violate user's *privacy*. Biometric characteristics are sensitive data that may contain a lot of personal information. The DNA (being the typical example) contains (among others) the user's preposition to diseases. This may be a very interesting piece of information for an insurance company. The body odour can provide information about user's recent activities. It is also told that people with asymmetric fingerprints are more likely to be homosexually oriented, etc.

Use of biometric systems may also imply loss of anonymity. While one can have multiple identities when authentication methods are based on something the user knows or has, biometric systems can sometimes link all user actions to a single identity.

Biometric systems can potentially be quite troublesome for some users. These users find some biometric systems *intrusive* or personally invasive. Even if no biometric system is really dangerous, users are occasionally afraid of something they do not know much about.

In some countries people do not like to touch something that has already been touched many times (e.g., biometric sensor), while in some countries people do not like to be photographed or their faces are completely covered.

Lack of *standards* (or ignorance of standards) may also posses a serious problem. Two similar biometric systems from two different vendors are not likely to interoperate at present.

6. Conclusions

Let us discuss where the use of biometric systems may be an advantage and where not. Biometrics are a great way of authenticating users. The user may be authenticated by a workstation during the logon, by a smart card to unlock the private key, by a voice verification system to confirm a bank transaction or by a physical access control system to open a door. All of these cases are typical and correct places where to deploy a biometric system.

Very promising are solutions where the cryptographic functions as well as the biometric matching, the feature extraction and the biometric sensor are all integrated in one (ideally also tamper-resistant) device. Such devices provide a very high protection of the secret/private key, as the biometric data as well as the secret/private key will never have to leave the secure device.

We believe that biometric authentication is a good *additional* authentication method. Even cheap and simple biometric solutions can increase the overall system security if used *on top* of existing traditional authentication methods.

Biometrics can be used for dozens of applications outside the scope of computer security. Facial recognition systems are often deployed at frequently visited places to search for criminals. Automated fingerprint systems (AFIS) are used to find an offender according to trails left on the crime spot. Infrared thermographs can point out people under influence of various drugs (different drugs react in different ways). Biometric systems successfully used in non-authenticating applications may but also need not be successfully used in authenticating applications.

6.1 Where not to use biometrics?

Although good for user authentication, biometrics cannot be used to authenticate computers or messages. Biometric characteristics are not secret and therefore they cannot be used to sign messages or encrypt documents. If my fingerprint is not secret there is no sense in adding it to documents we have written. Anyone else could do the same. Cryptographic keys derived solely from biometric data are nonsense, too.

Remote biometric authentication is not trivial at all. The assumption that anyone who can provide my fingerprint can also use my bank account in the home banking application is not a good idea. Remote biometric authentication requires a trusted biometric sensor. Will a bank trust your home biometric sensor to be sufficiently tamper resistant and provide trustworthy liveness test? Although remote biometric authentication may work in the theory, few (if any) current devices are trustworthy enough to be used for remote biometric authentication.

While using biometrics as an additional authentication method does not weaken the security of the whole system (if users do not rely on the biometric component so much to ignore the traditional authentication method, e.g., by using simple passwords), replacing an existing system with a biometric one may be more risky. Users as well as administrators and system engineers tend to overestimate security properties of biometric systems; such a decision must be based on and confirmed by a risk analysis. Particularly, reviewing the process of the biometric data capture and transfer is very important. Sometimes biometric authentication systems replace traditional authentication systems not because of higher security but because of higher comfort and ease of use.

False rejects – the unpleasant property of biometric systems causing authorised users to be rejected – may prevent biometric systems to spread into some specific applications, where inability of a user to authenticate herself (and run an action) may imply serious problems.

References

[1] Calabrese, C., *The trouble with biometrics* in ;login:, Vol 24, No 4, ISSN 1044-6397, 1999.
[2] Daugman, J., *Phenotypic versus genotypic approaches to face recognition*, in Face Recognition: From Theory to Applications, Heidelberg, Springer-Verlag, ISBN 3-540-64410-5, 1998.
[3] Jain, A., Bolle, R. and Pankanti S., *BIOMETRICS: Personal Identification in Networked Society*, Kluwer Academic Publishers, 1999.
[4] Mansfield, T. , *Biometric Product Testing – Final Report*, National Physical Laboratory, 2001, *http://www.npl.co.uk/*.
[5] Matsumoto, T., Matsumoto, H., Yamada, K., Hoshino, S., *Impact of Artificial "Gummy" Fingers on Fingerprint Systems*, SPIE Vol. 4677, Optical Security and Counterfeit Deterrence Techniques IV, 2002, *http://cryptome.org/gummy.htm*.
[6] Matyáš, V., Říha, Z., *Biometric Authentication – Security and Usability*, in Advanced Communications and Multimedia Security, Kluwer Academic Publishers, ISBN 1-4020-7206-6, 2002.
[7] Matyáš, V., Říha, Z., *Biometric Authentication Systems*, Technical report. *http://www.ecom-monitor.com/papers/biometricsTR2000.pdf*.
[8] Thalheim, L., Krissler, J., Ziegler, P.-M., *Body Check*, in c't magazine 11/2002, *http://www.heise.de/ct/english/02/11/114/*.

Legal Issues and Privacy

Security and Privacy in Advanced Networking Technologies
B. Jerman-Blažič et al. (Eds.)
IOS Press, 2004

Legal Challenges for Privacy Protection and Identity Management

Jos DUMORTIER & Caroline GOEMANS
K.U.Leuven – Faculty of Law
Interdisciplinary Centre for Law and ICT
http://www.law.kuleuven.ac.be/icri/

Introduction

Privacy protection and identity management are essential for the development of a digital economy. Over the last years, these issues have been tackled from a technological, social, economic and legal viewpoint in a considerable number of conferences, seminars, workshops, books, journal articles and research reports. From a legal perspective, the efficiency of the current regulatory framework has been thoroughly questioned. In parallel, platforms have been developed to open up the nature of the traditional legal framework through self-regulatory initiatives such as codes of conduct, industry guidelines, seal programs, standardization documents, etc. Up till today however, it is generally admitted that - in the field of on-line privacy - legal security for the public and private sector as well as transparency for citizens and consumers are not present yet at an acceptable level in Europe.

The objective of the present contribution is to present the most important challenges for the law in the area of privacy and identity management, building further on previous research and taking into account socio-economic and technological developments.

Our exercise begins with a recall of the current state of practice. Therefore, in a first section, we briefly describe the current legal drivers for governments to protect the privacy of their citizens and for enterprises to develop privacy policies.

In the following sections, two fields for legal action are proposed in this area. A first field relates to the possibilities of the law and other types of regulation, more in particular to the question how to find the right mixes of different types of regulatory instruments and mechanisms to ensure real impact on practices.

The second field of potential legal action relates to the link between regulation and technology developments. We suggest four potential streams related respectively to: 1) a screening of the European legal rules from a technological perspective, 2) how to avoid and monitor the development of privacy decreasing technologies and application fields, 3) regulatory issues concerning the use of privacy enhancing technology, and 4) the regulation concerning management and use of (multiple) identities.

It has to be underlined that a main 'transversal' task of legal experts in all future developments is to ensure that privacy and identity management technologies remain embedded into an adequate regulatory framework. The need for such an approach is clarified with examples in section 2.

1. Legal drivers for privacy protection

A roadmap for legal action in the area of privacy and identity management has to start with a short description of the present state of play. The present section briefly recalls the current legal drivers for governments and enterprises in the field of privacy protection and identity management.

1.1 The role of government: respect of the rule of law and development of a welfare state

The role of governments regarding privacy protection is twofold and therefore always ambiguous. Governments have to ensure the respect of the rule of law, but do also play a proactive role in the development of a welfare state. Finding a correct balance between these two roles of the modern State will always remain one of the core problems in the development of a regulatory framework in this area.

The essence of the 'rule of law' is an autonomous legal order. The rule of law requires the supremacy of laws and limits government arbitrariness and discretionary power. It is opposed to the 'rule of person' under which there is no limit to what governments, individuals or entities can do.

Regarding the right to privacy, governments are bound to ensure respect of compelling international and European instruments as well as constitutional obligations and domestic regulations. Those instruments protect the right to privacy of citizens, both against intrusions of other citizens and business and against state intrusions.

The right to privacy protection is being considered as a core value in a democratic society. It is not just 'a' regulation but it is recognized as a fundamental right in all major international treaties [1] and agreements on human rights and in the constitutions of most countries in the world [2], either explicitly or implicitly.

In Europe, the fundamental right to privacy is recognized in Article 8 of the European Convention of Human Rights and Fundamental Freedoms [3] which states that everyone has the right to respect for his private and family life, his home and his correspondence. The 'rule of law' is clearly present in Article 8, paragraph 2 that protects individuals against arbitrary intrusion of public authority. Privacy intrusions – for instance by interference or control of public authority - are tolerated only if the exceptional measure is explicitly provided for by law and necessary in a democratic society for matters touching on public order and on subjective rights of individuals.

With the development of information technology and its controlling potentials on data, the mere recognition of a fundamental and constitutional principle of privacy in general appeared to be insufficient to safeguard effectively the growing need to protect the right of privacy, with regard to processing of personal data. This explained the move towards the adoption of comprehensive national data protection laws - applicable both to the private and public sector -, enacted in a large number of countries since the start of the seventies in an attempt to structure knowledge and disclosure of an individual's personal information. The development of comprehensive national data protection law was also stimulated by the aim to comply with international policy instruments adopted in parallel with national initiatives, such as the OECD Guidelines and the Council of Europe's Convention No 108 [4]

The general Data Protection Directive 95/46/EC [5] pursues two closely linked objectives: on the one hand to ensure that the rights of the individual on his personal data have a uniform level of protection within the EU and, on the other hand, to ensure that such data can move freely within the Single Market created between the Member States of the European Union. It should be taken into account that the Directive provides for a general framework on processing of personal data and that much of the effectiveness of the protection of personal data depends - amongst other issues - on the various implementation mechanisms.

A second, more specific, Directive 2002/58/EC translates the principles of the general Directive into specific rules for the electronic communications sector, regardless of the used technology [6]. This Directive updates Directive 97/66/EC and regulates issues such as confidentiality of communications, status of traffic data, itemized billing, calling and connected line identification and unsolicited communications.

Beside their role of maintaining the rule of law, governments play a proactive role in the development of a welfare state. The public sector has to be run efficiently in its diverse activities and tasks, such as taxation, social security, health, voting, education, civil status, etc.

This role involves the automatic processing of huge amounts of personal data and thus identity management. For the effective implementation of their caring tasks, governments have to develop a highly complex information infrastructure - both at front office and back office level - taking into account the above-mentioned data protection regulations. The development of a caring and privacy friendly public environment is essential for the development of the Information Society as it will allow citizens to trust civil servants in the processing of their personal data and use of identities. This requires an approach whereby privacy issues and in particular identity management are taken into account at the earliest stage of the organization of the information infrastructure ('privacy by design') [7].

1.2 Legal drivers for privacy policies and identity management schemes

It is obvious that privacy legislation is an important driver for enterprises in respect to privacy and identity management. An important question is to know how legal rules have to be designed in order to stimulate organizations to develop effective privacy policies and identity management schemes that can be fluently integrated in their business practices.

Regular surveys and polls indicate that legal rules are by themselves not sufficient to achieve adequate compliance and implementation of data protection regulation from the side of business [8], especially of small and middle-sized enterprises. The need for more adequate legal incentives will be dealt with later in this paper.

Larger companies have fortunately realized that there is an inherent risk in not complying with data protection rules, following major court cases involving leading organizations such as GeoCities, Toysmart or Microsoft [9]. Still, most enterprises deal with data protection as a compliance issue and not as a business issue [10].

2. Finding the Most Effective Combination of Regulatory Mechanisms for Privacy Protection

This section proposes future action on the types of regulation [11] that are needed to ensure real impact on practices, in particular how to find the right blending of different types of regulatory instruments and mechanisms for effective privacy protection. Relevant elements in this analysis are rule development and implementation, the latter comprising communication, compliance control, dispute resolution, redress, prevention. The need for such actions is explained by assessed deficiencies of current types of regulation.

2.1. Current types of regulation for privacy protection

In most countries that endeavor to protect privacy most effectively, a number of different types of regulation are used simultaneously [12].

Comprehensive laws for privacy protection are the favored type of regulation in the European Union. The general EU Directive 95/46/EC on data protection constitutes a general framework regulation on the collection, use and transfer of personal data, underlining the obligations of the data controllers and the rights of the data subjects. Independent public supervisory authorities monitor compliance.

Countries such as the United States favor the adoption of sector-specific laws regulating, e.g. cable communication privacy, public records privacy, financial privacy, children's privacy [13]. In such cases enforcement is achieved through a range of mechanisms. In many countries with general data protection laws, sector-specific laws are used as a complement by providing more detailed protections for certain categories of information, e.g. law enforcement, consumer credit records, health records, electronic communication, etc.

Personal data protection can also be achieved through various forms of self-regulation, all based on co-operation and consensus between the interested parties and leading to voluntary accepted rules and guidelines.

One type is the so-called 'code of conduct' conceived in the EU Directive itself [14]. Recital 61 and Article 27 of the Directive state that the Member States and the Commission, in their respective spheres of competence, must encourage the trade associations and other representative organizations concerned to draw up codes of conduct so as to facilitate the application of the Directive. In the philosophy of the Directive the particular rules on personal data protection with regard to online commerce have to be developed in a dedicated code of conduct taking account of the specific characteristics of the processing [15].

A second type or self-regulation is standardization. Over the last year, standardization efforts have been initiated in the field of privacy [16]. In previous research, three areas of activity were suggested for privacy standardization, namely a general data protection standard or management standard, sector specific standards, and privacy tools, including privacy enhancing technologies [17]. The Initiative on Privacy Standardization in Europe (IPSE) reviewed the possible role of privacy standardization and issued a set of recommendations, amongst them the adoption of a European set of voluntary best practices for data protection, an inventory of data protection auditing practice, the conduct of a survey of web seals and an analysis of the impact of technologies on data protection [18].

A third example of self-regulation in the field of privacy is the use of *privacy seals* [19]. Privacy seals are trust marks certifying visitors of a website that the visited site has agreed to comply with certain principles of data protection and that it is successfully registered to the trust mark organization. Several studies have been carried out to analyze the development of privacy seals in the online market [20].

2.2 Assessment of the effectiveness of current types of regulation

It falls outside the scope of this paper to assess extensively the effectiveness of current types of regulation in the field of privacy protection and identity management. However, from previous research, we can deduce a consensus on assessed deficiencies regarding effective data protection, in the several types of regulation [21]. Research studies and regular polls also seem to indicate an inadequate compliance or understanding of data protection regulation from the side of the business and a lack of trust from the side of consumers. [22] However, as mentioned earlier, big enterprises have realised that there is an inherent risk in not complying with data protection rules, following major court cases. Nevertheless, privacy issues are mostly perceived as 'compliance' issues and not yet as a real priority in business.

Legislation in the European countries contains a comprehensive set of rules and procedures directly deducted from the EU Directive. Some rules are quite abstract and it therefore remains quite delicate to translate this general legal framework into specific, operational guidelines directly applicable to the context of electronic business [23].

Another difficulty is the fact that current legislation has no effective impact and is not adequate in respect with a growing global digital economy and its inherent complexities. It is generally admitted that enforcement and effective implementation are not optimal and that the margin of manoeuvre left to the Member States in the implementation of the EU Directive has lead to disparities, which are detrimental to business [24].

Privacy codes of all kinds have been developed with varying quality relating to enforcement mechanisms, redress and communication. Accordingly their adequacy is variable. [25]

Seal programmes are of diverse quality and are submitted to auditing methods following unequal quality standards. There is a lack of transparency: consumers are not in the position to appreciate the differences and understand what level of protection they offer [26].

Regarding standardization, the efforts have initially been welcomed with mixed feelings, depending on the addressed stakeholders. Its potential in the field of privacy is presently at the stage of useful recommendations formulated by IPSE [27], which will hopefully be implemented in future [28].

As a conclusion, we may say that each type of regulation, assessed separately, has its deficiencies or is still in its infancy. This leads us to further questions on how to improve regulation to ensure sufficient impact on business practices.

2.3 Which types of regulation are necessary for effectively protecting privacy?

Commonly assessed deficiencies in current types of regulation were listed in the previous section. The question often arises whether an entirely new approach should be adopted to ensure effective impact on practices or whether a mere review of the existing legal framework would be sufficient. In this report both approaches are tackled [29].

In section 3.1 of this paper, further legal action is proposed on the screening of the basic concepts used in the data protection EU Directives. In the present section however, the scope of proposed further legal action is much wider than a mere adjustment of existing legal framework.

In the light of commonly accepted deficiencies of current types of regulation, there is a need for finding the right "mixes" of different types of regulatory instruments and mechanisms that are required for effective data protection. More in particular there is a need to define the core components for any privacy regulation to have real impact on practices.

Core components are: rule development and implementation, the latter comprising communication, compliance control, enforcement and dispute resolution, prevention.

Privacy regulation involves various stakeholders. Their involvement in rule development can vary according to the type of regulation, namely legislation, self-regulation, co-regulation, and particularly EU Directives, national laws, codes of conduct or standards. As a matter of example, it has been mentioned above, that the EU general Directive 95/84 does not directly addresses information technology but rather focuses on organizations (data controllers) and individuals (data subjects). The IPSE report on the possible role of standardization states that consumer and civil society representatives are usually not well represented in rule development [30].

Furthermore measures taken outside the scope of data protection regulation, especially in the field of law enforcement [31], have direct effects on business which are acting within the scope of data protection regulation. The boundaries between both are currently quite vague.

In this respect, specific questions are, for example: Who are the stakeholders? Are they adequately involved in rule development to ensure the drafting of rules that are feasible, transparent and not too complex to implement? How do media, ngo's, academics, etc., influence rule development? How to anticipate the impact of regulation on other sectors (e.g. law enforcement and commerce)? Could an interface between both be developed? Rule development necessarily proceeds along a range of phases. As a matter of example, ISO standards follows a number of phases of standard development, such as the identification of the needs of the partners, collective programming, drawing up the draft standard by the interested parties, consensus, validation, approval. Rule development may proceed differently according to the type of regulation but should in all cases be better explicited and organised. Important questions, also for traditional legislators in this area could be : What are the different steps of rule development for effective privacy regulation? Are all the essential stakeholders sufficiently involved in the process ? How can we test and validate the impact of the regulation ? Is the regulation reviewed on a regular basis? How to develop positive legal incentives to comply with the regulation rather than punitive sanctions only?

The commonly accepted deficiencies of current regulation, mentioned earlier in this paper, indicate also the necessity for developing effective implementation strategies. For example, specific questions relate to how communication, compliance control, enforcement, dispute resolution and prevention should be incorporated in implementation strategies [32] of any type of privacy regulation. How are rules communicated to ensure effective implementation and compliance? Is an awareness or education campaign developed for all types of stakeholders? Who is in charge of the awareness campaign and how is it organised?

How is education for implementers organised? Are there compliance assistance schemes, especially for SME's? What techniques and methods are used for compliance control? How is it regulated? How is compliance measured? What are the potentials of seals, assessment, audits to improve compliance with the rules? What are the potentials of not-yet-explored techniques such as on-line compliance control or "PIRTs" (Privacy Invasion Response Teams)? By analogy with CERTs (Computer Emergency Response Teams) [33], the development of PIRTs (Privacy Invasion Response Team) could be promoted to tackle effectively ongoing privacy-threats [34]. National PIRTs could be linked to one another to facilitate cooperation throughout the world. It seems very likely that the creation of an international organisation that shares information on privacy threats and vulnerabilities and investigates transborder privacy incidents could offer high potentials for effective on-line compliance control.

Enforcement mechanisms are essential for effective implementation of any type of regulation. They can vary considerably, e.g. publication in a 'bad actors' list; verification procedures of business statements with subsequent cancellation of the right to use certifying trust marks; traditional enforcement mechanisms such as criminal court condemnation and payment of fines. Specific questions related to enforcement mechanisms are, for example: What are effective enforcement mechanisms in case of non-compliance? Are there affordable, independent recourse procedures for complaints with redress mechanisms? Could data protection rights be enforced as a collective right through class actions, for instance through powers given to consumer associations or trade unions?

What are the potentials of on-line dispute resolution (ODR) for negotiation, mediation and arbitration purposes? Is ODR compatible with the current national and international legal frameworks? How to map the different alternative dispute resolution arrangements within Europe, especially their different practices and normative basis of decisions [35] ?

The independent supervisory authorities of the Member States play an important role in the implementation of the Directive. However, the powers of the national supervisory authorities within the EU are not uniform. They can act as ombudsmen, auditors, consultants, educators, negotiators, enforcers, policy advisors [36] Moreover, for business and citizens it is not clear whether an advice or decision of a national supervisory authority may be relied upon for activities in another EU country. Consequently, it seems relevant to make an institutional analysis of supervisory data protection authorities and reflect on their role within a borderless internal market. The possibilities of "on-line" data protection authorities should also be further explored, as a way amongst others to develop rules and procedures for monitoring privacy threats.

3. Privacy protection in a new technological context

A recurrent conclusion of many studies and reports is that technology and regulation have no or little mutual impact on their respective developments and that mechanisms should be developed to bridge the gap between technology and regulation [37]. Initiatives from both the legal and the technological side and with mutual involvement should be taken in order to avoid a situation where technology rules de facto the processing of personal data.

3.1 Adapting the European regulatory framework to the new technological environment

The exercise to define potential legal action topics aimed at bridging the gap between privacy regulation and technology necessarily leads us - in a first stage - to the analysis of the European privacy law on data protection. In this respect we can pinpoint three important issues, related to respectively the screening of basic concepts of the European data protection directive 95/46/EC, the relevance of current case law of the European Court of Human Rights in the light of new technological developments and the privacy protection of vulnerable categories of individuals in society.

3.1.1 Screening basic concepts of the general data protection Directive from a technological perspective.

Open consultations on the implementation of the general data protection directive have taken place. We refer especially to the Conference on the Implementation of the Data Protection Directive, organised by the EU Commission on 30 September 2002, in Brussels [38]. Building further on the discussions in these forums, we think that there is a need to examine whether the basic concepts used in the general data protection Directive are still workable in a new technological environment.

Two examples can clarify the need for the proposed analysis.

1) The data subject's right of access to data (art. 12 Directive 95/46/EC): how can this right effectively be implemented in an on-line technological environment, which is quite different from the off-line model presented in the Directive? The exercise of the subject's right to access through e.g. the Internet asks for strong authentication to ensure that the applicant is really the data subject involved. The exercise of this right in the context of wireless communications or ubiquitous computing context seems even more difficult to realise in practice. There are also serious difficulties from the side of the data controller to fulfil in practice the obligation to grant access to personal data. Aggregation of personal data is the biggest threat to privacy intrusions, whilst the increasing strength of search engines is

commonly known. To provide fully access to personal data involves therefore not only the keeping of records but also the release of profiled patterns. Moreover, personal information is kept in different hands so that the access to this information should be efficiently organised.

2) Deletion of personal data (art.6e Directive 95/46/EC): the EU Directive rules that personal data may not be kept longer than is necessary for the purposes for which the data were collected or for which they are further processed. However, in practice it may not be feasible that an injunction to delete personal data will be implemented in all departments of a multinational company operating in different countries over the world. The data controller could only guarantee that while the data still exist 'somewhere' there is no route to trace them back or that there is no tangible link between the data and the data subject. The full destruction of personal data can rarely be guaranteed.

3.1.2 Analysis of the relevance of current case law in a new technological context.

The case law of the European Court of Human Rights contains several decisions related to privacy intrusions, for example for law enforcement purposes, operated through 'old' technologies such as telephone tapping [39].

As a matter of example, the Court ruled in the Kruslin case that "tapping and other forms of interception of telephone conversations represent a serious interference with private life and must accordingly be based on a 'law' that is particularly precise. The Court further stated that: "it is essential to have clear, detailed rules on the subject, especially as the technology available for use is continually becoming more sophisticated."[40]

Another example is the Malone case, where insufficient basis in domestic law [41] for justifying a privacy intrusion for law enforcement purposes was successfully alleged. The Malone case related to - amongst other issues - the practice of 'metering' of telephone calls [42]. The technology of metering involves the use of a device that registers automatically the numbers dialed on a particular telephone and the time and duration of each call. This process was designed for its own purposes, namely investigating complaints of poor quality service, checking possible abuse of the telephone service and ensuring that the subscriber would be correctly charged.

The question now is whether or not these cases are still relevant in the new technological environment, for instance for regulating retention of traffic data by electronic communications service providers. Therefore we recommend a legal analysis examining whether current case law of the ECHR related to privacy intrusions committed with 'old' technologies could be relevant for and be applied to new technologies. The analysis should focus on the basic conditions that have to be met to allow privacy intrusive measures, e.g. for law enforcement purposes, namely the existence of a clear legal basis, of a pressing social need, as well as the respect of the principle of proportionality, the latter requiring that the extent of interference is not excessive in relation to the legitimate needs and interests, which have occasioned the interference.

3.1.3 Privacy protection of vulnerable categories of persons in society

The general data protection directive distinguishes between several categories of data, the 'sensitive' personal data (for instance related to health, ideology, religion, sexual behavior, etc.) being submitted to a stricter data protection regime. However, vulnerable categories of persons in society are not addressed in the Directive. One could think of adapted privacy protection for children, prisoners, mentally impaired or elderly persons, hospitalized persons, students or employees.

For instance, children's natural curiosity and trustful nature heightens their vulnerability regarding the use of the Internet, especially when some benefits can be obtained by giving up their privacy (e.g. filling in a questionnaire on a full set of personal information regarding themselves, their parents, their family in exchange of a Lord of the Rings T-shirt). The protection of their privacy is involved in their relation with schoolteachers, parents and the outside world.

Particular privacy issues related to children are:

Verifiable parental consent [43]: how can parental consent be organized in terms of privacy and data protection? How can it best be verified that the consent is really coming from the child's parent? Should the verification methods be stricter for sites that disclose information to third parties or make it publicly available through chat rooms or other interactive activities? What if the consent is de facto impracticable or requires disproportionate effort? How to prevent the parental consent of becoming a mechanism to exercise control over a child in circumstances where the protection of the child's privacy does not require the parent's involvement? [44]

Definition/verification of a 'child' [45]: How to define a 'child' taking into account that children have not the same ability at the same age? How, in the on-line world, could a data controller know the age of a person accessing its website? Might the establishment of mechanisms to verify such details create privacy risks in other contexts?

As a starting point for this research one can refer to the US Children's Online Privacy Protection Act of 1998 (COPPA). Privacy protection of minors is also expressly mentioned in, for instance, the Dutch data protection act [46]. It should further be examined whether there is a need for specific data protection regulation for a number of vulnerable categories of persons, such as children, prisoners, mentally impaired or elderly persons, hospitalized persons, students, etc. Cooperation between ongoing projects focusing on on-line privacy awareness of vulnerable categories should be stimulated [47].

3.2 Framework for innovators

It has been raised earlier in this paper that the terms of the EU Directive 95/84 do not refer sufficiently to technology. The EU Directive mainly addresses organisations (data controllers) whereas the IT industry, a core stakeholder, is not directly addressed. Reference to technology is indirectly made, only in connection with security, namely in article 17 of the EU Directive 95/84 which rules that controllers and processors must implement appropriate technical and organizational measures to protect personal data against accidental loss and unlawful forms of processing.

However, Recital 30 of EU Directive 2002/58/EC on privacy in electronic communications encourages a closer mutual impact between regulation and technology as it states that 'systems for the provision of electronic communications networks and services should be *designed* to limit the amount of personal data necessary to a strict minimum.' Indeed, building privacy requirements into the design activity is a generally agreed approach. Further research is needed to develop 'rules' for the assessment and monitoring of privacy by design.

The two following questions could be regarded as illustrations of the general need for more regulatory mechanisms to improve mutual impact on respectively regulation and technology.

These questions are: how can we avoid the development of privacy decreasing technologies and how can we intercept them timely? The same question could be addressed regarding the development of privacy decreasing application fields.

3.2.1 How can we avoid the development of privacy decreasing technologies and how can we intercept them timely?

By way of examples of privacy decreasing technologies we can refer to Public Key Infrastructure (PKI) and Digital Rights Management (DRM).

Public Key Infrastructure (PKI) commonly provides four functions - authentication, integrity, non-repudiation and confidentiality - to guarantee security and reliability of electronic exchange of information. Whilst PKI applications can enhance privacy [48], there are serious privacy risks linked with the use of PKI [49] The following specific questions are relevant privacy issues.

- For the issuing of a digital certificate, evidence of identity must be registered. How to ensure that this process is not privacy intrusive and that the identification level is not excessive in relation to the specific application asked for?
- How to avoid potential profiling by means of personal information mentioned in publicly available certificates?
- How to avoid potential profiling by consulting published PKI directories? Do PKI applications necessarily require publication of PKI directories? If so, shouldn't clients be allowed to opt out having their public keys listed in the directory? How to avoid profiling of logs of accesses and online transactions?
- How to deal with the progressive accumulation of additional uses for certificates or associated personal information? How to avoid that the use of PKI becomes a de facto unique identifier system? How to deal with PKI applications, some of which requiring a higher level of identification than others? How to develop special purpose attribute certificates which simply represent the individual's eligibility for a service without identifying them? Are pseudonymous certificates as provided in the EU Directive on electronic signatures [50] a sufficient legal answer?

These privacy issues related to the use of PKI may justify the need for a regulatory framework, such as e.g. best practices related to the use of PKI [51]. It is our impression that regulators – including the European legislators - have thus far too much focused on the use of identity certificates, without sufficiently taking into account the possibilities of alternative techniques, such as the use of (anonymous) credentials, etc.

A second example of a technology with potential negative effects on privacy is Digital Right Management (DRM). DRM technologies are originally designed to protect the rights of copyright holders through technical detection of copyright law infringements and technical restriction of use of digital files [52]. However, DRM involves all aspects of content distribution, such as access control (frequency, length of views), control of certain uses, usage metering (to track frequency of access), payment processes, record keeping [53]. Clearly DRM technologies can potentially limit or even violate privacy rights of users. DRM technologies usually require identification to access copyright protected content and thus can prohibit anonymous access to information. Furthermore DRM technologies can exercise control over purchases and facilitate profiling of users preferences because of its strong search and profiling capacities, in the process of controlling the use of copyright protected works. Some DRM technologies are even designed to harm a user's system, e.g. by forcing a reboot of the user's computer or even crashing a user's computer [54]. Specific privacy questions remain open, such as e.g. how DRM technologies could recognize fair use rights of copyright protected works, e.g. for educational or cultural purposes.

Many DRM technologies have thus been developed without taking enough account of privacy issues [55] and, consequently, without incorporating privacy enhancing technologies although this appears to be technically feasible. Up to date however, a commonly accepted technical approach for meeting these legal privacy requirements seems to be lacking [56]. As a matter of example the development of the "Trusted Computing Platform" continues to be heavily criticized by privacy advocates [57].

The general legal protection of DRM technologies and rights management information, guaranteed by the EU Copyright Directive 2001/29/EC [58] on the one hand and, on the other hand, the mere statement in the EU Copyright Directive [59] that DRM systems should incorporate privacy safeguards in accordance with the EU data protection directive, do not seem to be sufficient to guarantee an effective balance of the involved rights.

3.2.2 How can we avoid the development of privacy decreasing application fields and how can we intercept them timely?

The development of e-government raises numerous privacy issues. The need for more transparency within administration has to be reconciled with privacy requirements. The examples below should provide some clarification.

Citizens have to identify themselves to benefit from a whole range of public services, such as e.g. health and other social services, or to fulfil certain obligations, e.g. taxation. Most public services have their own identification numbers and codes attributed to each citizen. One single identification number for accessing and using all these services would result in an important simplification both for citizens and administrations. The crucial question is how to incorporate guarantees from a data protection perspective.

The Article 29 Working Party held in its Opinion [60] on the use of unique identifiers in telecommunication terminal equipments that; for instance, the possible integration of an unique identification number in the IP address - as designed according to the new Internet protocol IPv6 - raises specific privacy concerns [61]. New systems of on-line authentication services, such as Microsoft's Passport identification and authentication services have also been examined by the Art.29 Data Protection Working Party [62].

- A large number of public services should be accessed anonymously in particular when there is no purpose for identification, such as gathering information or tax simulations. How will a citizen get the guarantee of a full anonymous access?

- In several countries initiatives are taking place to develop an electronic ID card. How to regulate the use of electronic ID cards for different functionalities, e.g. simultaneous control of identity and access to administrative services? [63]

- The integration of 'front office' and 'back office' seems quite complex. Is the integration of 'front office' and 'back office' feasible from a data protection perspective, particularly taking into account the purpose limitation and transparency principle? How to point out, for instance, who is the data controller?

Public/private partnerships can offer an added value, such as partnerships between interim-job offices and public administrations offering job opportunities or such as exchange of change of addresses between public administrations and banks, telephone companies, etc. Should those public/private partnerships be object of particular precautions from a privacy perspective?

A second example of an application field with potential risks for privacy is the area of law enforcement. The right to privacy as guaranteed by the European Convention on Human Rights, allows no interference by a public authority with the exercise of this right except if the interference is "in accordance with the law and is necessary in a democratic society for the protection of public order, ..., prevention of crime."[64].

With the increase and diversification of law enforcement activities, a considerable number of privacy decreasing regulations and technologies have been widely adopted the last years, for the sake of public security. New law enforcement policy trends that have been identified are: increased communications surveillance; search and seizure powers by reducing authorization requirements and oversight; increased data sharing, e.g. relating to traveller's information, financial information. These trends result in an increased profiling and identification [65]. As a matter of example, regulations on mandatory retention of traffic data have raised a lot of privacy concerns [66].

These policy measures are supported by a parallel development of new privacy decreasing technologies and systems such as the use of "black boxes" on ISP networks, key logger systems capable of circumventing encryption, sophisticated camera surveillance spotting patterns, satellite surveillance, etc. [67]. The recent US announcement of the Total Information Awareness (TIA) system - developed to 'revolutionize the ability of the United States to detect, classify and identify foreign terrorists and to decipher their plans' [68] - puts once again the balance between overall security requirements and individual privacy seriously in question.

Moreover, the additional threat with privacy decreasing technologies developed for law enforcement is their overall opacity for citizens. Consequently, questions to resolve are: How can developers of privacy decreasing technologies for law enforcement purposes be monitored timely to ensure a right balance between security and privacy? How to educate and control effectively implementers of law enforcement technologies or how to control 'the controllers'?

It should be underlined that legal action and reflections so far, have rather focused on data controller's compliance than on ensuring privacy protection requirements at the earliest framing of programs or services and in all successive activities. The consequence is that new privacy invasive technologies and applications are continuously dropped on the market without effective legal support. The legal impact is often limited to reactive measures, instead of providing a proactive regulatory input. The same could be stated regarding technology input in new regulation.

The improvement of mutual impact between privacy legislation and privacy decreasing technology is even more challenging when we consider the development of pervasive computing that uses mobile and ubiquitous systems and enables the exchange of information anytime, anywhere [69].

Further research should be focused on developing regulatory mechanisms to incorporate data protection compliance at an early stage of technology design. In this respect the development of guidelines to assist business in conducting systematically privacy impact assessments (PIA) could be stimulated.

PIAs provide a method of identifying privacy risks so that these can be addressed when potentially privacy decreasing technologies and applications are being designed, revised or extended. Those schemes bring together a variety of skills to identify and assess privacy implications of proposed programs or services, before they are allowed to be marketed. Legal expertise would relate to advice and recommendations with respect to data protection, to liability issues, procedural issues, controlling mechanisms etc[70]. In Canada for instance, the conducting of PIAs is - since May 2002- made compulsory for governmental departments and agencies in respect with new programs and services that raise privacy issues.

3.3 Using privacy technology

A third field of legal action related to the link between regulation and technology regards the rules for using privacy enhancing technologies (Privacy enhancing technologies).

It is likely that the role of Privacy Enhancing Technologies [71] will increase in future, even if it is admitted that Privacy enhancing technologies need more economic incentives and that the market for Privacy enhancing technologies should be more structured in order to ensure a better development [72]. The legal context of Privacy enhancing technologies has its basis in article 17 of the EU Directive 95/84 which rules that 'controllers must implement appropriate technical and organizational measures to protect personal data against accidental or unlawful destruction or accidental loss, alteration, unauthorized disclosure or access, ... and against all other unlawful forms of processing.' However, specific legal questions on the use of Privacy enhancing technologies need to be answered.

At least three major questions, listed below, would need further consideration.

3.3.1 How much identification do we need for each particular environment?

Privacy enhancing technologies allow prevention or reduction of identification (e.g. anonymizers). The effective need for identification varies considerably according to the type of service asked for. In the field of e-government for instance, the access to social security rights will require a high identification whereas a citizen should principally benefit from an anonymous access to tax simulations. In between, a whole taxonomy of identification and authentication degrees can technically be envisaged for different types of requests or activities. Up till now there is no regulatory framework to give guidance on the use of the appropriate level of identification and authentication according to the type of service asked for. In this context, the legal 'translation' of the use of credentials should be examined.

3.3.2 What will be the rules for privacy protection service providers?

Currently, the different functionalities and applications of Privacy enhancing technologies lack transparency and legal security, which make them less attractive and trustworthy towards users. This seems for instance essential for the further development of P3P [73]. One of the critics relating to P3P - putting aside the fact that a P3P compliant privacy policy is not necessarily a privacy policy that is compliant with the laws of the website owner and of the user - is the current inability of P3P vocabulary to replicate accurately human readable policies. One example is that financial institutions have used the word "may" in their privacy policies to indicate instances where action-using information may or may not be taken. Yet, in the current P3P language, 'may' means 'will' which results in an inaccurate interpretation of the human readable policy [74]. This creates legal uncertainty as to the legal value of P3P statements, as to liability issues [75]. The drafting of guidelines for user agents could overcome these difficulties and improve transparency towards users.

3.3.3 How free will individuals be to use privacy enhancing technologies?

Privacy enhancing technologies are being developed, but currently there are many obstacles to freely use some types of privacy enhancing technologies. For instance, how could we avoid that users of privacy enhancing technologies are not discriminated against in consulting websites (e.g. when using cookie blockers)? How to avoid that users of privacy enhancing technologies (e.g. when using anonymizers) are not discriminated against in criminal or civil investigations?

The emergence of obstacles to freely use some types of privacy enhancing technologies is not illusory. For instance, in some countries, such as Belgium, anonymizing services may be banned in future [76]. In this respect, further initiatives from the law enforcement sector may be expected. Service providers also have controlling rights and duties over traffic and/or content according to the type of services offered, particularly in respect with the EU Directive on electronic commerce. One could also question how the right to use cryptography will develop?

3.4 Regulation of identities

Citizens need an identity to distinguish themselves from others. Citizens are using their identity - an aggregation of unique characteristics - as 'evidence' for specific competences, roles, capacities, authorizations, rights, access to services. Sometimes the 'real' identity is used but this is often neither necessary nor desirable from a privacy perspective. A basic principle of data protection is indeed to process personal data only where necessary. In parallel with physical identity, the concept of 'digital identity' has emerged as a whole set of digitised personal data (PINs, accounts, multiple user names, passwords, tokens, smart cards). Individuals can also perform different roles and accordingly adopt multiple virtual identities. These new developments inevitably raise a number of legal issues.

3.4.1 Legal concept of on-line identities

The concept of on-line identity (digital identity, virtual identity) should not be taken for granted in a digital environment as it is in a physical environment [77]. The current legal framework does not provide for adequate, clear cut definitions. As a matter of example the notion of on-line 'identifiability' adopted in the EU Directive 95/84 is interpreted in different ways throughout Europe.

According to the Directive, an identifiable person is one "who can be identified, directly or indirectly, in particular by reference to an identification number or to one or more factors specific to his physical, physiological, mental, economic, cultural or social identity". The EU Directive specifies in its Recital 26 that to determine whether a person is identifiable, account should be taken of all the means likely reasonably to be used either by the controller or by any other person to identify the said person. Different interpretations of the concept of "identifiable" create legal uncertainty and make it difficult to adopt clear-cut definitions for new developments such as on-line identity.

Moreover, the refinement of the concept of on-line identity should be linked to the concept of on-line anonymity, which can be used in different degrees according to the context in which it is used. Interdisciplinary research shows that legal definitions do not necessarily match with technological concepts.

This is for instance the case for the concept of on-line anonymity. Currently there is no legal 'answer' to the whole taxonomy of technical properties and degrees of on-line anonymity (unlinkability, untraceable, unobservability, condition/unconditional on-line anonymity). In a legal context, the type of anonymity is usually not specified but limited to a mere ruling on an explicit or implicit authorisation or - on the contrary - a ban to use anonymity or pseudonymity. For instance, the EU Directive on electronic signatures provides for an express right of the signatory to mention a pseudonym instead of his real name (art.8), whereas - on the contrary - the specific European directive regarding privacy protection in the electronic communication sector bans explicitly the use of anonymity for sending commercial communications (art.13.4).

Consequently, legal answers should be found to define the core concepts of on-line identity, on-line anonymity, pseudo identity and pseudonymity [78], which should map the corresponding technological definitions. Related new risks, such as identity theft, should also be given legal attention.

An issue related to the clarification of the concept of on-line anonymity regards the conditions of its use. It is true that the need for on-line anonymity has been accepted by the Art. 29 Working Party in its Recommendation 3/97. However, in practice, the use of on-line anonymity is often controversial. This is partly due to a lack of refined and transparent rules on a controlled use of anonymity. Thus the question raises how to develop a more transparent, controlled use of on-line anonymity, in order to achieve a fair balance between anonymity and accountability.

3.4.2 Legal issues of multiple identities

It is generally known that opportunities to create fictitious virtual identities, potentially in fully fictitious environments are highly exploited in a digital context. The creation of virtual identities can be motivated by privacy and security concerns, convenience or leisure. Virtual identities may disappear without leaving traces. Consequently, the concept of these virtual identities is in contradiction with criteria of permanency and physical reality that are expected in any identification process linking a physical individual to a set of digital data [79].

Consequently the use of multiple 'virtual identities' will have to be regulated. In particular, legal questions raise regarding accountability, legal representation - for instance when minors adopt 'virtual' identities -, regarding contractual and tort liability, fair use, law enforcement issues.

Other legal issues relate to the question whether privacy rights - principally conferred to an identifiable individual - can be conferred to virtual identities: for instance, whether ownership of a virtual identity can be claimed or how evidence of theft of a virtual identity can be established? [80]

3.4.3 Rules for identity managers

Rules for identity managers refer to the concept of identity management. With the development of e-business, organizations need to manage secure access to information and applications spread over a wide range of network systems. Organizations also have to manage secure access to a great number of users, both inside and outside the organisation - such as customers, business partners, employees, suppliers, etc. - according to agreed authorizations and in respect with data protection regulation.

Identity management software has been widely developed [81]. It enables administrators to control user access and conducted business through authentication methods (passwords, digital certificates, hardware or software tokens) and authorization rights. Delegation of management of permission rights to business managers and partners is also made possible. It is generally admitted that improvement of identity management will enhance the benefits of a global economy.

One type of identity 'managers' is the business model of infomediaries or information brokers [82] that has emerged over the last years. Infomediaries will assist customers to articulate their determinations by protecting personal information (e.g. customers preferences) against abuse and by disclosing personal data only with the customer's specific permission ("permission marketing"). To this end the infomediary will offer both a "privacy tool kit" and a "profiling tool kit". The customer of an infomediary will have the choice either to remain anonymous or to allow his profile and his personal data to be given to vendors or direct marketers. [83].

In this business model, an essential component is clearly 'trust' taking when one considers the profiling capability of infomediaries who may collect sensitive data. In this respect, the International Working Party on Telecommunications compares the relation 'client-infomediary' to the relation 'client-attorney' or 'patient-doctor' [84].

It is recommended to examine whether the existing legal framework is still adequate for identity management business models. Clear rules should be developed and made available to the users.

Regarding infomediaries, specific legal questions raise whether the 'trust' relation between infomediary and client should be legally protected against search and seizure? Other specific questions are: how to ensure informed consent or free choice of the client; how to deal with liability, accountability issues in case of non-compliance of the infomediary.

3.4.4 Control instruments for identity holders

There is a tendency to move privacy protection into the hands of individual users and to find mechanisms to provide them real insight in the processing of his personal data. It is generally admitted that current access rights - mainly a right of information and correction according to the EU Directive - are rather theoretical and cumbersome to exercise in practice. Those rights have been elaborated in an offline context, which does not always seem adequate anymore. They will be even less adapted to upcoming phenomena such as ubiquitous computing that will provide commonly used tools for business and private activities.

An example of alternatives to the traditional access right is the introduction of a 'digital safe' for each citizen in his/her relation with public authorities [85]. Current access rights need to be reconsidered and it should be examined how to develop new schemes which offer maximal possibilities to users to manage their identity (or identities) and monitor on a permanent basis how their data are used [86]

Examples of specific questions that will have to be dealt with, are: Which requirements are needed to help users to make informed choices? Or how to define electronic consent? As a matter of example: is 'electronic consent' valid when the 'consent box' is pre-ticketed? Given legal and cultural differences between countries, shouldn't the user be able to choose between a number of default settings?

4. Conclusion

Reflecting on potential legal challenges in the area of privacy and identity management can best start with an analysis of the current state of play. Commonly assessed deficiencies in the current types of regulation raise often the question whether an entirely new approach should be adopted to ensure effective impact on practices or whether a mere review of the existing legal framework could be sufficient. In this report both approaches are tackled. In this paper a systematic screening of the basic concepts of the general data protection directive is suggested. To our view however, the core legal issue is the need for finding an adequate blending of different types of regulatory instruments and mechanisms for privacy protection. Core components in this analysis are: rule development and implementation.

A second main potential legal action field relates to the link between regulation and technology developments. Previous workshops in the field of privacy technology have recurrently come to the conclusion that technology and regulation have no or little impact on their respective developments and that mechanisms should be developed to bridge the gap between technology and regulation. Consequently, an important research challenge for the future is to enhance multidisciplinary involvement so as to avoid to reach a situation where technology would de facto rule privacy issues in the absence of appropriate regulation or vice versa. Any future legal action should, to our view, be intrinsically linked with technology.

In this respect, we proposed four further legal action topics. As mentioned above, the basic concepts of the EU directives should be carefully screened from a technological feasibility perspective. Vice versa, the development and timely monitoring of privacy decreasing technologies and application fields should be analysed from a legal feasibility perspective, in particular how an effective regulatory support could be built in at an early stage of design.

Furthermore, an adequate legal support for the 'free' use of privacy technologies will have to be developed so as to improve transparency and legal security. This seems to be lacking for the time being, which explains partly the perceived difficulties to increase the demand for those technologies.

Finally, technological developments which facilitate the use of on-line identities have not found an adequate legal answer yet, in particular on basic concepts of on-line identity, on-line anonymity, on the use of multiple identities, the regulation of identity managers and on control instruments for identity holders.

The potential legal action topics have been deliberately kept generic so as to ensure their relevance in the most varying contexts of electronic communication. It appears that one "use case scenario" may apply to various proposed topics. For instance, law enforcement measures may have an impact on other sectors, which is an element of concern at the stage of rule development. Law enforcement technologies have also been cited in this report as an example for the need to analyse the current case law on privacy intrusive 'old' technologies and to examine their potential relevance for 'new' technologies. Finally, the impact of law enforcement activities has also been raised as an example of a privacy decreasing application.

We could conclude by stating that the proposed legal challenges should necessarily remain open and flexible, as they have to be closely linked with and continuously assessed against ever progressing socio-economic and technological developments.

References

[1] Overview of the international instruments in the field of data protection: http://europa.eu.int/comm/internal_market/en/dataprot/inter/index.htm

[2] Overview of national legislation in over 50 countries: "An International Survey of Privacy Laws and Developments", Electronic Privacy Information Centre and Privacy International, http://www.privacyinternational.org/survey. Also: http://www.epic.org

[3] European Convention for the Protection of human rights and fundamental freedoms, Council of Europe, Rome, 1950, http://conventions.coe.int/Treaty/EN/CadreListeTraites.htm; See also article 7 of the Charter of Fundamental Rights of the European Union, O.J. C 364/1, 18.12.2000.

[4] The Guidelines governing the Protection of Privacy and Transborder Data Flows of Personal Data, promulgated by the Organisation for Economic Co-operation and Development's on 23 September 1980; the Council of Europe's Convention No 108 for the Protection of Individuals with regard to the Automatic Processing of Personal Data, adopted in 1981. See overview: http://europa.eu.int/comm/internal_market/en/dataprot/inter/index.htm

[5] Directive 95/46/EC of the European Parliament and of the Council of 24 October 1995 on the protection of individuals with regard to the processing of personal data and on the free movement of such data, O.J. L 281, 23 November 1995.

[6] Directive 2002/58/EC of 12 July 2002, concerning the processing of personal data and the protection of privacy in the electronic communications sector (Directive on privacy and electronic communication), O.J. L 201/37, 31 July 2002, replacing Directive 97/66/EC of the European Parliament and of the Council of 15 December 1997 on the processing of personal data and the protection of privacy in the telecommunications sector, O.J. L 53, 14 January 1998.

[7] TRUCHE P., GAUGERE J.P., FLICHY P., Administration électronique et protection des données personnelles, Livre Blanc, Paris, 2002; VERSMISSEN J.A.G., and DE HEUIJ A.C.M., Electronic government and privacy, protection of personal data in the information structure of the government, College Bescherming Persoonsgegevens, The Hague, July 2002, http://www.cbpweb.nl/en/index.htm.

[8] Forrester Research survey published in September 1999 found that 67% of respondents were either 'extremely concerned' or 'very concerned' about releasing personal information online; FTC annual privacy

surveys, http://www.ftc.gov/privacy/index.html ; see also Centre for Democracy and Technology, http://www.cdt.org/privacy/survey/findings/ ; EU Commission, D.G. Internal Market, Online consultation regarding citizens' and controllers' views on the implementation of Directive 95/46/EC, http://www.europa.eu.int/comm/internal_market/en/dataprot/lawreport/consultation_en.htm WALRAVE, M., ePrivacy Survey and ePrivacy Scan, www.e-privacy.be

[9] See Electronic Privacy Information Center and Privacy International, "An International Survey of Privacy Laws and Developments", http://www.privacyinternational.org/survey ; http://www.epic.org

[10] The RAPID issue paper on Privacy enhancing technologies in Enterprises mentions as negative 'business' drivers for privacy: not realised returns, lack of trust from the side of the user, damage of enterprise image. Positive 'business' drivers are: reduction of costs, more returns, enhancing trust, higher customer retention rates, Specific 'business' drivers for identity management are: reduction of operating costs, integration of the workflow process, improved security. See http://www.ra-pid.org

[11] The concept of 'regulation' used in this paper refers to types of legal regulation. It is obvious that social, cultural and economic 'regulation' also play an important role in privacy protection.

[12] Privacy and Human Rights 2002, An International Survey of privacy laws and developments , Electronic Privacy Information Center, Washington , DC, USA, Privacy International Londen, UK.

[13] Other examples are listed at http://www.publicrecordfinder.com/privacy_protection.html

[14] Privacy codes can be classified in different types: organizational, sector-specific, functional, technological, professional codes, see BENNETT, C., Implementing Privacy Codes of Practice: a report to the Canadian Standards Association, Canadian Standards Association (CSA), PLUS 8830, Rexdale, 1995; RAAB Ch., Privacy protection: the varieties of self-regulation, 24th International Conference of Data Protection and Privacy Commissioners, Cardiff, 9 - 11 September 2002.

[15] Examples are: http://www.icx.org ; http://www.iata.org ; http://www.fedma.org ; http://www.dma.org.uk/shared/PrefServices.asp

[16] Standardization differ from other types of self-regulation (all characterised by a consensus and voluntary nature) as the consensus on the voluntary rules is reached in the context of a recognized body. Further reading: DUMORTIER, J., and GOEMANS, C., Data Privacy and Standardization, Discussion Paper prepared for the CEN/ISSS Open Seminar on Data Protection, Brussels 23/24 March 2000, http://www.cenorm.be/isss/Projects/DataProtection/dp.default.htm .

[17] DUMORTIER, J. and GOEMANS, C., ibid.; reaffirmed in: Initiative on Privacy Standardization in Europe, IPSE, Final Report, 13 February 2002, http://www.cenorm.be/ISSS/Projects/DataProtection/IPSE/ipse_finalreport.pdf.

[18] Initiative on Privacy Standardization in Europe, IPSE, Final Report, 13 February 2002, http://www.cenorm.be/isss/Projects/DataProtection/dp.default.htm

[19] Examples are: TRUSTe, BBB Online, CPA Webtrust. See list of trustmarkprograms in appendix C, Final Report Initiative on Privacy Standardization in Europe, IPSE, http://www.cenorm.be/ISSS/Projects/DataProtection/IPSE/ipse_finalreport.pdf

[20] See e.g. CAVOUKIAN, A., and CROMPTON, M., Web seals: a review of online privacy programs, a joint paper by Ontario's Information and Privacy Commissioner and the Federal Privacy Commissioner of Australia, http://www.ipc.on.ca/english/pubpres/papers/seals.htm

[21] Initiative on Privacy Standardization in Europe, IPSE, Final Report, 13 February 2002, http://www.cenorm.be/isss/Projects/DataProtection/dp.default.htm ; Data Protection Conference on the implementation of Directive 95/46/EC, Brussels 30 September - 1 October 2002, http://europa.eu.int/comm/internal_market/en/dataprot/lawreport/index.htm

[22]Privacy surveys: Forrester Research survey published in September 1999 found that 67% of respondents were either 'extremely concerned' or 'very concerned' about releasing personal information online; FTC annual privacy surveys, http://www.ftc.gov/privacy/index.html ; see also: Centre for Democracy and Technology, http://www.cdt.org/privacy/survey/findings/ ; EU Commission, D.G. Internal Market, Online consultation regarding citizens' and controllers' views on the implementation of Directive 95/46/EC, http://www.europa.eu.int/comm/internal_market/en/dataprot/lawreport/consultation_en.htm ; eMarketer's eDemographics Weekly, Issue 17, 2001 - http://www.entrepreneur.com/Your_Business/YB_SegArticle/0,4621,290753,00.html ; WALRAVE, M., ePrivacy Survey and ePrivacy Scan, www.e-privacy.be

[23]Institute for Prospective Technological Studies Seville, Joint Research Centre European Commission, Future bottlenecks in the Information Society, Report to the European Parliament, Committee on Industry, External Trade, Research and Energy (ITRE), Joint Research June 2001, Sevilla.

[24] Conference on the implementation of Directive 95/46/EC (Data protection) organised by the European Commission in Brussels on 30 September - 1 October 2002.

[25] RAAB Ch., Privacy protection: the varieties of self-regulation, 24th International Conference of Data Protection and Privacy Commissioners, Cardiff, 9 - 11 September 2002, p.5.; IPSE report on Privacy Standardization, ibid. ,p. 43.

[26] IPSE Report, ibid.

[27] Conclusions IPSE Report, ibid.

[28] Some recommendations have been further developed, such as e.g. the identification of a common European set of voluntary best practices in the GUIDES project, http://eprivacyforum.jrc.it

[29] See e.g. Institute for Prospective Technological Studies Seville, Joint Research Centre European Commission, Future bottlenecks in the Information Society, Report to the European Parliament, Committee on Industry, External Trade, Research and Energy (ITRE), Joint Research June 2001, Sevilla.

[30] See IPSE Report, ibid., p.49.

[31] An obvious example are law enforcement regulations on mandatory retention of traffic data which have a direct and serious impact on business activities. There is presently no 'interface' between both boundaries to anticipate the impact of those regulations on both sides (law enforcement and business).

[32] See for instance in the field of regulation for environment protection: http://www.epa.gov/ttn/atw/mactstra.pdf

[33] One of the key roles of Computer Emergency Response Teams (CERT's) is to identify, evaluate, provide advice and notify about serious computer network threats and vulnerabilities which could harm the confidentiality, integrity or availability of organisations' network data and/or services.

[34] Alerts, advisories and updates to provide accurate, timely and trusted privacy information would be distributed through privacy bulletins.

[35] See Draft Recommendation on online alternative dispute resolution (ODR), United Nations Centre for Trade Facilitation and Electronic Business (UN/CEFACT), 6 June 2002, http://www.e-global.es/arbitration/papersadr/Legal_Group_UNCEFACT_ODR.doc ; see also: http://www.e-global.es/arbitration/papersadr/green_paper_eu.pdf

[36] BENNETT, C.J., The Data Protection Authority: regulator, ombudsman, regulator or campaigner?, presentation for the International Conference of Data Protection Commissioners, Cardiff, September 9-11, 2002, http://web.uvic.ca/polisci/bennett ; BENNETT, C.J., and RAAB, Ch., The Governance of Privacy: policy instruments in global perspective, Ashgate Press, Forthcoming, January 2003.

[37] Privacy and Identity in the Information Society: Systemic Risks, Brussels, 5-6 February 2002, organised by the Institute for the Protection and Security of the Citizen (IPSC) of the European Commission's Joint Research Centre (JRC), http://dsa-isis.jrc.it/Privacy/index.html.

[38]Conference on the review of the EU Directive 95/46 EC held in Brussels on 30 September - 1 October 2002, http://www.europa.eu.int/comm/internal_market/en/dataprot/lawreport/programme_en.htm .

[39] Cases related to telephone tapping are: Klass v. Germany, ECHR, 6 September 1978; Huvig v. France, ECHR, 20 April 1990; Niemietz v. Germany, ECHR, 23 November 1992; Halford v. U.K., ECHR, 25 June 1997; Lambert v. France, ECHR, 24 August 1998 Rotaru v. Romania, ECHR, 4 May 2000; Amann v. Switzerland, ECHR, 16 February 2000, to be consulted at: http://www.echr.coe.int/Hudoc.htm.

[40]Kruslin v. France, ECHR, 24 April 1990, to be consulted at: http://www.echr.coe.int/Hudoc.htm.

[41] One of the conditions ruled in article 8 par.2 of the European Convention on Human Rights to tolerate privacy intrusions for law enforcement purposes is that the intrusion is 'in accordance' with the law.

[42] Malone v. U.K., ECHR, 2 August 1984, 87, to be consulted at: http://www.echr.coe.int/Hudoc.htm

[43] Any reasonable effort to ensure that a parent receives notice of the operator's personal information collection, use and disclosure practices, and authorizes the collection, use and disclosure, as applicable, of

personal information and the subsequent use of that information before that information is collected from the child. (Section 1302 (9) COPPA)

[44] The Internet Content Rating Association is an international, independent organization that empowers the public, especially parents, to make informed decisions about electronic media by means of the open and objective labelling of content. http://www.icra.org/_en/about. By analogy parents could be given the possibility to disallow access to web sites based on the objective information declared in the privacy policy and the parents' subjective privacy preferences. (Link with P3P) . http://www.microsoft.com/security/articles/safe_harbor.asp ; Kids Passport is a parental consent service used by the .NET Passport service and some .NET Passport participating sites. It allows parents to give parental consent for the collection, use and sharing of children's (ages 12 and under) personal information online. http://www.passport.net/consumer/kidsprivacypolicy.asp?lc=1033

[45] In the Dutch Data Protection Law (article 5) children are defined as minors younger than 16. Their protection is especially mentioned. http://www.cbpweb.nl/asp/CBPPrint.asp

[46] See http://www.ftc.gov/ogc/coppa1.htm ; COPPA defines children as those younger than 13 years of age. Compare with the Dutch Data Protection Law (article 5) in which children are defined as minors younger than 16. Their protection is especially mentioned. http://www.cbpweb.nl/asp/CBPPrint.asp .

[47] Special attention should be paid at the objectives of the SAFT project which are twofold: gaining knowledge on risk behaviour and information needs of children, their parents, educators and create an awareness campaign. The Consortium of the SAFT project consists of seven partners from five countries (Norway, Denmark, Iceland, Sweden and Ireland). Online awareness programs have been developed, e.g. http://www.consumerfed.org/internet_brochure.html , http://www.consumerfed.org/internet_brochure1.html , http://wwwkids.mcafee.com/guardnet/adultguide.asp . The "Guard Your Net" program heightens awareness of Internet Safety & Privacy issues by providing adequate information to parents, children, teachers and guardians.

[48] e.g. the use of digital certificates reduces the ever recurring need to provide basic evidence of identity (date of birth, address,etc.) and guarantees confidentiality of communications through encryption of messages.

[49] The privacy issues listed below are extensively discussed in: The Office of the Federal Privacy Commissioner, Privacy and Public Key Infrastructure: Guidelines for Agencies using PKI to communicate or transact with individuals, http://www.privacy.gov.au/government/guidelines; International Working Group on Data Protection in Telecommunications, Working Paper on data protection aspects of digital certificates and public-key infrastructures, 28 August 2001, Berlin, http://www.datenschutz-berlin.de/doc/int/iwgdpt/pubkey_e.htm.

CLARKE, R., Privacy requirements of PKI, paper presented at the IIR IT Security Conference, Canberra, 14 March 2000, http://www.anu.edu.au/people/Roger.Clarke/DV/PKI2000.html and CLARKE, R., PKI position statement, 6 May 1998, http://www.anu.edu.au/people/Roger.Clarke/DV/PKIPosn.html

[50] Directive 1999/93/EC if 13 December 1999 on a Community framework for electronic signatures, O.J. L 13/12, 19.01.2000.

[51] See e.g. the Guidelines developed by the Office of the Federal Privacy Commissioner http://www.privacy.gov.au/government/guidelines

[52] Examples of DRM systems are: http://www.perimele.com; http://www.contentguard.com ; http://www.macrovision.com ; http://www.midbartech.com/cactus.html ; http://www.microsoft.com/presspass/features/2002/jul02/0724palladiumwp.asp ; see also http://www.idrm.org IDRM is an IRTF (Internet Research Task Force) Research Group formed to research issue and technologies relating to Digital Rights Management (DRM) on the Internet.

[53] See KOELMAN K., and HELBERGER N., Protection of Technological measures, Copyright and Electronic Commerce (ed. Hugenholtz P.Bernt, ISBN 90-411-9785-0, Kluwer International, 2000).

[54] See http://www.epic.org/privacy/drm/.

[55] This issue is analysed in BYGRAVE, Lee A., and KOELMAN, Kamiel J., Privacy, Data Protection and Copyright: their interaction in the context of electronic copyright management systems, Copyright and Electronic Commerce (ed. Hugenholtz P. Bernt, ISBN 90-411-9785-0, Kluwer Law International, 2000).

[56] KORBA, L., and KENNY, S., Towards meeting the privacy challenge: adapting DRM, 2002 ACM Workshop on DRM,Washington, 18 November 2002, http://www.crypto.Stanford.edu/DRM2002/progr.html .

This paper examines the prospect of adapting systems designed for Digital Rights Management for the purpose of Privacy Rights Management for EU application.

[57] For example : http://www.againsttcpa.com; the homepage of the Trusted Computing Platform is http://www.trustedcomputing.org

[58]Article 6 of Directive 2001/29/EC of 22 May 2002, (O.J. L 167/10 of 22 June 2001), introduces a legal protection for "technological measures" defined as "any technology, device that is designed to prevent or restrict acts, in respect of works, which are not authorized by the right holder of any copyright provided for by law." Article 7 of the Directive also introduces a legal protection of the so called "rights management information" which are defined as 'any information provided by rightholders which identifies the work, the author or any other right holder, or information about the terms and conditions of use of the work, and any numbers or codes that represent such information.'

[59] Recital 57 of Directive 2001/29 of 22 June 2001, O.J. L 167/10.

[60]Art.29 Data Protection Working Party, Opinion 2/2002 adopted on 30 May 2002 on the use of unique identifiers in telecommunication terminal equipments: the example of IPv6, http://www.europa.eu.int/comm/internal_market/en/dataprot/wpdocs ; DINANT, J.M., Les risques majeurs de IPv6 pour la protection des données à caractère personnel, Droit et Nouvelles Technologies, http://www.droit-technologie.org. . For another example of privacy concerns regarding the use of unique identifiers, see INTEL' s unique Processor Serial Number (PSN), http://www.bigbrotherinside.org/#notenough , http://www.intel.com/support/processors/pentiumiii/psqa.htm

[61] In this respect the Working party "regrets that it has not been consulted prior to the adoption of the communication and it expresses the wish to be involved in the coming works taking place on IPv6 at European level.", Opinion 2/2002 adopted on 30 May 2002 on the use of unique identifiers in telecommunication terminal equipments: the example of IPv6, http://www.europa.eu.int/comm/internal_market/en/dataprot/wpdocs

[62] Art. 29 Data Protection Working Party, First orientations concerning on-line authentication services, 2 July 2002, http://www.europa.eu.int/comm/internal_market/en/dataprot/wpdocs

[63] TRUCHE P., GAUGERE J.P., FLICHY P., Administration électronique et protection des données personnelles, Livre Blanc, Paris, 2002.

[64] European Convention for the Protection of Human Rights and Fundamental Freedoms, Council of Europe, 4 November 1950, http://conventions.coe.int/Treaty.

[65] For more details see privacy and human rights 2002, EPIC and Privacy International, http://www.privacyinternational.org/survey/phr2002/phr2002-part1.pdf

[66] The appropriateness of further legal action on this topic is dealt with in the section III.1.2. Screening the EU Directives from a technological perspective; opinion of the Data Protection WP29 on mandatory retention of traffic data, http://www.europa.eu.int/comm/internal_market/en/dataprot/wpdocs/index.htm ; more about this issue: GOEMANS C., and DUMORTIER J., Mandatory retention of traffic data: possible impact on privacy and on-line anonymity, in Anonymity on the Internet, Asser series, (in press).

[67] A list of law enforcement technologies can be found at: http://www.privacyinternational.org/survey/phr2002/phr2002-part1.pdf ; See also http://www.lawenforcementtechnologies.com

[68] More about the TIA system is explained at http://www.darpa.mil/Iao/TIASystems.htm .

[69] See the excellent report of the IPTS, Security and Privacy for the Citizen in the Post-September 11 Digital Age : A Prospective Overview, European Commission, Joint Research Centre, July 2003, http://fiste.jrc.es/pages/detail.cfm?prs=1118

[70] Canadian Privacy Impact Assessment Policy: http://www.tbs-sct.gc.ca/pubs_pol/ciopubs/pia-pefr/paip-pefr_e.html and http://www.privcom.gc.ca/media/nr-c/02_05_b_020424_e.asp ;.

[71]Privacy enhancing technologies are generally divided in two main categories, namely Privacy enhancing technologies used to prevent or reduce identification and/or Privacy enhancing technologies used to prevent unlawful processing of personal data. For an inventory of Privacy enhancing technologies: http://www.epic.org/privacy/tools.html. Working party on Information Security and Privacy, OECD, Inventory of Privacy Enhancing Technologies, 7 January 2002, DSTI/ICCP/REG (2001)1/FINAL, http://www.oecd.org/EN/home/0,,EN-home-43-nodirectorate-no-no-no-13,00.html .

[72] Discussions held at the technical Privacy enhancing technologies workshop, Conference on the review of Directive 85/84, Brussels, 28-29 September 2002.

[73] Platform for Privacy Preferences, developed by World Wide Web Consortium (W3C), that is designed to give users more control over their personal data by allowing P3P enabled browsers and servers to analyse privacy 'policies'; see http://www.w3.org/P3P

[74] BITS, Financial services roundtable, Position paper W3C Workshop on the future of P3P, November 12-13? 2002Dulles Virginia, USA.

[75] CRANOR Lorrie Faith and REIDENBERG Joel R.,"Can user agents accurately represent privacy notices?", paper presented at TPRC2002, http://intel.si.unich.edu/tprc/archive-search-abstract.cfm?PaperID=65.

[76] In Belgium, a new provision, inserted in the text of a law of 21 March 1991 on the reform of certain economic public companies gives power to the King (i.e. the Federal Government) to fully or partly forbid the rendering of telecommunication services which make impossible or could hinder the identification of the user or the interception of telecommunications by law enforcement agencies. The new law opens, in other words, the possibility to publish a Royal Decree that simply forbids offering anonymity services.

[77] Institute for Prospective Technological Studies Seville, Joint Research Centre European Commission, Future bottlenecks in the Information Society, Report to the European Parliament, Committee on Industry, External Trade, Research and Energy (ITRE), Joint Research June 2001, Sevilla.

[78] The concept of pseudonymity refers originally to the context of copyright law, but is used in many other contexts in the digital world.

[79] BOGDANOWIVZ, M., and BESLAY, L., Cyber-security and the future of identity, IPTS report, September 2002.

[80] BOGDANOWICZ, M. and BESLAY, L., ibid.

[81] Examples of Identity Management (web access) software are IBM Tivoli's Policy Director (www.tivoli.com), Netegrity's SiteMinder (www.netegrity.com), Entegrity's AssureAccess (www. entegrity.com), RSA Security's ClearTrust (www.rsasecurity.com), Oblix's NetPoint (www.oblix.com), Baltimore Technologies's SelectAccess (www.baltimoretechnologies.com) or Entrust's GetAccess (www.entrust.com); see also: http://www.bitpipe.com .

[82] E.g. PrivaSeek, Yenta.com and others.

[83] International Working Group on Data Protection in Telecommunications, Common Position on Infomediaries, 4-5 May 2000, Rethimon, http://datenschutz.berlin.de/doc/int/ingdpt/find_en.htm.

[84] See International Working Group on Data Protection in Telecommunications, ibid.

[85] TRUCHE P., GAUGERE J.P., FLICHY P., Administration électronique et protection des données personnelles, Livre Blanc, Paris, 2002; VERSMISSEN J.A.G., and DE HEUIJ A.C.M., Electronic government and privacy, protection of personal data in the information structure of the government, College Bescherming Persoonsgegevens, The Hague, July 2002, http://www.cbpweb.nl.

[86] This is one of the objectives of the European « PRIME » project ; see http://www.prime-project.eu.org/.

Security and Privacy in Advanced Networking Technologies
B. Jerman-Blažic et al. (Eds.)
IOS Press, 2004

213

Privacy-Enhancing Technologies

Vanja SENIČAR, Tomaž KLOBUČAR, Borka JERMAN-BLAŽIČ
Jožef Stefan Institute,
Jamova 39, 1001 Ljubljana, Slovenia

Abstract. In this paper we discuss privacy threats on the Internet and possible technical solutions to this problem. Examples of privacy threats in the communication networks are identity disclosure, linking data traffic with identity, location disclosure in connection with data content transfer, user profile disclosure or data disclosure itself. Identifying the threats and the technology that may be used for protection can provide satisfactory protection of privacy over general networks that are building today the information infrastructure. In general these technologies are known as Privacy-Enhancing Technologies. This article analyses some of the key Privacy-Enhancing Technologies, such as remailers or anonymous communication systems, and provides view in the projects developing these technologies.

Introduction

In today's society, computers have penetrated almost in all parts of our lives. Nearly every daily routine is carried out either through or with the help of the computers. Everywhere we use information services, we leave traces making it possible for anybody interested enough to collect, organise and analyse our personal data. The nature of on-line business and e-commerce led over the Web, where personal information is transferred in digital form, has led to the situation where privacy is threatened every day. The lack of privacy on the Web makes us susceptible to many abuses, which are now starting to be better understood and well publicised. There are many good reasons to be concerned about privacy on the Web and on the communication networks. Possibilities range from distaste for targeted, junk e-mail to the desire for search of certain topics in private. For example, we may have a health condition that we do not wish to share with others, and there may be a wealth of information available on the Web left after a search of data related to particular health condition.

In this article, we take a look at several approaches, all with technological background and supported by legislation, that are aiming towards creation of privacy-protected services. The review is based on the on-going work in the field of privacy-enhancing technology development. The focus of the article is oriented towards last developments and implementation of technical tools and methods being developed, as we are aware, that the way to achieve trustworthiness that is required in the construction of well-designed systems is long and far from perfection and is still a subject of development.

1. What Does Privacy Mean?

There exist many definitions of privacy in the literature. Ross Anderson defines privacy as "ability and/or right to protect our personal secrets, the ability and/or right to prevent invading our personal space" [1]. Probably the most often used definition is the one by Alan Westin, i.e. privacy is the right of individuals to determine for themselves when, how, and to what extent information about them is communicated to others [2]. A person has privacy when two factors are in place; first, she must have ability to control information about herself, and second, she must exercise that control consistent with her values. The first factor goes to the existence of choice — the legal power to control the release of information — not how pleasant the choice is. In the commercial world, people almost always have the ability to control information about them. If we exclude pure commercial transactions, they can decide absolutely who is entitled to receive information about them. Exercising control of information — the second factor that delivers privacy — is difficult to be achieved. Many users, just browsing over the Internet or receiving unconsolidated mail, are unaware of how the Information Economy works and that they are unintentionally a part of it. Information about particular user behaviour is collected without user awareness. Good user education about the threats of the new world can help them to understand what is happening on the net and how personal data could be abused. There are users or consumers that have the highest sensitivity to disclosure of information. However, this is not always of big help to them as companies still rarely offer in their services an appropriate range of information practices regarding privacy protection to them. These unsatisfactory choices make the second factor in privacy protection hard to be achieved. Other users or consumers of information may have a higher tolerance for information sharing or they may have senses of privacy that point toward information that are not yet touched by commerce. Their privacy may be entirely unaffected by even the broadest commercial information sharing. Good example where information must be protected is medical privacy [3].

There is no question that protection of privacy in the commercial world using electronic way of doing business is hard. But it is also important to note, that besides commerce there is another big player in the information highways that may be considered as potential data abuser – the government. Protecting privacy from public administration or governmental bodies is almost impossible. For example when citizens apply for licenses or permits, fill out forms for regulators, or prepare tax returns, they do not have the power to control what provided information will be shared. They must submit information the government requires. The first factor in privacy protection — power to control personal information — is almost totally absent in the governmental context.

To identify the privacy-enhancing technology, we need first to identify privacy threats in the communication networks and afterwards we may continue with study how privacy-enhancing technologies can improve the privacy itself. Although the Internet is rapidly becoming "the" only widely accessible communication network, because of its origin and development it has not been engineered to preserve certain types of privacy. Simone Fischer-Hübner identifies four ways that privacy protection can be achieved [4, 5]:

- Protection by government laws;
- Self-regulation for fair information practise by codes of conduct promoted by businesses;
- Privacy education of consumers and IT professionals;
- Protection by privacy-enhancing technologies.

We will discuss in this article just the last way.

2. Threats

To get a better look at the privacy-enhancing technologies that enable policy implementation and protection of data as stated usually in legislative acts, it is necessary to look at the privacy threats in the communication network, such as identity disclosure, linkability of data, observability of data, location disclosure in mobile networks, or data disclosure. In this section we provide a brief overview of specific threats to privacy that arise in the Internet. We will use here some terms as defined in Common Criteria [6]: anonymity, pseudonymity, unlinkability and unobservability. Anonymity ensures that a subject may use a resource or service without disclosing its user identity. Pseudonymity ensures that a user may use a resource or service without disclosing its identity, but can still be accountable for that use. Unlinkability ensures that a user may make multiple uses of resources or services without others being able to link these uses together. The requirements for unlinkability are intended to protect the user identity against the use of profiling of the operations. Hiding the relationship between different invocations of a service or access of a resource will prevent this kind of information gathering. Unlinkability differs from pseudonymity that, although in pseudonymity the user is also not known, relations between different actions can be provided. Unobservability ensures that a user may use a resource or service without others, especially third parties, being able to observe that the resource or service is being used. In this case, the intent is to hide the use of a resource or service, rather than to hide the user's identity. Other users should not be able to observe that a service, for example a learning service, is being used.

2.1 HTTP Chattering

The most often used service on the communication networks is web browsing enabled by the HTTP protocol. Unless a user takes deliberate steps to hide her personal data, she is considered to be anonymous during a web browsing session. The underpinning web protocol for a browsing session, i.e. HTTP, relies upon the exchange of personally traceable information between the remote user and the host web server. To establish a web session a set of default data variables are transmitted from the user's machine to the remote server. By default most servers log IP addresses, and HTTP chattering indicates the operating and browsing environment, as well as the URL location the user was at before loading the current web site. Thus, this information is automatically transmitted without the explicit consent (and often knowledge) of the browser. Using these IP addresses along with technology for tracing a route of TCP/IP packets, an approximate geographical location can be deduced. Because of the fact that IP addresses are unique to every node on the Internet, this information allows for individuals to be traced using ISP (Internet Service Provider) records, in cases where such effort is warranted. With the advent of IPv6, which contains much more explicit geographical positioning information in HTTP headers, this is likely to become even more of a threat to privacy. Similar considerations apply to other Internet protocols (e.g. SMTP for e-mail, or FTP for file transfer).

Hence, in the Internet there are mechanisms available to e-business administrators to identify, either by name or by IP address, a user that is visiting a site, regardless of whether the user has carried out any processing at the e-business web site or filled in any data submission forms. This identification mechanism, in addition to the web technology called a cookie, can be used to provide mechanisms for tracking, profiling and monitoring the activities of a user. A user cannot entirely disable this HTTP 'chattering' process. However, users may use anonymizing services or write browsers which will only send vital headers (not including the referrer).

2.2 Cookies and E-privacy Threats

Cookies are at the core of many e-privacy incidents. The HTTP cookie is a file mechanism that creates the opportunity for more automated interaction between a web server and a client -

it provides the remote server with a 'memory' of a user's identity. Cookie files may typically store information about a user's personal ID, recent activities at a web site, credit card details, or site password information. Cookies can also provide some automation or 'intelligence' in e-commerce applications such as 'shopping carts' and management of user preferences. Cookies are a powerful technology for enhancing web site interactivity. However, cookies are also a technology that has a number of inherent flaws that pose additional threat to personal privacy, e.g.:

Security failures: Sensitive information is often stored in cookies, which are passed openly over the Internet. The contents of a cookie are, in theory, accessible to anybody capable of intercepting the cookie on the Internet or maliciously gaining remote access to a networked computer. For that reason cookies should be encrypted when containing personal data, but a user hardly has any control over the security measures being taken with cookie file transfer and storage.

Monitoring: Many people believe that user identification via cookies is an invasion of their personal privacy. People are at liberty to enter a retail store in the physical world with anonymity and without their purchases or activities being recorded or monitored. Privacy advocates feel that the same choice for anonymity should be available during on-line browsing. Cookies may also permit a third party to investigate the activities of an individual if they have access to their computer and their cookie files.

Data Disclosure: An e-commerce site that has personal information about a user, stored via cookies, may exchange this data with other sites (for example, related business partners or sites that buy advertising space from them). This sharing of data may extend as far as cookies being synchronised for a group of businesses. This implies that personal information supplied voluntarily at one site may be used to track or identify an individual at other sites where they have never intentionally disclosed such information.

Limited control: End-users have very little control over the content and use of cookies; in fact to most users they are a totally invisible technology. Some web browsers provide the user with an option to disable cookies (i.e. to not accept them). However, this can often make some sites totally inaccessible. For those who do decide to accept cookie files there are no browser mechanisms that inform the user as to what use is being made of the cookie or what data is being stored within it.

Collecting data: One way of using cookies for collecting personal data invisibly or for assigning users a unique identifier is via links to a mechanism typically described as a Web Bug. A Web Bug is a graphic on a web page or in an e-mail message that is designed to monitor the user of the web page or reader of the e-mail message. Web Bugs are typically 'invisible' on a web site because they are usually defined as a blank image that is 1-by-1 pixels in size, and are represented as HTML image (IMG) tags. Remote third parties typically place the Web Bugs on a web site to indirectly monitor the activities of the web site users. Another use of Web Bugs is to provide an independent accounting of how many people have visited a particular web site. Web Bugs are also used to gather statistics about web browser use at different places on the Internet. Web sites that are invisibly hyperlinked (which are unconsented link diversions for instance in combination with a banner) can place cookies and collect typed keywords [7].

2.3 E-Profiling

E-profiling is the process of building databases that contain the preferences, activities and characteristics of users. It is a practice that has long been part of the off-line commercial sector, but which has developed significantly with the growth of e-commerce. It is common for the profiling databases to hold references to millions of web clients. Many e-commerce web sites (including on-line search engines) have associations with commercial information brokerage companies. These sites make use of cookies to monitor client's activities at the host site and record the data that was provided to the web server. Users' interests, browsing patterns and buying choices are stored as a profile in a database without their knowledge or consent. This profile information is used to decide which advertisements or services will be offered at the affiliated web sites. The information is typically collected and stored without a user's knowledge or, more importantly, consent. The information collected is purported to be non-personally-identifiable. However, where a user provides personal data to a web server (e.g. name and address) it is possible to correlate the data with e-mail addresses, IP addresses and demography, to create a far more personalised profile.

Organisations involved in e-profiling activities stress that these activities are in the interest of the user; providing more customised and directed services through the Web. However, many see e-profiling as a violation of basic privacy rights because data is collected and distributed without the user's consent.

2.4 Embedded Software

Besides the browser mechanisms described above, which permit collecting personal data, there are also privacy threats posed by new programming paradigms. Powerful programming languages have been developed for web-based applications, which have increased the complexity and capability of the Internet by many orders of magnitude. These languages include Java, JavaScript, XML, and Active X. They permit remote servers to run applications on a client's PC. These languages may be exploited in the commercial sector to allow an e-business to gain access to the user's personal computing environment and the data held within it. Typically users are totally unaware of the privacy risks posed by Internet enabled software applications running within their computing environment. These privacy risks are more and more significant because the Internet is becoming a widespread channel for the entertainment industry (audio, video, gambling, etc.).

3. Protecting Privacy

Privacy can be protected by measures that include proper legislation and use of privacy-enhancing technologies and mechanisms. In this section, we will give an overview of known privacy-enhancing technologies.

Several decades of legislative lobbying have yielded an impressive number of laws and regulations aimed at privacy protection, but in the eyes of most observers, these haven't stopped its erosion. As a response to the shortages of legislation as well as to general changes in the technological set-up of our societies, a new approach to the protection of personal privacy has emerged in the last couple of years. A new breed of technologies, so-called Privacy-Enhancing Technologies (PETs), has been developed to help individual users control what personal information they disclose in an on-line transaction. These technologies promise to enable individuals to take control over how their data is being collected. The goal is to restore the balance of power between the individual who wants to retain privacy and many actors in the on-line environment who want to gather personal information. The final goal of these initiatives is to make informational self-determination a practical reality and to implement emerging policy frameworks – legislation and self-regulation – aimed at minimising the occasions in which violations of privacy are attempted by restricting certain practices. Their ideal is a situation in which the individual's privacy is protected by default and individual acts of transgression can be dealt through policy framework enabled by implementation of appropriate mechanisms.

These, ideally, allow individuals to take action to protect their own privacy against frequent and unknown attempts to infringe upon it. Rather than relying on the state – or some industry association – to deal with the problem on a collective level, these technologies are designed to support action by the individual for the individual. The approach recognises that electronic communications have massively increased scope of surveillance and thus the development of the solution is aimed to remedy this situation on the same technological level: a technological fix for a technological problem.

There are many different privacy-enhancing technologies available to Internet users. Certain programs allow users to manage the cookies that web sites place on their hard drives. Others provide the ability to surf on the Internet anonymously so that advertisers cannot track a user's shopping habits. These tools provide certain privacy to the users of the Internet, so that they can take full advantage of the technology. In the following, the most important technologies and mechanisms are briefly discussed.

3.1 Encryption and Steganography

One of the oldest security mechanisms that can be used for provision of data confidentiality (data protection) is encryption. Encryption is the transformation of data into some unreadable form. Its purpose is to ensure privacy by keeping the information hidden from anyone for whom it is not intended, even those who can see the encrypted data. The reverse process of encryption is decryption, the transformation of encrypted data back into some intelligible form.

Usually, encryption is not enough. A user may also need to cover the fact that the data is encrypted. This can be done by steganography, the art of hiding signals inside other signals. This basically comes down to using necessary bits in an innocent file to store the sensitive data. This way, users not only hide the message itself, but also the fact that they are sending that message. Steganography includes a vast array of techniques for hiding messages in a variety of media [8].

3.2 Blind signatures

A blind signature scheme is a variant of the digital signature scheme, where the content of the message being signed is not revealed to the person signing it. Paper-world analogue example is a document in a closed carbon envelope. A signatory applies her signature on the envelope without seeing the document's content. Later, the document owner can open the envelope and get a signed document. The scheme was first introduced by David Chaum [9], and has had many uses since then. One can receive, for example, a timestamp of the document, without revealing the document. Probably the most known example of blind signatures use is in electronic cash schemes, e.g. in Ecash. In this case, blind signatures are used for preventing traceability of electronic money. A bank specifies a money value and applies a blind signature on a blinded electronic banknote generated by a user, without knowing its serial number.

3.3 Credentials

Whenever a user accesses an electronic service or resource, she has to show some sort of digital credential, such as a token or public key certificate, to establish either a claimed identity or the authorisations of the use. Similarly to non-electronic environment, use of different types of credentials may represent different privacy threats. Subway tickets or coins, for example, do not reveal any information about a holder, but still allow her to use the service. Equivalent digital credentials that allow their holders to prove certain certified attributes in an anonymous and unlinkable way are thus needed for privacy protection.

Today, access control decisions are too often identity based. A service provider first authenticates the user, and grants or denies access to a service or resource according to user's identity information, such as a name. An example of an identity based credential is an X.509 public key certificate which binds user's identity with her public key. A public key certificate can be seen as an identity card or passport. Such credentials pose a threat to the user's privacy, as they can be easily traced and used for linking together different uses. If the user's identity in the certificate is represented by her real name, one can easily compile user's dossier. A better solution is to use pseudonyms and different public-key certificates with pseudonyms for different services, so that different service uses can not be linked together.

In many situations, an identity may not be needed as a criterion for service access control decision. Attributes such as a role or group membership should rather be the basis for granting or denying access. X.509 Recommendation introduces attribute certificates that are more appropriate for storage of authorisation information, as they bind a set of attributes to the user's identity [10]. However, X.509 attribute certificates are linked to public key certificates. This means that the users can still be traceable unless they use different public-key certificates with pseudonyms. An attribute certificate should also not contain more attributes than necessary. For example, if an access control decision is based on user's age, only this information should be included in the credential, or revealed to a verifier. Zero-knowledge systems have developed Private Credentials that can be used for disclosure of a specific portion of the data in the credential, without revealing any other information. Private Credentials can also be presented in such a way that the verifier is left with no evidence at all of the disclosed property [11]. Blind signatures are the basis for these credentials. Camenisch and Lysyanskay describe an anonymous credential system in [12]. In this system, users can demonstrate possession of a credential as many times as necessary without involvement of the issuing organisation, and transactions carried out by the same user can not be related. The credentials also allow anonymity-preserving credential revocation, and can provide protection against credential sharing.

3.4 Trust Centres

Trust centres are needed for the realisation of certain security services on the entire IT structures. The way in which such a trust centre works is often compared with that of a notary, i.e. a neutral, non-involved body. As a rule, that body must be able to satisfy all those involved (that is, the user and any communications and business partners, and the operator of the I/C systems (information and communications systems) used if necessary) that they are doing their job correctly. The user, for instance, has faith that her true identity will remain confidential when using a pseudonym and that, if her identity is lawfully revealed, she will be informed without delay about who it will be disclosed to and why. The operator of the I/C system has faith that the user's real identity will be disclosed in defined, agreed cases of need (such as detecting abuse of power) to safeguard her legitimate interests. As well as a commercial or public trust centre (called Trusted Third Parties - TTPs), the job of a trust centre may also be done by the Personal Trust Centre (PTC) which is under control by users, e.g. 'intelligent' security tokens such as smart cards. The tasks, which a trust centre may perform, fall into four main areas:

- Key management: Generating and revoking keys, storing (public) keys, distributing and deleting/disabling keys
- Certification services: Issuing certificates for public keys, personalising keys: allocating them to users (identity or pseudonym), registering users (confirming identity and allocating pseudonyms if necessary), personalising PTCs, certifying/admitting PTCs
- Trustee functions: Acting as trustees for lodging, personal data, e.g. ID data, keys for data security, etc.
- Server functions: Providing information to the security infrastructure on-line, such as lists of (public) user keys, authenticating information, time stamps, and warnings of security-critical events.

Ensuring that trust centres are as trustworthy as possible requires a considerable amount of reliability and specialist knowledge. The neutrality and independence that a trust centre has to have must not be compromised by conflicts of interest; such problems may arise as the result of inappropriate combinations of a number of the (sub)tasks or roles above. It is not recommended that tasks, where a high level of security is required, are carried out by a single trust centre; rather, they should be spread amongst them. Trust centres are expected to work in accordance with a published policy, which states their tasks, and security requirements are clear and are as user-verifiable as possible. Not all tasks of a trust centre above are suitable for minimising the data abuse and hence to help ensure individual privacy, for example generating keys and holding public keys with identities. Examples of trust centres are First Virtual and public-key certification authorities.

3.5 Identity Protector

According to the definition of the Netherlands Data Protection Authority an identity protector can be seen as a system element that controls the exchange of the identity between the other system elements. [13]. One of its most important functions is to convert a user's actual identity into a pseudo-identity — an alternate (digital) identity that the user may adopt when using the system. Pseudo-identities may be persistent (lasting over a period of time) or used only once.

In the privacy-protective systems of the future, the identity protector would most likely take the form of a smart card controlled by the user, which could generate pseudo-identities as desired. An identity protector performs the following functions [13]:

- Generates pseudo-identities as needed;
- Converts pseudo-identities into actual identities (as desired);
- Combats fraud and misuse of the system.

Since the identity protector is under the control of the user, she can set it to perform a variety of functions such as revealing one's actual identity to certain service providers but not to others. When an identity protector is integrated into an information system, the user may use the services or engage in transactions anonymously, thereby elevating privacy to an all-time high.

3.6 Cookie Management Tools

Another tool for protecting user's privacy is dealing with cookies. As we already specified in the first part of this article, a cookie is a data file that sits on user's computer hard disk. It is placed there by a remote web server that the user has visited using a web browser (e.g. Netscape Communicator, MS Internet Explorer). Whilst being a very powerful technology for enhancing web site interactivity, cookies are a technology that can be misused in ways that present an abuse of personal privacy. Sensitive information is often stored in cookie files (passwords, credit card details), which passes openly over the Internet, and cookies can be used to trace the user in the Web. The contents of the cookie would be, in theory, accessible to anybody capable of intercepting the cookie on the Internet or maliciously gaining remote access to the user's computer. Cookie files should be encrypted when containing personal data, but as a client, the user has no control over the security measures being taken with cookie file transfer and storage.

One of the remedies can be disabling HTTP Cookie Files. HTTP cookie files are one of the major privacy threats associated with web-based browsing or interactions. As a result a number of organisations (both commercial and public) have issued tools and mechanisms for managing cookies. Cookie management software allows cookies to be deleted routinely. These tools allow a user to:

- Disable cookie files - preventing cookie files being stored on your machine;
- Selectively accept cookie files - allowing a user choice of who they accept cookie files from;
- View Cookie files - allowing a user to search the contents of cookies and establish what information is being stored.

3.7 Remailers

Secure e-mail mechanisms such as S/MIME protocol are mainly concerned with confidentiality, authenticity and integrity of e-mail messages. In some cases, for example when communicating with a doctor who is a specialist in infectious diseases, such as AIDS, this may not be sufficient. An electronic mail system that also hides communicating parties is needed. A user must be able to send an e-mail without disclosing her identity. Identity should be protected against third parties, or also against an e-mail recipient. In the last case, the recipient must be able at the same time to respond without knowing the identity of the originator of the message.

There are several re-mailer services running on the Internet that aim at providing anonymity. The simplest are the programs that accept mail, strip off information that would identify the origin of the message, and resend the mail to the designated recipient. This scheme alone, however, is insecure if the anonymous re-mailer becomes compromised (or if the remailer was set up by an untrustworthy party in the first place). Whoever controls the remailer will have access to the identities of senders and recipients. The best known example of such, so-called Type 0 remailer was the anon.penet.fi service. Similar role play web-based e-mail servers that allow users to set up anonymous e-mail accounts. Each anonymous account is assigned a unique ID so that recipients can respond to an anonymous e-mail message.

More secure remailers are based on Chaum's mix networks [14]. In mix networks a message passes through a number of mix nodes (mixes). Each mix node collects a number of messages, mixes them, and sends to other nodes. Chaining remailers won't help a user much without encryption. Everyone can read the entire message and see who is sending what. If the user is applying, for example, public-key cryptography on her messages to the remailers, that is no longer possible. Each remailer will only know where the message came from and where it is going to, but not who else are in the chain or what the actual message is. An attacker eavesdropping the network will also not be able to find the correspondence between input and output messages. Flaws of Type 0 remailers were addressed by contributors to the Cypherpunk mailing list (Cypherpunk anonymous remailer). Later, Cottrell implemented the Mixmaster system or Type II remailer, which introduced constant length message to prevent passive correlation attacks, improved message reordering and provided defenses against replay attacks. [15] The latest, Type III re-mailer Mixminion maintains Mixmaster's flexibility while addressing some flaws and adding new features, such as single use reply blocks, exit policies, integrated directory servers, dummy traffic and key rotation. [16].

3.8 Anonymisers on the Web

Anonymising services are needed on the Web to enable users browsing the Internet anonymously and without fear of losing privacy. Many such services have been proposed so far, for example anonymous web proxies. Besides browsing, anonymity is sometimes desirable also for documents publishing. A user should have a possibility to store a document on the server without disclosing her identity. Similar requirements apply for web servers. Sometimes, users should not be able to find out exactly from which web server the document was retrieved.

The principle of anonymous proxies is simple - an account is created with a 'trusted' Internet Service Provider. Number of pseudonyms or 'aliases' can be created, which the user can use whilst carrying out transactions on the Web. The weakness of those systems is establishing the credibility and trust of the third party provider.

Under anonymizers we can also understand proxies and firewalls. Proxies and firewalls are barriers between a computer and the Internet. Communications are only allowed under certain circumstances and certain types of communications can be blocked entirely.

Services that enable anonymous publishing are not that numerous. An example of a system where publishers can put their documents on the server without revealing their identities is Publius [17]. TAZ (temporary anonymous zone) servers system allows a web server where the document is published to remain anonymous at retrieval time [18].

3.8.1 Crowds

Crowds is a system for protecting user privacy while browsing the Web [19]. For example, Crowds prevents a web server that a user visits from learning information that could identify her. The system Crowds operates by grouping users into a large and geographically diverse group (crowd) that collectively issues requests on behalf of its members. Web servers are unable to learn the true source of a request because it is equally likely to have originated from any member of the crowd, and indeed collaborating crowd members cannot distinguish the originator of a request from a member who is merely forwarding the request on behalf of another. Crowds provides a mechanism for hiding user's identity from others while obtaining the information that she desires. A proxy running on user's local machine (or another machine you trust) executes the Crowds protocol on her behalf. Participating in a Crowd simply requires that the user starts this proxy and sets her browser to use it as the browser's proxy.

3.9 Anonymous communication systems

Apart from the e-mail and World Wide Web, anonymous communication is also required in other environments. An example of a general purpose infrastructure for private communication over public networks is Onion routing [20]. Onion routing is based on Chaum's mix networks, and uses a distributed network of onion routers (mixes) to provide anonymous connections that are resistant to eavesdropping and traffic analysis. Onion routers are under control of different administrative domains so that no single router can breach user's privacy. The anonymous connections can be used anywhere a socket connection can be used. In distinction to the mix-based remailers described in Section 3.7, where a user chooses her route freely from all mixes, an application proxy selects in Onion routing a suitable route (chain of onion-routers). Onion routing received its name from the layered packets that look like an onion. The packet specifies properties of the connection at each point along the route, e.g. cryptographic control information. Each onion router "peels of" a surface layer of the packet and forwards the rest to the next router from the route. The Onion router prototype network (http://www.onion-router.net/) is off-line as of January 2000. According to that web page, testing of the next generation system is pending.

Existing P2P networks offer different degrees of anonymity to their users. Freenet, a fully decentralized P2P file-sharing system, for example, aims at permitting publication, replication, and retrieval of data while protecting the anonymity of both authors and readers [21]. As in most cases explained so far, privacy in Freenet is achieved by a variation of mix networks. Each Freenet participant runs a node that provides the network some storage space, and each node in the message-travel chain knows only about its immediate neighbours. Freenet offers lower degree of anonymity than Type II or Type III remailers as users can not control the routing of data (select a chain of nodes).

4. Projects

There are several on going projects that are researching and developing privacy-enhancing technologies. We are presenting here briefly the most known.

4.1 P3P

P3P (Platform for Privacy Preferences) [22], developed by W3C, is a standard, designed to provide Internet users with a clear understanding of how personal information will be used by a particular web site. The P3P is designed to enable users to communicate simply and automatically. It is based on a web site's stated privacy policies, and how they compare with the user's own policy preferences. The P3P specification brings ease and regularity to web users wishing to decide whether and under what circumstances to disclose personal information. User's confidence in on-line transactions increases as they are presented with meaningful information and choices about web site privacy practices. P3P does not set minimum standards for privacy, nor can it monitor whether sites adhere to there own stated procedures. It just enables to the user good view on the possibilities of its privacy protection on the Web. Addressing all of the complied, fundamental issues surrounding privacy on the Web require appropriate combination of technology, a legal framework and self-regulatory practices to be applied all together.

Despite its original and far-reaching plans, P3P 1.0 is in its essentials a language for privacy policies. Although P3P developers, and some supporters, rightly and honestly acknowledge the limitation of P3P, some vendors have made grandiose promises about what P3P can do to solve on-line privacy problems. Whether P3P will be adopted, remains to be seen. As technologies like P3P comes and goes, it is necessary for these tools to be evaluated critically.

Here are some references to P3P implementations, utilities and services that have been developed so far:.

- Netscape 7.0 introduces two new privacy-related features based on the P3P standard:
    - Know privacy practices of web sites with the P3P Privacy Policy;
    - Viewer is informed about cookies with P3P Cookie Management.
- JRC P3P Proxy Version 2.0 acts as an intermediary agent (the middleman) that controls access to remote web servers dependent upon the privacy preferences a user has specified. A new version has now been released with improved speed, user interfaces, identity management, special P3P menu integrated into every HTML page, and a complete toolkit for exploring P3P. There is also a local version of agent, which does not require a separate proxy server and can work in conjunction with a company proxy.
- Internet Explorer 6 helps protect user privacy on the Web by giving the user more control over cookies and more information on a web site's privacy policy.
- The AT&T Privacy Bird will help Internet users stay informed about how information they provide to web sites could be used. The tool automatically searches for privacy policies at every web site a user visits. The user can tell the software about her privacy concerns, and it will tell her whether each site's policies match her personal privacy preferences by using bird icons.

4.2 RAPID

The RAPID (Roadmap for Advanced Research in Privacy and Identity Management) project from the 5. Framework Programme of European Union has developed a strategic roadmap for applied research in the area of privacy and identity management [23]. The research topics identified within RAPID were grouped within two areas, technology and non-technology research topics. In this section, we will briefly present the essential technical research challenges related to privacy-enhancing technologies that have been identified in the Multiple and Dependable Identity Management (MIM), Infrastructure and Enterprise areas. The timeframes within the RAPID roadmap are short-term (0-3 years), mid-term (3-5 years), and long-term (5-10 years).

The most essential research issues in the multiple and dependable identity management area are focused on providing multiple and dependable identities life-cycle management capabilities to end users. Privacy-enhancing technologies related to this area thus need to be implemented on the user's side. In short-term users should be able to efficiently obtain and create identities, and revoke them when they become obsolete or not applicable anymore. Development of user-side architecture for multiple identity management is needed, as well as prevention of identity proliferation and identity theft. Management of user profiles is also an essential research issue. This research topic includes as well personal mobile identity management devices and media, integration of MIM with other services, e.g. authentication services, and distributed registration and certification authorities.

For efficient privacy protection some of the mechanisms need to be integrated into or supported by the infrastructure. Identified essential infrastructure research topics are address privacy, location privacy, and service access privacy. All of them are envisaged as short-term topics. A number of privacy-enhancing technologies that support these functions are already available and were described in Section 3. However, the technologies are not yet mature enough, user friendly and widely deployed. With regard to address privacy more research is needed in new anonymising routers, dynamic IP address allocation and privacy preserving ad hoc networking. Topics for location privacy are location logging by mobile operators, location based services, data minimisation, and need-to-know principle in pervasive computing. Anonymous access to the services shall be enabled by more advanced anonymity proxies and development of techniques for privacy policy negotiation. Among identified medium-term topics we can find anonymous credential schemes and anonymous communication and its relation to the needs of billing and charging

The third area covers research issues of privacy and identity management on the enterprise side. Essential short-term research challenges for enterprise service systems comprise federated and end-to-end identity management systems, PET functions in privacy friendly access control, and development of identity management and privacy ontology and policies.

4.3 PISA

The Privacy Incorporated Software Agent (PISA) project supported by the European Union aimed at demonstrating privacy-enhancing technology as a secure technical solution to protect the privacy of citizens when they are using intelligent agents in e-commerce or m-commerce applications [24]. The developed solution takes into account the EC Directives on privacy.

An intelligent software agent is defined as a piece of software that is capable of performing tasks autonomously on behalf of its user. The PISA agent protects privacy in two ways. First, it protects user's personal data that is stored within the agent, and controls the internal processing of these data and the exchange of the data with authorized users and agents according to the applied legislation. Second, the agent also protects the data about others that it collects. The whole solution, as well as an overview of privacy-enhancing technologies, is described in the project deliverable Handbook of privacy and privacy-enhancing technologies for ISATs [25].

4.4 GUIDES

The EU GUIDES project (principal partners Joint Research Centre and Price Waterhouse Coopers) was funded by DG Enterprise and completed in April 2002. The aim of the twelve-month GUIDES project was to develop a set of guidelines on a European level for assessing the compliance of Internet-based data processing technologies to the EU Data Protection Directive (95/46/EC) - DPD.

The GUIDES project used case study analysis of typical web information processing systems in the areas of e-commerce, health and government in order to characterise the Internet-based data handling practices, particularly those pertinent to personal data. Subsequently, these practices were assessed within the context of the principles for privacy protection defined within the DPDs. The mechanisms that are being used to exploit personal and private data were analysed and categorised in relation to the EU DPD. In addition, the mechanisms, that are being developed or proposed to support the implementation of privacy principles, particularly technologies such as P3P, digital signatures and anonymous agents, were assessed to identify how closely they satisfy the requirements of the DPDs. The outcome of the project was the production of a set of guidelines that clearly elaborate on the privacy issues relevant to current data processing practices based upon Internet and WWW technologies.

The GUIDES set of guidelines is advisory only. The guidelines are drafted in a manner that is technology-neutral and gives an e-business a 'quick guide' to helpful information about DPD 95/46/EC. The purpose of the guidelines is to assist an e-business in Europe to adopt best privacy practice and comply with DPD in respect to their web sites and related back-offices. Whilst there are many valid privacy concerns for other Internet services and Internet service providers (that result from their role as intermediaries) these are considered outside the scope of GUIDES. The GUIDES set of guidelines could be used as a template for other sector specific guidelines (e.g. e-payment, e-health, HRM applications, on-line advertising etc.).

The final set of guidelines has been defined in consultation with representatives from the standardisation, industry, government and academic privacy field. The main Guides document contains an introductory section, a section on applicability issues of DPD 95/46/EC and the main section with the e-commerce guidelines on DPD 95/46/EC. The guidelines section consists of best practices illustrated with examples (using fictional entities).

During the latter stages of the GUIDES project the European Commission was formulating the new legislation covering the e-commerce sector and telecom sectors. Unfortunately it was not possible to address it within GUIDES, and perhaps a useful follow-up to GUIDES would be to integrate the new legislative issues within the guidelines [26].

5. Conclusion

Over the last 35 years, legislation has not been able to stop the continuous erosion of privacy, and PETs, more recently, have shown to be useful only in very narrow domains. The failure of the first PETs developed specifically to prevent invasions of privacy that occur even more frequently on-line, shows that we have barely begun to integrate the Internet into everyday life. There is little indication that the boundary between the private and the public is not blurring. It will still take a lot of effort to develop the kind of PETs that will suffice the needs of users and protect their privacy on the Internet.

Acknowledgment

This paper is based on a paper previously published in Computer Standards & Interfaces, Vol. 25, 2003, pages 147-158, under the title "Privacy-Enhancing Technologies – approaches and development". The paper, published with permission from Elsevier Science, incorporates major revisions and updates to the material from the original paper.

References

[1] Ross Anderson, Security Engineering: a guide to building dependable distributed system, Wiley Computer Publishing, 612 pp., 2001.
[2] Alan F. Westin: Privacy and Freedom. Atheneum, New York NY, 1967.
[3] Matt Curtin, Developing Trust: Online Privacy and Security, Apress, 2002.
[4] Simone Fischer-Hübner in D.Thomas, Privacy and security at risk in the Global Information Society, B.Loade (Eds.): Cybercrime. – London: Routledge, 2000.
[5] Simone Fischer-Hübner, Privacy-Enhancing Technologies (PET), Course description, Karlstad University Division for Information Technology 2001.
[6] Common Criteria for Information Technology Security Evaluation, Part 2: Security functional requirements, August 1999, Version 2.1.

[7] Jean-Marc Dinant, ESPRIT Project 27028, Electronic Commerce Legal Issues Platform, 1999.

[8] Duncan Sellars, An introduction to Steganography, Computer Science Department, 1999.

[9] David Chaum, Blind signatures for untraceable payments, Advances in Cryptology - Crypto '82, Springer-Verlag (1983), 199-203.

[10] ITU-T Recommendation X.509 | ISO/IEC 9594-8: Information Technology. Open Systems Interconnection. The Directory: Public-Key and Attribute Certificate Frameworks.

[11] Zero-Knowledge Systems, Inc. Private Credentials, 2000.

[12] Jan Camenisch, Anna Lysyanskaya. Efficient Non-transferable Anonymous Multi-show Credential System with Optional Anonymity Revocation. In Advances in Cryptology - Eurocrypt 2001, Vol. 2045 of LNCS, pages 93-118, Springer Verlag, 2001.

[13] Ronald Hes, John Borking (Eds.), Privacy-Enhancing Technologies: The path to anonymity. Revised edition. Achtergrondstudies en Verkenningen 11. Registratiekamer The Hague, August 2000.

[14] David Chaum, Untraceable electronic mail, return addresses and digital pseudonyms. Communications of the ACM, 24 (2): 84-88, 1981.

[15] Lance Cottrell. Mixmaster and remailer attacks, 1994. http://www.obscura.com/~loki/remailer/remailer-essay.html.

[16] George Danezis, Roger Dingledine, Nick Mathewson, Mixminion: Design of a Type III Anonymous Remailer Protocol, IEEE Security & Privacy 2003.

[17] Marc Waldman, Aviel D. Rubin, Lorrie Faith Cranor: Publius: A robust, tamper-evident, censorship-resistant, web publishing system. Proc. 9th USENIX Security Symposium, pp. 59-72, 2000.

[18] Ian Goldberg and David Wagner, "TAZ Servers and the Rewebber Network Enabling Anonymous Publishing on the World Wide Web", University of California, Berkeley, 1997.

[19] Michael K. Reiter and Aviel D. Rubin, Crowds: Anonymity for Web Transaction, AT&T Labs-Research, 1997.

[20] David M. Goldschlag, Michael G. Reed, and Paul F. Syverson: Onion Routing for Anonymous and Private Internet Connections. Communications of the ACM, vol. 42, num. 2, February 1999.

[21] Ian Clarke, Scott G. Miller, Theodore W. Hong, Oskar Sandberg, Brandon Wiley: Protecting Free Expression Online with Freenet. IEEE Internet Computing, pp. 40-49, January-February 2002.

[22] W3C, Platform for Privacy Preferences, P3P 1.0, 2002.

[23] Jan Huizenga (Ed.), Deliverable RD3.0 – Overall Roadmap 'Privacy and Identity Management', Final report, RAPID project, http://www.ra-pid.org, 2003.

[24] Privacy Incorporate Software Agent (PISA), Building a privacy guardian for the electronic age, 2000, http://www.pet-pisa.nl/pisa_org/pisa/index.html.

[25] PISA Consortium. Handbook Privacy and PET for ISATs. Deliverable D8, 2003.

[26] GUIDES Project, Final Report: Deliverable D5.2, 2002.

Security Applications

Security and Privacy in Advanced Networking Technologies
B. Jerman-Blažic et al. (Eds.)
IOS Press, 2004

Austrian Citizen Card: A Bottom-Up View

Herbert LEITOLD

A-SIT, Secure Information Technology Center – Austria

Karl C. POSCH

*IAIK, Institute for Applied Information Processing and Communications,
Graz University of Technology*

Abstract. This paper discusses several aspects of building successful e-government services. As an example, it uses the concept of the Austrian Citizen Card as a focal point. The paper briefly sketches ongoing work for implementing e-government in Austria, addresses data-protection compatible unique identification, emphasizes the importance of open standards and open interfaces by describing the security-layer interface, and finally discusses some of today's problems around implementing cryptographic hardware.

1. Introduction

This presentation uses the Austrian Citizen Card as an example for discussing problems arising around the implementation of e-government. It discusses the influence of side-channel attacks on smart cards, the fair distribution of responsibilities by introducing the security-layer interface, and by briefly sketching the organisational structure in Austria.

The "Austrian Citizen Card" ("Bürgerkarte", [1]) is a project of the Austrian government. It has been initiated by an government council end of 1999 and should enable substantial simplifications in bureaucratic procedures between offices (government to government) as well as between citizens and administration (citizen to government). The citizen card may be used as a kind of ID card in administrative procedures, processed over the Internet for instance. In technical terms, it is a signature-creation device holding the secret signature-creation data linked to the owner of the card. Data that uniquely identifies the citizen all her life, independent from the validity period of digital certificates or alike, is kept as well.

Currently, the most obvious instantiation and cost efficient implementation of this card is a smart card. But, other devices like mobile phones, USB devices, or PDAs might also be a technical means to implement the function of the citizen card. Thus, the Austrian Citizen Card is a concept and not the physical device. This concept defines requirements for the secure electronic procedures over some communication media.

In this presentation, we will mainly use smart cards as an example implementation for the citizen card, even though a mobile phone provider has as well announced to implement the citizen card functions. We will walk through several topics which are crucial for the correct and secure functioning of services where individuals need to identify themselves over the network. The overall idea is to emphasize some of the risks showing up outside the scope of pure cryptography, and to show how to cope with those risks. The topics span from the European Directive on Electronic Signatures to the vulnerability of smart cards against attacks.

Section 2 briefly sketches the Austrian e-government setup. The role of unique identification and electronic signatures is addressed, where particular attention is paid to data protection concerns. The distribution of responsibilities between the certification service provider and the general user is described in section 3. In section 4 we shed light on the vulnerability of smart cards which are typically used as signature creation devices. Finally, we draw conclusions.

2. e-Government in Austria

Austria's e-government is currently rapidly evolving. Its strategy is based on three fundamental concepts [2]: A simple, yet clear framework of laws, secure systems in order to promote trust of the citizens, and the use of sustainable technology supported by open standards and open interfaces.

The European Directive on Electronic Signatures [3] has been implemented through the Austrian Signature Act [4] and the Austrian Signature Ordinance [5]. Several other laws like the Data Protection Act [6] and laws defining administrative procedures have been modified. At the time of this writing, an e-government law has just been ratified by the parliament and enters into force in 2004 [7]. This law inter alia lays down the legal basis for the citizen card, defines how identification in e-government services shall be carried out, or how notified delivery of records or deeds can be carried out electronically.

A typical problem in e-government applications is the electronic identification of the participants in some administrative procedure. One might assume that electronic signatures already serve as a means of identification. Even though a digital certificate is unique and thus identifies the owner of the related private key, this does not suffice the e-government needs: A digital certificate expires and the citizen needs to have an identifier that is valid beyond that period, e.g. in real estate proceedings. The data in the certificate, usually the name, thus not uniquely identify a person, such as several John Smiths'.

A solution to the identification problem is a central registry for natural persons and for legal entities like companies. While such registries exist in Austria, such as a central resident register or the commercial register, using the unique identifiers in all e-government processes raises some data protection concerns: The introduction of e-government shall not introduce a sentiment of increased control. To introduce unique identifiers might lead to the suspicion that cross-search between unrelated cases is enabled.

In order to comply with data protection aspects, a concept referred to as sector-specific identification is followed. As a first step, the unique identifiers undergo a strong encryption process to ensure that the source identifiers are not stored. The result – a so called "Stammzahl" ("base identifier") – is processed by the "Stammzahlregisterbehörde" ("Base Identifier Authority") which is the Federal Data Protection Authority.

An administrative process must never store the unique personal base identifier obtained, but rather a hash value of a combination of this personal identifier and the administrative process ID. We refer to this number as process-specific identifier. Moreover, the unique personal base identifiers must not be stored outside the citizen card, they are generated on demand from the central registry. In this way, the (usually illegal) comparison of the various data bases does not become any easier than it has been up to now. In addition to unique base identifiers, also typical basic data about the person like date of birth or nationality may be stored on the citizen card. With this, many administrative procedures between citizens and the administration become simpler, as persons do not have to add such documents to some application.

Citizens identify themselves electronically by using a token containing their personal identifiers that are used to derive the process-specific identifiers. Moreover, for authentication the tokens contain the citizens' signature creation data, i.e. their secret signing key. As these tokens will change with advances of technology, an abstraction of such tokens has been defined. This abstraction is known under the name "Bürgerkarte" ("citizen card"). Currently, a typical implementation of this token might be a smartcard capable of computing public key cryptographic algorithms. In addition, there exists also a slightly different concept under the name "Bürgerkarte Light." Here, the mobile phones serve as tokens, and the mobile phone system is used together with the Internet for creating electronic signatures.

Instead of contacting the administration personally, a citizen can authenticate herself electronically through qualified certificates issued by a certification service provider. Austrian certification service providers need to comply with the Electronic Signature Act. The Telekom-Control Commission[1] acts as the national supervisory authority for electronic signatures. In addition, the Secure Information Technology Center[2] serves as designated body for the conformity assessment of secure signature-creation devices according to the European Directive on Electronic Signatures.

Access to all e-government services is provided by a portal. The portal plays no role in the administrative process itself, but rather serves as a guide to services. The Austrian online government portal[3] has recently won the e-Europe Award 2003 at the European e-government conference in Como. This portal integrates information about federal administration, provincial administration, cities and municipalities.

The use of open standards and open interfaces is a prerequisite for building sustainable services. It provides the base for the integration of heterogeneous systems nationally as well as internationally. Among these standards are the citizen card concept, the security-layer interface described in section 3, registry services, and directory services. These specifications are publicly available from the Federal Chief Information Office web[4]. In the following we will concentrate on one of these open standards, the security-layer interface.

3. Security-layer Interface

When establishing a citizen's electronic identity by means of the citizen card concept, a central role is held by certification service providers: During the registration process, a citizen is identified on a high quality level by using an identity document. Digital certificates are created for her public signature keys which serve as electronic attestation and link signature-creation data stored with the citizen card to the citizen's identity. Usually two signature keys are created and certified, one for electronic signatures that are legally equivalent to handwritten signatures, and one for signatures that do not need that legal recognition. Moreover, the means to uniquely identify a citizen based on the federal residents register needs to be established. Therefore, a so-called persona binding that links the citizen's unique identifier to her public signature key is signed by the federal ministry of interior and is stored with the citizen card. Thus, the basic data the citizen card holds are the persona binding, the signature keys, and the certificates.

---

[1] http://www.signatur.rtr.at/en/supervision/index.html

[2] http://www.a-sit.at/signatur/bestaetigungsstelle/bestaetigungsstelle.htm

[3] http://www.help.gv.at

[4] http://www.cio.gv.at

Even though devices such as smart cards already represent the state of the art in safeguarding the citizen's electronic credentials, a number of further components are security-relevant during the signature-creation process: The viewer component may not display the document to be signed in any deceptive manner or the document may not be tampered with when communicated to the citizen card. In addition, the I/O device to enter the citizen's authorization data or the card acceptor device need to ensure that pass phrases or PINs to trigger electronic signatures can not be intercepted. In order to achieve a clear separation of the components that are security-relevant with respect to the Austrian Signature Act, we combine these components to a logical entity that we refer to as a security capsule.

By combining the components involved into the signature-creation process, the e-government application can delegate the identification and authentication processes to a single entity – the security capsule. This is straightforward from a system design perspective and allows for defining the application's interface on a high abstraction level. The basic functions to be provided by such an interface are to electronically sign a document, to verify an electronic signature, or to store or retrieve data in the information containers provided by the citizen card. This interface is called the security layer.

The security layer is implemented as a set of commands that are encoded in extensible markup language (XML). Several communication paths are defined to access the security layer of which the hypertext transport protocol (HTTP) is to be accented as fitting the requirements of the application of choice – the Web browser. In this approach, the security layer acts as a rudimentary Web server running on the citizen's PC. The citizen carries out her official process by accessing a portal, such as filling a Web form. When completing the form, techniques such as HTTP redirect or javascript can be employed to forward the result to the security layer. The security layer is than in charge of displaying the result to the citizen for final inspection and to create an electronic signature. A major advantage is that no changes to the Web browser are required and that the citizen is readily familiar with the application.

A further advantage of the security-layer approach is technology neutrality. The e-government application does not need to integrate a certain type of smart card, or to support a certain cryptographic algorithm. As further technologies emerge, like PDAs or USB tokens, they can be easily integrated into the citizen card concept by providing the security layer. This also keeps the approach open for the market: Citizen cards are readily offered by the private sector, such as by certification service providers. The financial sector has announced to follow the concept and to issue banking cards as citizen cards, the public sector is supposed to issue identity cards or health insurance cards as citizen cards, etc.

4. Side-Channel Attacks

Probably the most important element of modern information security is cryptography. We make use of cryptographic algorithms and protocols in order to achieve security goals like confidentiality, data integrity, authentication etc. The strength of these algorithms against attacks is usually challenged by cryptanalytical methods. If one can find ways to derive information about the secret key from the clear text and/or the cipher text, we consider such an algorithm as weak or even broken.

If we think of physical implementations of these algorithms on microchips, there exists another class of threats to the secret information: An attacker can exploit information leaking through some side channel of the physical device. In the case of smart cards executing some cryptographic algorithm, there are two major leaking side channels. These are the consumption of electrical current, and the electromagnetic field generated by the device while executing some algorithm. Both typically contain information about what is going on inside the device. If this information depends on the secret key used for computation, then the attacker can exploit this side channel and potentially derive the secret key. We currently distinguish between the following different types of side-channel attacks:

- Timing attacks
- Differential- and simple power-analysis (SPA & DPA) attacks
- Differential- and simple electromagnetic-analysis (SEMA & DEMA) attacks

In principle, the attacker makes a hypothetical model of the device to be attacked, makes assumptions about the implementation and the power consumption, and tries to predict the output characteristics of some side channel. This output is compared with results from real measurements. This comparison is done through a statistical analysis, and the model can be improved after obtaining some knowledge about the secret key involved in the computation. For more details on these attacks refer to [8] or [9].

The importance of the threat of side-channel attacks rises with the ubiquity of cryptographic devices. It is not so much the threat itself – in the case of the loss of a signature card the legitimate owner can usually always detect the loss of her card and revoke its corresponding certificate easily – but the mere existence and knowledge about these attacks could well hinder the acceptance of cards as a means for holding signature creation data, and thus severely inhibit the growth of trust in e-government applications.

We therefore need awareness about this fact, and we also need to improve counter measures against side-channel attacks. Currently, side-channel attacks and countermeasures against these are a highly active research area. A strong indication for this fact is that at last year's conference on Cryptographic Hardware and Embedded Systems (CHES 2003) in Cologne, Germany, almost one third of all presentations dealt with this topic [10]. We also see an increasing interest of the VLSI design community to take care of this problem by coming up with appropriate design methods and tools for implementing side-channel counter measures on microchips. Up to now, counter measures have always been implemented using ad-hoc approaches in each design. It is now the time to incorporate knowledge about side-channel attacks in the chip design flow in a similar manner as attributes like speed, area, or energy consumption are dealt with.

5. Conclusions

This presentation combines topics from a rather broad area, from legal issues down to microchip design. With this mix we want to emphasize the many aspects of designing a framework for electronic government services. Apparently, it also takes this variety of expertise, including law, politics, network security, cryptology, software design, and microchip design in order to successfully build e-government services. Only by pulling together knowledge from all parts of this broad spectrum, we are able to establish state-of-the-art e-government services which will have sufficient quality for earning the people's trust.

References

[1]   http://www.buergerkarte.at
[2]   Federal Chancellery – Bundeskanzleramt Wien: "e-Government in Österreich", 2003;
       http://www.cio.gv.at/service/conferences/graz_2003/e-Gov_Broschuere.pdf
[3]   Directive 1999/93/EC of the European Parliament and of the Council of 13 December 1999 on a
       Community framework for electronic signatures;
       http://www.signatur.rtr.at/repository/legal-directive-20000119-en.pdf

[4]   Austrian Signature Act; "Bundesgesetz über elektronische Signaturen (Signaturgesetz - SigG)",
        BGBl. I Nr. 190/1999, BGBl. I Nr. 137/2000, BGBl. I Nr. 32/2001.
        http://www.a-sit.at/signatur/rechtsrahmen/2001A152.pdf
[5]   Austrian Signature Ordinance; "Verordnung des Bundeskanzlers über elektronische Signaturen
        (Signaturverordnung - SigV)", StF: BGBl. II Nr. 30/2000.
        http://www.a-sit.at/signatur/rechtsrahmen/SigV2000.pdf
[6]   Federal Act concerning the Protection of Personal Data; "Datenschutzgesetz 2000" BGBl. I Nr.
        165/1999
        http://www.bka.gv.at/datenschutz/dsg2000e.rtf
[7]   Federal E-Government Act; "Bundesgesetz über Regelungen zur Erleichterung des elektronischen
        Verkehrs mit öffentlichen Stellen, (E-Government-Gesetz – E GovG)", 2004.
[8]   Aigner M., Oswald E.: Power Analysis Tutorial; Institute for Applied Information Processing and
        Communications, 2002. Available from http://www.iaik.tu-
        graz.ac.at/aboutus/people/oswald/papers/dpa_tutorial.pdf
[9]   Oswald E.: On Side-Channel Attacks and the Application of Algorithmic Countermeasures. PhD
        Thesis, Graz University of Technology, 2003.
[10]   Colin D. Walter, Çetin K. Koç, Christof Paar (Eds.): Cryptographic Hardware and Embedded
        Systems – CHES 2003; 5th International Workshop Cologne, Springer LNCS 2779, Germany, 2003.

Security and Privacy in Advanced Networking Technologies
B. Jerman-Blažic et al. (Eds.)
IOS Press, 2004

Provision of Security Services in Government and Public Administration

Hubert GROßE-ONNEBRINK

Fraunhofer Institut für Sichere Telekooperation SIT
Schloß Birlinghoven, D-53754 Sankt Augustin, Germany
hubert.grosse-onnebrink@sit.fraunhofer.de

Mechthild STÖWER

Fraunhofer Institut für Sichere Telekooperation SIT
Schloß Birlinghoven, D-53754 Sankt Augustin, Germany
mechthild.stoewer@sit.fraunhofer.de

1. Introduction

With the exponential growth of the Internet and related commercial services, governments have found it impossible to ignore the possibility that the Internet and private networks can provide a means to carry out government business. The way we are governed in Europe is undergoing great change, to which the introduction of Information and Communications Technology is making its own powerful contribution, hand-in-hand with other societal trends. This makes eGovernment one of the biggest challenges currently facing Europe as it touches on so many aspects of our personal, family, community, working and business lives. The following pages will provide an introduction to eGovernment paying special attention in security measurements.

1.1 Definition of eGovernment

Stated simply, electronic government (eGovernment) is the use of information technology to support government operations, engage citizens, and provide public services. eGovernment can support more streamlined and responsive service, wider public participation, and more cost-effective business practices at every level of government.

It ranges in complexity from basic access to official information to radically redesigned public processes:

- **Publish**
  Information available online
- **Interact**
  Two-way communication
- **Transact**
  Transaction handled online
- **Integrate**
  Process, system and organizational integration
- **Transform**
  Entirely new services delivered cross-agency through a centralized enterprise portal

However, while e-government offers the opportunity to innovate, it also presents substantial policy, management, and technology challenges. Effective eGovernment initiatives require a realistic and comprehensive view of these challenges as well as a compelling vision of the benefits.

1.2 Why eGovernment?

There are a number of reasons to consider implementing eGovernment:

Pervasiveness of the World Wide Web
Turning on the radio or television or opening a magazine or newspaper and, chances are, one will see an advertisement or story about the Web. Today, most organizations, including state agencies and local governments, maintain websites.

Growing online population
More and more customers have access to the Web at home, work, school and other locations. With an increase in your citizens using the Web, one will see that one have reached the critical mass necessary to make eGovernment service delivery viable. There are still, however, those that do not have access to the Web.

Reduced cost
Typically, traditional over-the-counter transactions cost more than those conducted via the Internet. Counter transactions often consume more staff time and more paper supplies (including printing) than electronic transactions. Internet transactions can be less expensive but they entail costs of their own.

Increased public expectations
As the online population grows and more eCommerce is conducted online, customers expect governments to have an Internet presence and online transactions. Surveys (option polls) are often an effective method of determining citizen's characteristics and what type of eGovernment applications the citizen's desire.

Increased public frustrations
Customers have more demands for their time. Commuting times and distances to work have increased. The prevalence (occurrence) of dual-income families has increased too. Thus, customers are not often able to visit government offices during normal office hours. Customers want access to government services when it is convenient to them, particularly after regular working hours, and 24/7 (twenty-four hours a day / seven days a week), eGovernment may be the solution to this problem.

1.3 Benefits

Enhanced access to government
eGovernment allows, providing a variety of services around the clock. One can provide customers with a new means of communication while still allowing customers to access information and services via traditional means (e.g., phone, mail, fax, etc.). With the flexible hours and the ability to access the Internet via any computer, the eGovernment services are often more convenient for citizens.

Happy and informed citizenry
The citizens will be pleased by the improved service. The customers also become better citizens as they are better informed about and more involved in the activities of government. The government will thus become more accountable to its citizens. Important is, to keep in mind that the goal is to make it easy for citizens to help themselves.

Streamlined business process and improved efficiency
Before any eGovernment application is undertaken, a business process analysis should be conducted in order to determine the best applications to convert to the Web and most efficient way to provide that service online. Since eGovernment applications are automated, one will also be able to be more efficient in the work.

Increased productivity and integrated operations
By design, eGovernment integrates operations, even across jurisdictions. Departmental boundaries become blurred as eGovernment fosters cooperation. This integration of operations thereby helps to increase productivity and efficiency.

1.4 Obstacles to eGovernment

Lack of resources
Implementing eGovernment can be expensive. Besides ensuring that one have enough money for start-up costs, one will need to ensure that one have adequate money set aside for the remainder of the project and for maintenance in the future. One will also need to consider resources such as staff expertise and IT infrastructure. Some of these resources one will have in place and others one will need to invest in.

Incomplete planning
Careful planning ahead of time is essential. Before starting an eGovernment project, one needs to have a comprehensive plan in place. It is important too that one have adequate drive and vision to sustain throughout the project. eGovernment is a long-term commitment that requires constant monitoring and revision.

Insufficient partnerships
If one haven't partnered with the right people; one may have left an essential element out of the planning. Excluding certain partners, whether deliberate or not, could also cause bad feelings.

Incomplete cultural change and training
The staff will be the people most directly involved in the daily operations of eGovernment. Thus, it is key that the staff adapts to the new ideas and functions of eGovernment and is skilled in handling the eGovernment applications.

Inadequate policy maintenance
Even if one has information or eGovernment policy in place, one will need to maintain and monitor it. Technology is constantly changing, so the policy should also be regularly revised to reflect these changes.

Lack of management or citizen support
If the management and the citizens do not support the eGovernment initiatives, the chances of success are slim. Why are these two groups so important? Management often provides leadership and money. Citizens are the primary customers for many of the eGovernment initiatives.

Digital divide
The digital divide refers to the gap of opportunity between those who have access to personal computers and the Internet and those who do not. One need to determine how one will address this issue to ensure that one have the means of reaching all the citizens.

2. Information security and eGovernment

One of the biggest concerns to citizens (and government) is security on the Internet. There are a number of reasons why information security is an issue for eGovernment:

- Dependency on information systems
- High degree of information sharing
- Increase use of remote access
- Challenges of controlling information
- Laws relating to information security
- Dealing with highly sensitive citizen's and business data
- National security

One can mitigate the risk of security and privacy by implementing appropriate measures, developing policies, training the staff and carefully monitoring the system.

2.1 Security Risks

There are five primary categories of security risks:

1. **Electronic.** Internal perpetrators, such as disgruntled employees, or external perpetrators, such as hackers or spoofers, cause this type of risk. Hackers often break into computer systems or networks for the thrill or notoriety. Spoofers break into computer systems as well by deceitful means.

2. **Malicious code.** There are several different types of malicious code. Viruses, worms, and Trojan horses are three of the most common.

   a. Virus is a program or piece of code that is loaded onto a computer surreptitiously to carry out either mischievous or destructive activities against your computer system.

   b. Worm is a type of virus or replicative code that propagates itself across computers, usually by creating copies of itself in each computer's memory.

   c. Trojan horse is an apparently harmless computer application that sneaks a computer virus onto a computer system.

   It is often difficult to prevent these attacks from occurring, but staff can take simple precautions such as not opening e-mail attachments from outside sources before running them through virus-checking software. Once an attack has occurred, you can usually obtain patches for your software from the major software vendors within a few days.

3. **Physical / human.** Computer equipment or systems can be compromised by natural disasters, such as fire, flooding, electrical surges, etc. If computer equipment is not secured properly, it is susceptible to theft.

4. **Privacy.** One could face legal actions or public embarrassment by releasing sensitive or non-public information about employees, customers or corporations.

5. **Downtime.** Downtime can be caused by a variety of factors, including computer errors, viruses or bugs, denial-of-service attacks or disasters. A denial-of-service attack is an incident in which a user or organization is deprived of the services of a resource they would normally expect to have on the Internet because of a massive, automated coordination of bogus requests to a website. Natural and human disasters (e.g., power outages, civil unrest, etc.) may also cause computer systems to fail. Regardless of the factors involved, one should avoid downtime as it compromises citizens' trust. And if it is a frequent occurrence, citizens may stop visiting the website altogether.

2.2 Risk Management

Risk is the possibility of something adverse happening. Risk management involves technical and legal factors. The process of risk management involves three steps:

- **Analysis of risk**. What are the potential benefits of the eGovernment application? One should weigh the risk against potential benefits. In good risk management, the potential benefits should outweigh the risks.
- **Consideration of alternatives**. Is there a less risky alternative? There will always be some risk involved in any application. The goal is to reduce the risks to an acceptable level. When considering the options, one should keep in mind that not all risks are equal.
- **Implementation of best option**. The best option will help you to maintain a consistent level of risk.

2.2.1 Determining Risk

Risk can be determined by using a simple formula:

$$RISK = THREAT * VULNERABILITY * COST$$

Directions for using formula:
First, examine the possible threats, vulnerabilities and costs. Assign a number from 0 to 10. A zero signifies no threat, vulnerability or cost, a ten means the highest possible threat, vulnerability or cost and any number in between signifies different gradations of trouble. Multiply your determined figures for threat, vulnerability and cost. If your answer is close to zero, you have a low risk. If your answer is closer to one thousand (the highest possible score), you have a high risk.

Threat is the likelihood that an event will occur in a given period of time. This figure will vary according to geographic location and other factors. One have the least control over this.

Vulnerability is the likelihood that threat will disrupt the government or application. One have the most control over this factor as one can modify the system or site if one find vulnerabilities.

Cost is dependent on the threat and vulnerability levels. When the threat has successfully penetrated the vulnerable systems, one has a security event and costs. In order to reduce the costs, it is necessary to reduce the threat and vulnerability. Costs can be monetary, but they could also include matters, such as downtime, lost productivity, etc.

Over time, risks, threats and vulnerabilities will change. There is a need to re-examine these risk management items periodically and revise the eGovernment application accordingly.

2.3 Interrelated levels of eGovernment security

In order to ensure the highest level of security for your eGovernment applications, a multi-level approach is recommended. Security breaches can be caused by problems with the technological systems that you use, but they can also be caused by negligent staff. There are three primary interrelated levels of security:

- **Telecommunications network**. A secure telecommunications networks that agencies and local governments can use is the Virtual Private Networks (VPN). A VPN is a network that retains privacy over a public telecommunications network by using encryption and other security mechanisms to ensure that only authorized users can access the network and that the data cannot be intercepted.

- **Information systems.** Protection is not only necessary on the network on which the data is transmitted, but also on the computer systems within the office. Governments often require staff to use logins and passwords to access their computers or local area networks (LANs). The rooms in which computer equipment is kept, especially those that are essential to the operation of the website and those that contain private information, should be secured. Computers are storage devices for electronic records and as such, should be subject to the same degree of security as the paper records.
- **Staff.** The best security system is worthless if their users are not well-trained and when appropriate policies are not implemented. The staff should also be familiar with the security policies and procedures. For instance, if a staff member leaves their computer terminal without logging off, someone could gain access to restricted information or e-mail. Staff should be warned against opening attachments and executable files sent via e-mail as these have been the origin of many accidental downloads of viruses.

2.4 Security and privacy policies

Before engaging in eGovernment, one needs to have a security and privacy policy in place. The staff should be made aware of the policy and one should consider posting a similar policy on the website for the citizens.

2.4.1 Authenticating transactions

In order for eGovernment to work, there must be an assurance of authenticity. It is important to be able to verify who you are conducting business with. If one can't ensure that the transactions are honest, then one is putting the government at risk, both legally and financially.

2.4.2 Monitoring security

It is crucial to maintain tight security procedures and policies. The bigger one get and the more private information one maintain online, the more of a target one become to hackers. Hackers may be after the private information, but they may also be after the satisfaction that comes with cracking your site.

2.4.3 Maintaining privacy and maintaining trust

One can gain the trust of the citizens, if one is able to assure them that one is capable of securing their private information online. Many people are wary of conducting financial transactions online as they fear that their credit card information will be compromised. Indeed, there have been reports of credit card or confidential personal information accidentally being posted to government and other organizations' websites.

2.5 Security measures

How can one prevent or minimize the threat of security risks? There are various methods that one can use. These methods work best when they used together as part of an integrated strategy. Remember, however, that none of these security measures is foolproof. One will need to constantly monitor and revise one's security practices.

Firewalls. A firewall is hardware and/or software that controls information entering one's computer system or network.

Intrusion detection software. This type of software detects unauthorized intrusions into the computer system.

Encryption. Encryption is a security method that transforms information into random streams of bits to create a secret code. There is software-based encryption such as Public Key Infrastructure (PKI) and Secure Sockets Layer (SSL). Hardware-based encryption, such as smart cards, is another type of encryption. PKI is the combination of software, encryption technologies, and services that enables enterprises to protect the security of their communications and business transactions on the Internet. SSL is a program layer created by Netscape for managing the security of message transmissions in a network. A smart card is a plastic card resembling a credit card that contains a computer chip, which enables the holder to perform various operations, such as mathematical calculations, paying of bills, and the purchasing of goods and services.

Digital signatures or electronic signatures. A digital signature is sometimes referred to as an electronic signature, but is more accurately described as an electronic signature that is authenticated through a system of encryption logarithms and electronic public and private keys. A digital signature is often described as an envelope into which an electronic signature can be inserted. Once the recipient opens the document, the digital signature becomes separated from the document and the document can be modified. Thus, a digital signature only preserves the integrity of a document until it is opened.

Secure networks. There are a variety of secure networks currently available. The most common networks are Virtual Private Networks (VPNs), closed networks such as Wide Area Networks (WANs) or Local Area Networks (LANs). VPN is a network that retains privacy over a public telecommunications network by using encryption and other security mechanisms to ensure that only authorized users can access the network and that the data cannot be intercepted.

Training. Even if one have implemented all possible safety measures, they are useless if the staffs do not know how to properly use them. Training can range from formal, structured classes to informal memos.

Policy and oversight. In order for one's security to be effective, one needs to develop a security policy and a method of monitoring staff adherence to it. If one have a good policy in place and one is able to prove that staff follow it, one may avoid legal problems in the future.

2.6 Privacy Guidelines

The importance of having privacy guidelines is to protect against invasions to citizens' privacy and to show citizens one is working to protect their privacy. The following is a list of recommended privacy guidelines for both state agencies and local governments:

- **Get informed consent when you collect data**: It is important to explain to citizens how one plan to use the data that one have collected.
- **Collect only the data one need**: By collecting only what one need, one protect citizens' privacy as well as preserve storage space and avoid wasting the time.

- **Allow customers to view and correct data**: If customers have questions about their personal data, allow them to look at your records and make any corrections.
- **Obtain consent for additional use**: If it is wanted to use data for purposes other than originally intended, one need to obtain consent from the citizens.
- **Use cookies only when appropriate**: A cookie is a text file stored on your computer by a website and contains information gathered during a visit to the site. Cookies are often used for facilitating quick logins, processing transactions and personalizing information. Cookies can also be abused; some monitor customers' routes on the Internet and they are often used to personalize ads to send to users. In light of the negative press about cookies the federal government it is recommended to ban cookies from the agencies' websites.
- **Keep private data confidential**: The demand is ensuring that the private data one is maintaining remains private. That is why it is important to establish security policies and install security equipment. Of concern to many is the potential for government employees to misuse personal information.
- **Respect customer's concerns**: In the past, public records were usually only accessible to those who visited the office in person. Increasingly, however, governments are posting public records on the Internet. Some citizens are concerned about public records being readily available to anyone on the Internet, while others want more and more records posted on the Internet for their convenience. Depending on the community's views, one will need to decide how much and what type of information should be posted on the website.

3. Implementation Guidelines developed within the EU funded transfer-project E-MuniS

3.1 E-Munis targets and project approach

The main objective of E-MuniS is to adapt and transfer the best practices of the EU municipalities to municipalities in South East Europe through pilot development and implementation of IT applications in the field of administrative work and provision of services to citizens.

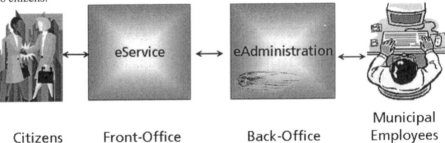

| Citizens | Front-Office | Back-Office | Municipal Employees |

E-MuniS considered in particular the "eAdministration" - the Back Office, and the "eService" - the Front Office and their interaction as shown in the following figure:

The project aimed then at achieving results for:
1. E-Municipality office, consisting of three adapted and improved pilot prototypes of IT applications:
   a. Electronic Document Management System providing tools for automated document workflow within the municipality.

b. Interface tool to external information resources (Citizen's Register, legal, statistical and other governmental data bases).
c. City Mayor's office information network based on the development approach of the executive information system utilising the previous two systems.

2. On-line services to citizens to be achieved through the transfer and adaptation of IT applications as city portal, citizens' information system, eServices and tools to connect front and back office applications.

More information about the project, the consortium and the project outcomes you find on the E-MuniS Internet site: www.emunis-ist.org

3.2 Recommendation for Implementation of local eGovernment applications

Regarding the risks and objectives of implementing Internet based front-end and back- end applications the following strategy was developed within the E-MuniS project:

1. All local e-Government activities should start with implementation or improvement of the city portal! It is the "visiting card" of every municipality and central access point for information and service to citizens, business, tourists and other administrations. E-MuniS layout and contents recommendations are oriented on European best practice applications. Improvement efforts for the City portal show results very soon and have an enormous benefit for all target groups.

2. A "Citizens Information System" must be integrated! These systems achieve transparency concerning the city administration and all municipal procedures. Citizens that are informed about the procedure of their requests save time and internal administration is not harassed with faulty claims. E-MuniS provides an approved solution.

3. A technology concept has to be developed regarding hard- and software infrastructure. Open source software should be used where possible.

4. The E-MuniS front end application "Service manager" is an appropriate instrument to use eServices. It offers a simplified and comfortable access to eServices with additional function for citizens.

5. Applications that have high security and legal requirements should be realised later! A very expensive infrastructure and know-how is necessary to implement and use these applications.

6. Back office procedures should be connected to the front-end applications. E-MuniS tools are helpful.

7. E-MuniS implementation process should be used to improve workflow and organisational structure.

8. A qualification push for employees that have to implement, maintain and update eGovernment applications must be started. Internet technologies will be very important for future development of IT applications. The personnel must have appropriate skills.

9. eGovernment applications must be accessible in an easy way by citizens and business! In particular the implementation of public Internet access points is very useful to increase the usage of Internet and to accelerate the provision of eServices in countries with low dissemination of private Internet access facilities. This is one of the key success factors in particular for the target countries of E-MuniS project. The following measures support this task:
    -   E-MuniS applications avoid specialised hard- or software applications. They require only a standard browser.

-   Applications must be available 24 hours a day.
-   Different ways to access e-Services must be provided as:
    -   PC at home or office
    -   Unattended public internet access point in central public buildings
    -   "Citizens' office" with attended public internet access point

References

[1] The Federal Office for Information Security (BSI), Germany, http://www.bsi.de/english/imprint.htm
[2] eGovernment in Europe,
http://europa.eu.int/information_society/eeurope/2005/all_about/egovernment/index_en.htm.
[3] Maximizing Revenues and Saving Costs Through E-Government: Success Stories in the Public Sector,
The National Electronic Commerce Coordinating Council, http://www.ec3.org/Downloads/2003/RevMax.pdf.
[4] Guide to eGovernment, An introduction to the UK's system of government, including the role of the
legislature, the executive, the judiciary and the Monarchy. http://www.open.gov.uk/Home/Homepage/fs/en.
[5] Access eGovernment, An Educational Program, http://www.access-egov.info/index.cfm?xid=PA.
[6] Global Survey of eGovernment. http://www.unpan.org/egovernment2.asp.
[7] Information about the E-MuniS project, the consortium and the project outcomes: http://www.emunis-
ist.org.

Author Index